Graphics Programming in C++

Springer
London
Berlin
Heidelberg
New York
Barcelona
Budapest
Hong Kong
Milan
Paris
Santa Clara
Singapore
Tokyo

Mark Walmsley

Graphics Programming in C++

Writing Graphics Applications for Windows 98

 Springer

Mark Walmsley, BSc, PhD
greengrass@btinternet.com

ISBN-13:978-1-4471-1231-0   Springer-Verlag Berlin Heidelberg New York

British Library Cataloguing in Publication Data
Walmsley, Mark
    Graphics programming in C++ : writing graphics applications
    for Windows 98
    1.C++ (Computer program language) 2.Computer graphics
    I.Title
    006.6'633
    ISBN-13:978-1-4471-1231-0
Library of Congress Cataloging-in-Publication Data
Walmsley, Mark, 1964-
    Graphics programming in C++ : writing graphics applications for
    Windows 98 / Mark Walmsley.
        p.   cm.
    Includes index
    ISBN-13:978-1-4471-1231-0   e-ISBN-13:978-1-4471-0905-1
    DOI: 10.1007/978-1-4471-0905-1

    1. Computer graphics. 2. C++ (Computer program language)
    3. Microsoft Windows (Computer file)   I. Title.
    T385.W353 1998
    006.6'633--dc21   98-20520

Typesetting: Camera Ready by author

34/3830-543210 Printed on acid-free paper

Contents

Preface

This is a book about computer graphics. It is aimed primarily at anyone wishing to develop graphics applications for Windows 98 and attempts to provide a quick and clear introduction to the subject without encumbering the reader in a mass of extraneous details. The application of object oriented techniques to graphics programming is a principal theme throughout the text and most of the software is written in C++ so a familiarity with C/C++ will be helpful — for a fuller introduction to the C++ language than is possible here consult the book *'Programming in C++'* (ISBN 0 85934 435 5). Beyond this only a general background in computing and/or mathematics is assumed and whenever new ideas are encountered they are fully explained with the aid of line-drawings and illustrative coding examples. For those brave enough chapter 10 also introduces the topic of 80x86 assembly language programming — without dedicated graphics hardware this is still the best way to produce really snappy animation code. The material covered by the book may be divided into three main categories:

— graphics facilities provided by Windows 98
— 2D drawing algorithms
— simulation of a 3D virtual world

These correspond roughly to chapters 1-6, chapters 7-10 and chapters 11-15 respectively although there is some overlap — more specifically the book is laid out according to the following plan:

Chapters 1 and 2

An introduction to message-based programming under the Windows 98 operating system — the basic procedure for creating and managing a window is also detailed here.

Chapter 3

Object oriented programming is a revolutionary approach to handling complexity in computer software design — this chapter discusses the application of object oriented techniques to graphics programming.

Chapters 4 to 6

These chapters cover the graphics facilities provided by the Windows 98 Graphics Device Interface — the key graphical items available under Windows 98 include pens, brushes, bitmaps and palettes.

Chapters 7 to 9

A selection of 2D drawing algorithms for generating bitmapped, wire-frame and polygon-fill images are described here — in particular, animated bitmap images are used to implement computer sprites.

Chapters 10 and 11

A technical and mathematical interlude that introduces assembly language programming and 3D vector geometry — these are important topics for many graphics applications.

Chapters 12 to 15

The last chapters of the book describe the process of projecting an image of a 3D object onto a 2D screen — hidden pixel removal, colour shading, texture mapping and 3D computer animation are all explained.

The book is written in incremental fashion and it is recommended that earlier chapters are well digested before later ones are tasted — so to begin at the beginning ...

MW
March 1998

1. Message-Based Programming

The first step in writing a graphics application for Windows 98 is to understand the message-based programming style which the operating system demands. A Windows 98 program must operate by processing the messages that it is sent — these messages originate with user input and are subsequently translated by the operating system before being passed to the program. The message-based approach contrasts strongly with the more traditional technique of allowing the program to dictate step-by-step the range of acceptable inputs — the Windows 98 operating system gives the user much more control. This chapter describes the following essential concepts:

- generation of messages from user input
- message queues and the program's message loop
- handling messages with callback functions
- Windows 98 messages

A number of important Windows 98 functions and data types are also introduced — subsequent chapters will describe in more detail how to use them in a graphics application.

1.1 Windows 98 Programming

Windows 98 is a message-based operating system — this demands a new style of programming. Traditionally the interaction of computer and user is principally dictated by the program — at every step in its execution the program limits the range of input which it will accept from the user. However, in a Windows environment the user is given much more control. Whenever the user performs an action such as typing a key or moving the mouse, a message is generated by the operating system and passed along to the program. In response to this message the program must execute code which is appropriate to the user's action — the code is known as a 'message handler'. The following figure demonstrates the procedure:

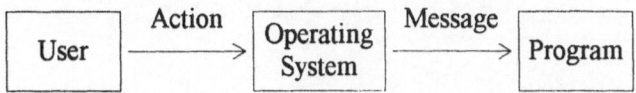

User actions are not the only way in which messages may be generated. As the program executes it must sometimes make requests of the operating system for various services — these requests can also generate messages which are then passed back to the program to initiate further processing. Indeed some operating system requests are designed specifically to send messages. The program can send messages to itself or to other programs currently running on the system — conversely, other programs provide a new source of incoming messages. The full picture is illustrated below:

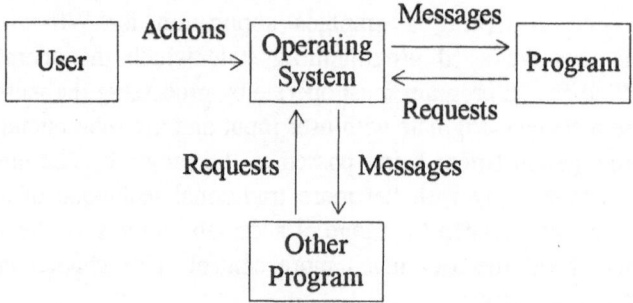

In summary, the role of a Windows 98 program is to respond to messages sent to it by the operating system. A program is implemented as series of message handlers — each handler performs processing for its own message and keeps direct interaction with other handlers to a minimum.

1.2 Window Components

The principal components of a window are the title bar, the menu bar, the window frame and the drawable area — these window components should all be familiar to any Windows user. The following figure illustrates the various window components:

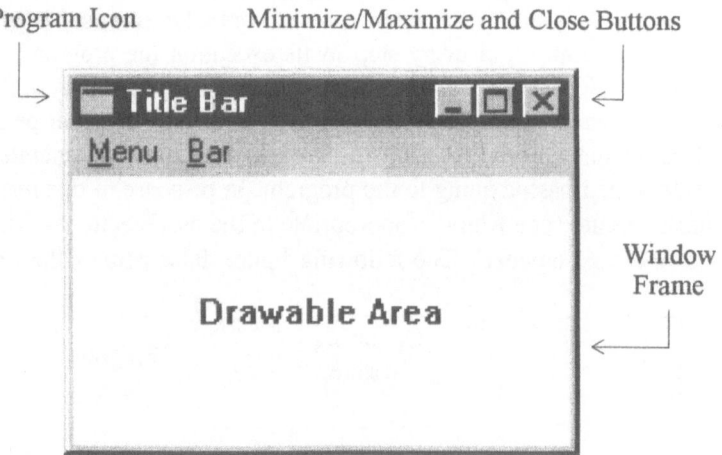

The title bar displays the name of the program to which the window belongs and clicking on the title bar allows the window to be dragged around the screen — the buttons at the right-hand side of the title bar permit the window to be minimized, maximized or closed. The menu bar typically provides a series of menus from which individual items may be selected — clicking on the program icon at the left of the title bar makes the system menu appear. The window frame allows the user to resize the window and the drawable area displays the output of the program.

As the user interacts with these components using the mouse or keyboard a whole host of messages are produced — the title bar and frame generate messages to move and resize the window, the menu bar generates messages when menus are opened or items are selected, and the drawable area generates messages as the mouse pointer moves over it. Messages are also generated if a mouse button is clicked whilst the mouse pointer is over the window or if a key is pressed whilst the window has the keyboard focus (with its title bar highlighted). Finally, as the user works with a collection of windows, messages may be generated to refresh the window's contents whenever other windows are removed that were previously overlapping it. All these messages are eventually processed by the program that created the window — the next section discusses how the program actually receives its messages.

1.3 Message Queues

Whenever a message is generated for a window it is eventually processed by a message handler in the program which created the window. Sometimes a deluge of messages are generated in quick succession and the program cannot be expected to handle them all at once. Clearly, whilst the program responds to the first message there must be some way to delay the arrival of the later messages. The solution is to provide each program with a 'message queue'. When messages are first delivered to the program they are placed in the message queue — as soon as the program finishes the processing for one message, it takes another message from the queue and starts to execute the appropriate message handler. A message is retrieved from the head of the queue by calling the function GetMessage() — if the queue is empty the GetMessage() function will wait for a message to arrive. In general, messages are taken from the queue in the same order that they arrive — however, requests to redraw a window are held until all other messages have been processed so that the window is not continually updated. Messages are placed into the queue by two activities:

1. User Input
2. Requests to the operating system

As noted in section 1.1 each message generated directly by user input (from the keyboard or mouse) may result in requests to the operating system that cause a number of secondary messages to enter the message queue. For example, the PostMessage() function can be called to place a message into the message queue — as soon as the function returns the new message is already in the queue. Each of these secondary messages will be dealt with before another primary message from the user can arrive in the queue. The flow of messages into and out of the message queue is depicted in the following figure:

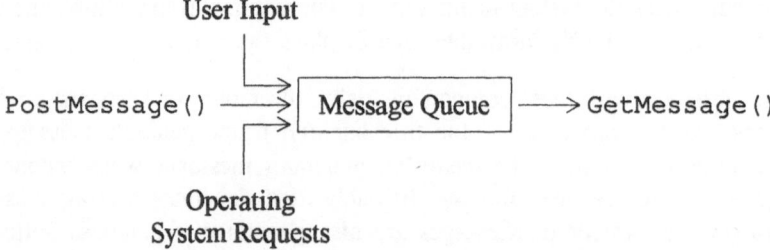

Finally, note that the message queue is associated with the program and not the window — if a program creates several windows then messages for all of them will be intermingled in the same message queue. The next section describes the message handling procedure in more detail — in particular it discusses how individual messages are associated with the correct window in a multi-window application.

1.4 Window Callback Functions

A program typically manages its message queue with a message loop — messages are repeatedly extracted from the queue with the `GetMessage()` function and dispatched for processing elsewhere. The following figure illustrates the interaction of the Windows 98 message functions with the message queue:

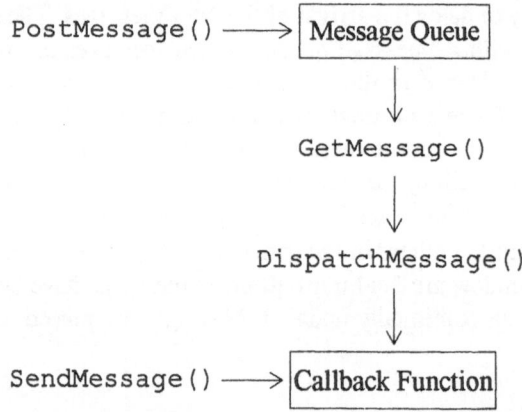

Whenever a new window is created it must specify a function known as a 'window callback function' and this function contains the code for all of the window's message handlers. For each message processed by the program's message loop, the `DispatchMessage()` function determines which window should receive the message and then forwards it to the corresponding callback function. After the callback function completes its processing, the `DispatchMessage()` function returns and the message loop continues. Hence, the program's message loop alternately calls `GetMessage()` and `DispatchMessage()` for each message in the queue and the message is handled by code within a window callback function.

An alternative procedure is to send a message directly to the callback function by calling the `SendMessage()` function — in contrast to using the function `PostMessage()` this approach by-passes the message queue altogether. Some other requests to the operating system also cause messages to be sent directly to the callback function rather than being posted in the message queue.

1.5 The `WinMain()` Function

A Windows 98 program may define several window callback functions but it must also contain a `WinMain()` function. This function must manage all the processing performed by the program — control passes to the `WinMain()` function when the program is started and the execution of the program ceases whenever the `WinMain()` function eventually returns. The value returned by the function is passed back to the operating system and acts as an exit code for the program — a zero value typically indicates that the program completed without error. The `WinMain()` function contains the following three steps:

1. Initialization
2. Message Loop
3. Finalization

Amongst other things the initialization step creates the program's main window — the destruction of the window brings the message loop to an end. The finalization step releases any resources still held by the program and returns an exit code to the operating system. The `WinMain()` function has the following parameter format:

```
int WINAPI WinMain(HINSTANCE instance,
                   HINSTANCE previous,
                   LPSTR arguments,
                   int code);
```

The `WINAPI` prefix indicates that `WinMain()` is a Windows API (Application Programming Interface) function — the prefix specifies a particular function calling convention but the details are not important. The `WinMain()` function receives four parameters from the operating system and returns an integer result. The first two parameters are of type `HINSTANCE` — the H stands for 'handle' and `INSTANCE` refers to a particular 'instance' or invocation of the program. Every time that a Windows 98 program is run by the user, a new instance of the program begins to execute — under `16-bit` versions of Windows the program's instance handle identified the location in memory of the data associated with that instance but `32-bit` programs each have their own memory address space and the instance handle is usually `0x00400000`. The `previous` parameter is also a hangover from 16-bit days and it is always zero for 32-bit programs. The `arguments` parameter is a pointer to a character string containing the command line arguments. Unlike the `argv` array of the C language `main()` function, the `arguments` parameter does not supply the program name at the beginning of this string — instead the `GetCommandLine()` function will return the whole command line including the program name. Finally, in 16-bit versions of Windows the `code` parameter recommended the initial status of the program's main window — for example, it could indicate that the program should start as an icon. However, this information is now provided as part of a `STARTUPINFO` structure that the operating system holds for each new program instance.

1.6 Windows 98 Messages

Within the program's message loop the `GetMessage()` function returns a `MSG` structure — the most important fields contained by this structure are as follows:

```
struct MSG {
    HWND hwnd;
    UINT message;
    WPARAM wParam;
    LPARAM lParam;
        .
        .
};
```

A `HWND` variable is a 'window handle' — unlike the program instance handles each window receives a unique handle value. The `hwnd` field of the `MSG` structure specifies the window to which the message should be forwarded by the `DispatchMessage()` function. The `message` field (an unsigned integer) holds a code value that indicates the type of message — most of the common message types are discussed in the next section. Finally, the `wParam` and `lParam` fields contain additional information that is specific to a particular type of message — they are of types `WPARAM` and `LPARAM` respectively. These types are another hangover from the 16-bit Windows era and refer to WORD (16 bit) and LONG (32 bit) parameters — in Windows 98 both types are 32-bit quantities. The `MSG` structure is broken apart by the function `DispatchMessage()` and the individual fields appear as separate parameters to the window callback function:

```
LRESULT CALLBACK WindowProc(HWND window,
                            UINT message,
                            WPARAM wparam,
                            LPARAM lparam);
```

The CALLBACK prefix identifies `WindowProc()` as a callback function — just like `WINAPI` this prefix specifies a particular function calling convention. The callback function returns a value of type LRESULT — for messages that are handled directly by the program the return value is nearly always required to be zero. Many messages are handled by passing them along to the function DefWindowProc() which the operating system supplies.

1.7 Some Important Messages

This section describes the various types of message that can be specified by the message parameter to the window callback function. There are many categories of messages including the following:

1. Control messages
   WM_CREATE, WM_CLOSE, WM_DESTROY, WM_QUIT
2. Window messages
   WM_MOVE, WM_SIZE, WM_PAINT, WM_COMMAND
3. Mouse messages
   WM_MOUSEMOVE, WM_*BUTTONDOWN, WM_*BUTTONUP
4. Keyboard messages
   WM_KEYDOWN, WM_KEYUP, WM_CHAR
5. Timer messages
   WM_TIMER

The control messages determine how long an individual window or the program as a whole continue to exist. The following figure illustrates the lifecycle of a window:

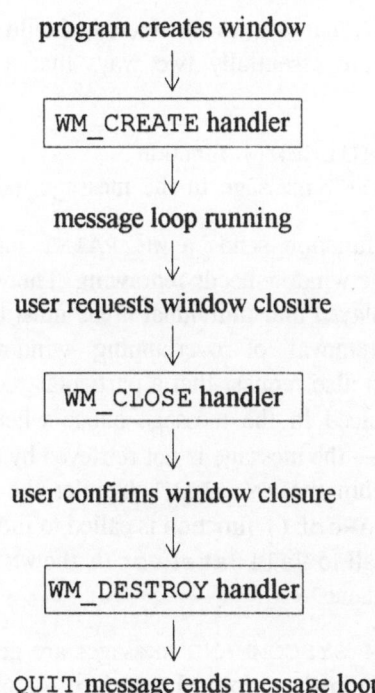

program creates window
↓
WM_CREATE handler
↓
message loop running
↓
user requests window closure
↓
WM_CLOSE handler
↓
user confirms window closure
↓
WM_DESTROY handler
↓
WM_QUIT message ends message loop

When the window is created a WM_CREATE message is sent directly to its callback function — the program message queue is not used for WM_CREATE messages. The message handler for a WM_CREATE message typically acquires the resources that a window will need to function properly. The program now enters the message loop in its WinMain() function and starts to dispatch messages to the window. When the user finally attempts to close the window, a WM_CLOSE message is posted to the message queue. In the WM_CLOSE message handler the user can be asked to confirm the closure request before the window is destroyed with a call to DestroyWindow(). The DestroyWindow() function sends a WM_DESTROY message directly to the callback procedure before destroying the window — the WM_DESTROY message handler may be used to release any resources still held by the window. At this point the window is destroyed but the message loop is still running. To terminate the loop a WM_QUIT message should be placed in the message queue — a call to the PostQuitMessage() function in the WM_DESTROY message handler will ensure that the message loop exits and the program can end.

Messages such as WM_MOVE, WM_SIZE, WM_PAINT and WM_COMMAND are received by the window callback function whilst the message loop is running. The WM_MOVE and WM_SIZE messages are sent whenever the window is moved or resized — a WM_MOVE message indicates the current screen position of the top left corner of the window's drawable area whilst a WM_SIZE message gives the width and height of the area.

A window receives WM_PAINT messages whenever it should redraw the contents of its drawable area. There are essentially two ways that a WM_PAINT message handler can be invoked:

1. directly by the UpdateWindow() function
2. by processing a WM_PAINT message in the message loop

The UpdateWindow() function sends a WM_PAINT message directly to the handler if any portion of the window needs redrawing. The whole window must be drawn when it is first displayed and individual areas must be redrawn when they are uncovered by the removal of overlapping windows — the function InvalidateRect() can also request that a particular rectangle be redrawn. A WM_PAINT message is placed in the message queue whenever any part of the window requires updating — the message is not retrieved by the message loop until the queue is emptied. Within the WM_PAINT handler the appropriate areas are redrawn and the ValidateRect() function is called to indicate that the image is up-to-date — without the call to ValidateRect() the WM_PAINT message will reappear in the message queue.

The WM_COMMAND and WM_SYSCOMMAND messages are generated whenever the user interacts with the window's graphical interface — possible user activities include clicking the minimize, maximize or close buttons and also selecting items from the various menus. The WM_SYSCOMMAND messages are usually passed along to the DefWindowProc() function for processing whilst the program deals explicitly with WM_COMMAND messages.

Keyboard and mouse messages relay input from the user. Whenever a key is pressed a WM_KEYDOWN message is generated — when the key is released this is followed by a corresponding WM_KEYUP message. The parameters passed to the message handler indicate the actual key pressed and released. To ensure uniform processing for a wide range of keyboards, the keys are coded using 'virtual key codes' — for example, the escape key is assigned the VK_ESCAPE virtual key code. The virtual key codes can be converted into ASCII representations by the TranslateMessage() function — this will generate WM_CHAR messages between the WM_KEYDOWN and WM_KEYUP pairs.

The number of messages associated with the mouse is larger than for the keyboard — there are messages for mouse movement (WM_MOUSEMOVE) and for clicking the mouse buttons. When the left mouse button is pressed a WM_LBUTTONDOWN message is generated and when it is released this is followed by a WM_LBUTTONUP message. Many windows can detect mouse double-clicks — for such a window two pairs of button messages are sent for each double-click but the second WM_LBUTTONDOWN message is replaced by a WM_LBUTTONDBLCLK message. There are corresponding messages for the middle and right mouse buttons — these replace the WM_L prefix with WM_M and WM_R respectively. All the mouse messages supply parameters for the current state of the mouse buttons and the position of the mouse pointer.

Finally, some programs require a regular heart-beat to drive them along — this mode of operation can be implemented by handling WM_TIMER messages sent from a timer. The timer must be created using the SetTimer() function and destroyed with the KillTimer() function — typically the window's WM_CREATE message handler creates the timer and the WM_DESTROY message handler destroys it. Whilst alive the timer may be programmed by the SetTimer() function to send WM_TIMER messages at some fixed interval.

1.8 Summary

The message-based nature of the Windows 98 operating system demands a new programming style. Each Windows program executes by processing a sequence of messages — the messages are generated either by user input or by function call requests made to the operating system. Whenever the program creates a window, the messages belonging to the window enter the program's message queue. The program provides a message loop within the WinMain() function to collect messages from the message queue and then dispatch them to a window callback function for further processing. The callback function contains code designed to handle only those messages which are needed to implement the window's functionality — any messages which are not explicitly processed should be passed to the DefWindowProc() function supplied by Windows 98. The chapter also described a number of important Windows 98 messages — these include window management messages such as WM_CREATE, WM_PAINT and WM_DESTROY as well as hardware input messages from the keyboard, mouse and timer.

2. Window Management

In Windows 98 a 'window class' provides a template that describes the general functionality supported by all windows of that class — before a window of a particular window class can be created the class must be registered with the operating system. The most important piece of information supplied by the registration process is the name of a window callback function — the function contains the message handlers for all windows created from the class. This chapter presents the programming details needed to create a window — the topics covered include:

— registering and unregistering a window class
— creating a window of a user-defined class
— building a program message loop
— implementing the callback function and message handlers

The chapter concludes with a discussion of the program framework that is common to every Windows 98 application. The code is cast into a form that will simplify the transition to an object oriented programming style.

2.1 Window Classes

Every window belongs to some window class — each window class defines a window callback function that handles messages for all windows in the class. Since the windows from a particular window class share a common callback function they each exhibit similar behaviours. For example, Windows 98 defines some standard window classes for items such as list boxes, buttons and scroll bars — each of these items is represented by a window class and the windows from each class generally behave in the same manner. Of course, individual windows from the same class can be treated slightly differently by the callback function. One technique is to specify a window style for each window — for example, both horizontal and vertical scroll bars are available through an appropriate choice of window style. Another possibility is to make certain processing decisions in the callback function on a window-by-window basis — the window associated with each message can be determined from the window handle passed to the callback function. This approach is more common for user-defined classes which will generate only a few specific windows — an extreme case is to generate only one highly-specialized window from a window class.

Each new window class must be registered with Windows 98 before any windows from the class can be created. The new class is specified by filling in the fields of a

WNDCLASS structure and passing this structure to the RegisterClass()
function. For example:

```
void Register(HINSTANCE instance) {
  WNDCLASS windowclass;
  LPCTSTR icon,cursor;
  HBRUSH brush;
  icon = MAKEINTRESOURCE(IDI_APPLICATION);
  cursor = MAKEINTRESOURCE(IDC_ARROW);
  brush = (HBRUSH)GetStockObject(WHITE_BRUSH);
  windowclass.lpszClassName = "windowclassname";
  windowclass.hInstance = instance;
  windowclass.lpfnWndProc = WindowProc;
  windowclass.style = CS_HREDRAW|CS_VREDRAW;
  windowclass.lpszMenuName = NULL;
  windowclass.hIcon = LoadIcon(NULL,icon);
  windowclass.hCursor = LoadCursor(NULL,cursor);
  windowclass.hbrBackground = brush;
  windowclass.cbClsExtra = 0;
  windowclass.cbWndExtra = 0;
       .
       .
```

The lpszClassName field is set using a string containing the name of the new
class — the callback function for this class is specified by the hInstance and
lpfnWndProc fields. The hInstance field contains the instance handle
received as the first parameter to the WinMain() function and the
lpfnWndProc field is assigned a pointer to the WindowProc() callback
function — the WindowProc() function must be defined elsewhere within the
program. The remaining fields are set to various default values — in particular,
each window in this class will have no menu bar, a standard application icon, an
arrow-shaped mouse cursor and the background of the drawable area will be
painted white. The choice of class style (CS_HREDRAW|CS_VREDRAW) ensures
that the windows will be redrawn whenever they change size. The cbClsExtra
and cbWndExtra fields allow extra bytes of storage to be associated with the
window class as a whole or with individual windows — the next chapter illustrates
one use for extra bytes. Finally, to register the new class the WNDCLASS structure
must be passed to the RegisterClass() function — this completes the
Register() function:

```
       .
       .
  RegisterClass(&windowclass);
}
```

The WNDCLASS structure may now be discarded — the whole procedure is an example of a common technique in Windows 98 programming:

1. Fill in a structure describing a new item
2. Pass the structure to a function to create the item
3. Discard the structure and use the item

Here a `WNDCLASS` structure is used to create a new window class. Any number of windows can now be created from the class template — this is the topic of the next section. The new class is associated with the program instance that registers it — the class will be automatically unregistered whenever the program eventually exits. However, it can also be explicitly unregistered by calling the function `UnregisterClass()`:

```
void Unregister(HINSTANCE instance) {
  UnregisterClass("windowclassname",instance);
}
```

Both the program's instance handle and the class name are required to identify which class to unregister.

2.2 Creating a Window

With the `Register()` and `Unregister()` functions defined it is now a simple matter to create a window — all that is needed is a call to the `CreateWindow()` function. Whereas the window class registration procedure involved the use of a `WNDCLASS` structure descriptor, the `CreateWindow()` function demonstrates the other common method of creating new items in Windows 98 — this involves passing a (long) list of parameters to a function. For example:

```
HWND Create(LPCTSTR title,HINSTANCE instance) {
  DWORD style = WS_OVERLAPPEDWINDOW;
  HMENU menu = NULL;
  HWND parent = NULL;
  LPVOID params = NULL;
  return CreateWindow("windowclassname",
                      title,
                      style,
                      LEFT,TOP,WIDTH,HEIGHT,
                      parent,
                      menu,
                      instance,
                      params);
}
```

The window class is identified by the program's instance handle and the window class name. A window style (`WS_OVERLAPPEDWINDOW`) is chosen that provides a window similar to that shown in section 1.2. The window has a title bar displaying the character string supplied by the `title` parameter and comes complete with minimize/maximize and close buttons as well as a system menu — however, since neither the window class nor the window itself specify a menu there is no menu bar. Four parameters determine the position of the window's top left corner and its width and height — these values refer to the total extent of the window and not to the smaller drawable area which the window contains. Here the window is initially positioned using the constants `LEFT`, `TOP`, `WIDTH` and `HEIGHT` defined in a program header file — the window can be moved by dragging the title bar and there is a window frame which allows the user to resize the window. The `parent` parameter is set to `NULL` to indicate that the window is a top-level window — windows exist in a hierarchy and may have either a 'parent window' or an 'owner window'. Child windows are clipped to the drawable area of their parent whilst owned windows always overlay their owner and are hidden when their owner is minimized — both child and owned windows are destroyed when their parent or owner window is destroyed. Finally, the `params` parameter can be used to pass initialization data to the `WM_CREATE` message handler — the next chapter examines this possibility in more detail.

Once the window has been created it is still invisible — to make the window visible a call to the `ShowWindow()` function is required:

```
void Show(HWND window) {
  ShowWindow(window,SW_SHOW);
}
```

The `SW_SHOW` flag generally just makes the window visible — however, the effect is more complicated if this is the first call that the program has made to `ShowWindow()`. In this case the program is generally attempting to display its main window and the window status is set using the `STARTUPINFO` structure that the operating system holds for this program instance. The wShowWindow field of the `STARTUPINFO` structure contains the default value for the second parameter of `ShowWindow()` — this value replaces the `SW_SHOW` flag in the first `ShowWindow()` call and may, for example, cause the program to start as an icon. The default value can be used in subsequent calls to `ShowWindow()` by passing the `SW_SHOWDEFAULT` flag instead of the `SW_SHOW` flag. An alternative method of making a window visible is to include the `WS_VISIBLE` flag in the window style parameter passed to the `CreateWindow()` function — however, the default value from the wShowWindow field of the `STARTUPINFO` structure is still used.

2.3 `WinMain()` Revisited

The processing required to register a window class, to create a window from the class and to display the window typically form part of the program initialization performed by the WinMain() function. For example:

```
int WINAPI
WinMain(HINSTANCE instance,HINSTANCE,LPSTR,int) {
  Register(instance);
  HWND window = Create("Test Program",instance);
  Show(window);
    .
    .
  return 0;
}
```

This code produces a single window with the name Test Program appearing in the title bar. Only the instance parameter to WinMain() is used — the others (previous, arguments, code) are effectively obsolete for 32-bit Windows programs and need not be declared explicitly. The previous parameter is always zero whilst the arguments and code parameters have been superceded by the GetCommandLine() function and the STARTUPINFO structure respectively. The program instance handle is required by many different function calls to the operating system and is currently passed in to the Register(), Create() and Unregister() functions as a parameter. Treating the instance handle as a global variable looks like a better approach but such variables are generally a bad idea — the next chapter examines a possible compromise. A zero value is returned to the operating system by the WinMain() function as the program's exit code.

The final ingredient of the WinMain() function is still missing — it is the message loop. Here is a complete listing:

```
int WINAPI
WinMain(HINSTANCE instance,HINSTANCE,LPSTR,int) {
  Register(instance);
  HWND window = Create("Test Program",instance);
  Show(window);
  MSG message;
  while (GetMessage(&message,NULL,0,0))
    DispatchMessage(&message);
  return message.wParam;
}
```

Each message is collected from the program's message queue by the GetMessage() function — the NULL parameter to this function retrieves messages for all windows created by the program whilst the twin zeros ensure that every type of message is included. As noted in chapter 1 the internals of the message are ignored here and the message is passed intact to the DispatchMessage() function for dispatch to the appropriate callback function. The message loop will continue until the GetMessage() function returns a FALSE value — this occurs whenever a WM_QUIT message is taken from the message queue. At this point the **while** loop ends and the WinMain() function returns — instead of passing back zero the exit code is now taken from the wParam field of the WM_QUIT message.

2.4 Message Handlers

The only other piece of code necessary to make a Windows 98 program work is a definition for the callback function WindowProc() — as described in section 2.1 this function was registered as the window class callback function with a call to RegisterClass(). The easiest way to implement the WindowProc() function is simply to pass each message to the DefWindowProc() function supplied by Windows 98 — this function provides default handlers for all the messages a window might receive.

```
LRESULT CALLBACK
WindowProc(HWND window,UINT message,
            WPARAM wparam,LPARAM lparam) {
  return
     DefWindowProc(window,message,wparam,lparam);
}
```

The program can now be built and run — a standard window will appear and perform all the usual window activities like minimizing and maximizing as well as moving and resizing when dragged by the mouse. The biggest problem arises when the window is closed — the window will be destroyed but the program continues to run. The message loop is still executing — it is looking for a WM_QUIT message that will never arrive. The problem is easy to solve by adding a WM_DESTROY message handler as follows:

```
LRESULT CALLBACK
WindowProc(HWND window,UINT message,
            WPARAM wparam,LPARAM lparam) {
  if (message == WM_DESTROY)
    return Destroy(window,message,wparam,lparam);
  return
     DefWindowProc(window,message,wparam,lparam);
}
```

The actual message handler code is placed within the Destroy() function:

```
LRESULT Destroy(HWND window,UINT message,
                WPARAM wparam,LPARAM lparam) {
  PostQuitMessage(0);
  return 0;
}
```

The WindowProc() callback function checks for the WM_DESTROY message which is sent when the program's window is destroyed — upon receipt of this message the `Destroy()` message handler is invoked to post a WM_QUIT message to the message queue. The parameter passed to the `PostQuitMessage()` function appears as the `wParam` field of the WM_QUIT message and is eventually used as the program's exit code. The `DefWindowProc()` function does not post a WM_QUIT message by default since there may be occasions when a window is destroyed but the program should continue — a multi-window application is a good example.

2.5 The `Hello` Program

Nobody is really happy with a new computer language or operating system until they have produced a `Hello` program using it. For Windows 98 this milestone is only a step away — all that is needed is a WM_PAINT message handler to display the `"Hello!"` string. The code to implement this function follows:

```
LRESULT Paint(HWND window,UINT message,
                   WPARAM wparam,LPARAM lparam) {
   PAINTSTRUCT paint;
   HDC dc = BeginPaint(window,&paint);
   RECT rect;
   GetClientRect(window,&rect);
   UINT flags = DT_CENTER|DT_VCENTER|DT_SINGLELINE;
   DrawText(dc,"Hello!",-1,&rect,flags);
   EndPaint(window,&paint);
   return 0;
}
```

All the redrawing operations are bracketed by calls to `BeginPaint()` and `EndPaint()`. Chapter 4 discusses this pair of functions in more detail — however, note here that the `BeginPaint()` function is responsible for calling `ValidateRect()` to ensure that the WM_PAINT message does not reappear in the message queue.

The `DrawText()` function actually draws the `"Hello!"` string. As well as its string parameter, the function is also passed a `RECT` structure and some drawing flags (`DT_CENTER` and `DT_VCENTER`) that tell it to centre the text string in the middle of the window — the `GetClientRect()` function fills in the fields of the `rect` structure with the current size of the window's drawable area. Windows 98 uses `RECT` structures to describe a variety of rectangles such as window extents — each `RECT` structure has the following layout:

```
struct RECT {
   LONG left;
   LONG top;
   LONG right;
   LONG bottom;
};
```

To ensure that the WM_PAINT messages reach the Paint() handler, the
WindowProc() callback function must be updated to explicitly test for these
messages:

```
LRESULT CALLBACK
WindowProc(HWND window,UINT message,
           WPARAM wparam,LPARAM lparam) {
  if (message == WM_PAINT)
    return Paint(window,message,wparam,lparam);
  if (message == WM_DESTROY)
    return Destroy(window,message,wparam,lparam);
  return
    DefWindowProc(window,message,wparam,lparam);
}
```

Whenever the window is resized it is automatically repainted — the WM_PAINT
handler is invoked to reposition the string at the new window centre. The following
figure depicts the typical appearance of the window:

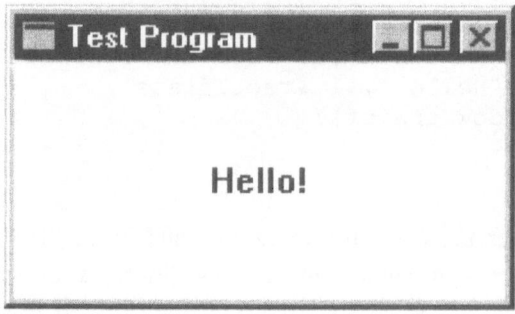

This is hardly a graphics application yet but all the fundamentals are already
present.

2.6 Windows 98 Program Framework

This is a good point to discuss the layout of the C++ source code within a
Windows 98 program and the use of C++ header files. The next chapter will detail
the changes which are necessary to move to an object oriented design — the
discussion presented here is designed to help smooth the transition. A group of
functions may be identified which are used to register a window class, to create
windows of that class, and to process messages sent to these windows — the code
for these functions will be placed in the window.cpp source file and its
window.h header. The header file defines the four constants LEFT, TOP, WIDTH
and HEIGHT which fix the initial position of a window — a more general design
would permit these window creation parameters to be modifiable but a simple

approach will suffice here. The header file also contains the relevant function declarations:

```
window.h:

  const int LEFT = 0;
  const int TOP = 0;
  const int WIDTH = 200;
  const int HEIGHT = 150;

  void Register(HINSTANCE);
  void Unregister(HINSTANCE);
  HWND Create(LPCTSTR,HINSTANCE);
  void Show(HWND);
  int Run(void);

  LRESULT CALLBACK WindowProc(HWND,UINT,WPARAM,LPARAM);
  LRESULT Paint(HWND,UINT,WPARAM,LPARAM);
  LRESULT Destroy(HWND,UINT,WPARAM,LPARAM);
```

The header file must be included by the window.cpp source file with a compiler include directive — the system header windows.h also needs to be included. The window.cpp file contains the definitions of the functions declared in the window.h header — in particular, there are functions to manipulate a window class and its associated windows:

```
window.cpp:

  #include <windows.h>
  #include "window.h"

  void Register(HINSTANCE instance) {
       .
       .
     RegisterClass(&windowclass);
  }

  void Unregister(HINSTANCE instance) {
     UnregisterClass("windowclassname",instance);
  }

  HWND Create(LPCTSTR title,HINSTANCE instance) {
       .
       .
     return CreateWindow(...);
  }

  void Show(HWND window) {
     ShowWindow(window,SW_SHOW);
  }
```

The `window.cpp` file also contains code for processing messages sent to the window:

```
int Run(void) {
  MSG message;
  while (GetMessage(&message,NULL,0,0))
    DispatchMessage(&message);
  return message.wParam;
}

LRESULT CALLBACK
WindowProc(HWND window,UINT message,
           WPARAM wparam,LPARAM lparam) {
  if (message == WM_PAINT)
    return Paint(window,message,wparam,lparam);
  if (message == WM_DESTROY)
    return Destroy(window,message,wparam,lparam);
  return
    DefWindowProc(window,message,wparam,lparam);
}

LRESULT Paint(HWND window,UINT message,
              WPARAM wparam,LPARAM lparam) {
    .
    .
  return 0;
}

LRESULT Destroy(HWND window,UINT message,
                WPARAM wparam,LPARAM lparam) {
  PostQuitMessage(0);
  return 0;
}
```

The code in `window.cpp` forms a framework for all Windows 98 programs and comprises the following functionality:

— window class registration
— window creation
— message loop dispatcher
— assorted message handlers

The next chapter discusses how this functionality can be packaged into a C++ class — the benefit will be that the framework code need not be duplicated for each new project.

Finally, the `WinMain()` function is contained in the `main.cpp` file:

```cpp
#include <windows.h>
#include "window.h"

int WINAPI
WinMain(HINSTANCE instance,HINSTANCE,LPSTR,int) {
   Register(instance);
   HWND window = Create("Title",instance);
   Show(window);
   return Run();
}
```

The `Register()`, `Create()`, `Show()` and `Run()` functions are made available by including the `window.h` header file — in the next chapter these functions are replaced by C++ class functions and the `window.h` file becomes a class header file.

2.7 Summary

This chapter has filled in many of the programming details omitted from the introductory discussion of the previous chapter. Every window created by a Windows 98 program must belong to some window class — the window class defines the window callback function which handles messages for all windows belonging to the class. Before a window can be created its window class must be registered — this is achieved by filling in the fields of a `WNDCLASS` structure and passing this structure to the `RegisterClass()` function. Any window classes registered by a program are automatically unregistered when the program exits but a class may also be unregistered by an explicit call to the `UnregisterClass()` function. The program's message loop is implemented by alternately invoking the `GetMessage()` and `DispatchMessage()` functions — the `GetMessage()` function returns a `FALSE` value when it retrieves a `WM_QUIT` message and thereby ends the message loop. Many of the messages dispatched from the message loop to the window callback function are simply passed along to the `DefWindowProc()` function supplied by Windows 98. The `DefWindowProc()` function provides default handling for any message that a window might receive. However, one message handler that must be explicitly defined is the `WM_DESTROY` handler — this handler should call `PostQuitMessage()` to place a `WM_QUIT` message in the message queue and so stop the message loop. To create a `Hello` program the only other message handler required was the `WM_PAINT` handler — when the window is redrawn this handler places the `"Hello!"` string in the middle of the window with a call to the `DrawText()` function. Finally, the framework of the basic Windows 98 program was examined and cast into a form that will make the transition to an object oriented style easier.

3. Object Orientation

Object oriented programming is a technique for managing complexity by breaking a large program into a collection of interacting objects. These objects communicate by passing messages from one object to another — each object only has to concern itself with handling the messages it receives and then sending out suitable replies. The process is very similar to the way in which windows operate under Windows 98 and so it is natural to associate each window with a corresponding C++ object. This chapter introduces the essential notions of object oriented programming and discusses how to convert the program framework code developed in chapter 2 to an object oriented model. The main topics include:

— separation of object implementation and interface
— encapsulation and polymorphism
— C++ inheritance and virtual functions
— associating C++ objects and graphical components

The chapter also introduces messages boxes and popup menus as means of communicating with the user — these items can be especially valuable whilst debugging a graphics application.

3.1 Object Oriented Programming

In an object oriented design the fundamental elements of a problem are identified and each element is represented by a different type of object. The problem may then be modelled as a collection of interacting objects and a solution can be expressed in natural terms. For a graphics application some of the important elements include windows, bitmaps, palettes, sprites and scenes. Each of these elements will be represented by a different type of C++ object — this chapter describes the object representation of a window whilst later chapters deal with the other object types.

The essence of object oriented programming is the separation of an object's functionality into two distinct parts:

1. Implementation
2. Interface

This section explains the meaning of these two terms as interpreted in a C++ context. The object's implementation describes exactly how it will perform its function — the data structures and processing algorithms used by an object define its implementation. These implementation details are hidden within the object and are not visible to the outside world — this is the notion of 'encapsulation'. For the outside world to utilize the functionality provided by the object it must make requests to the object by sending it messages through a well-defined communications interface. In C++ an object's interface is defined as a series of functions and a request is sent to the object by invoking the relevant function — the object may send back a reply as the return value of the function. The following figure illustrates the separation of implementation and interface:

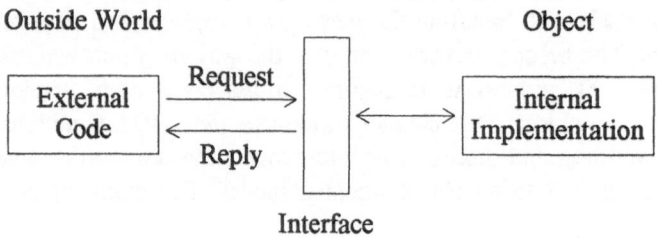

This approach means that the internal implementation can be updated without affecting the external code — the external code continues to make the same function calls. An interface provides the necessary isolation between an object and the outside world to ensure that objects become interchangeable — any object which supports the same interface as the original object can be substituted for it. If the functionality specified for an interface is sufficiently general then the range of interchangeable objects can include a variety of different forms — this is the notion of 'polymorphism'. For example, an interface for a sprite object may require that the object draw an image to the screen when its Draw() function is invoked — some sprite objects will consistently draw the same image but others will update the image in an animation loop.

In summary, the separation of implementation and interface permits both encapsulation and polymorphism — these are the key concepts in object oriented programming.

3.2 The Manager Object

The management of the instance handle for a Windows 98 program will serve as an example of the object oriented approach. The program's instance handle is required in many different calls to the operating system and therefore must be made available throughout the program. In chapter 2 the instance handle was passed around as a parameter to various functions which needed it — treating the handle as a global variable looked to be a better option. However, global variables can be modified by any code in the program and this can lead to bugs that are difficult to track — the problem becomes worse when multiple threads are all executing concurrently. The solution is to centralize the management of the global data and this is clearly the job for an object. The previous section stated that an object's implementation must define the following two items:

1. Data structures
2. Processing algorithms

Hence an object contains not just data but also the code to manipulate this data —
in the case of the instance handle, the data is simply the handle itself whilst the
associated code will set and retrieve this value.

In C++ every object belongs to some class — each class defines the general
characteristics of all the objects within the class. Here is a class specification for the
instance handle example:

```
class MANAGER {
public:
  void SetInstance(HINSTANCE);
  HINSTANCE GetInstance(void) const;
private:
  HINSTANCE Instance;
};
```

The **private** keyword declares the Instance data field as hidden — the result
is that the outside world cannot manipulate the data directly. Instead external code
must invoke the SetInstance() and GetInstance() functions which form
the interface of objects in the MANAGER class. In addition to the private data field
the implementation of a MANAGER object is provided by its function definitions:

```
void MANAGER::SetInstance(HINSTANCE instance) {
  Instance = instance;
}

HINSTANCE MANAGER::GetInstance(void) const {
  return Instance;
}
```

The **const** keyword indicates that the GetInstance() function will not modify
the state of the MANAGER object — hence any code can safely call this function
without corrupting the global data. The use of a MANAGER object is illustrated by
the following code:

```
MANAGER Manager;
Manager.SetInstance(instance);
       .
       .
HINSTANCE handle = Manager.GetInstance();
```

The . operator is used to associate each function call request with a particular
object — here the Manager object is the only one involved. An alternate approach

involves C++ pointers:

```
MANAGER* Manager;
Manager = (MANAGER*) new Manager;
Manager->SetInstance(instance);
     .
     .
HINSTANCE handle = Manager->GetInstance();
     .
     .
delete Manager;
```

Here the `Manager` object is created dynamically with the **new** keyword and a MANAGER* pointer to the new object is obtained — the object is later destroyed with the **delete** keyword. Whilst the object exists the functions in its interface may be invoked using the -> operator instead of the . operator.

In a multi-threaded environment functions such as `SetInstance()` and `GetInstance()` can be extended with the provision of thread synchronization code — this code ensures that if several threads attempt to simultaneously manipulate the global data held by the object then no corruption is possible. The advantage of an object oriented approach is that the synchronization code is centralized and closely associated with the data which it protects.

The following figure illustrates a typical arrangement of source and header files for a C++ program — the source files (with a .cpp extension) contain the program code whilst the header files (with a .h extension) hold class specifications and define various constants:

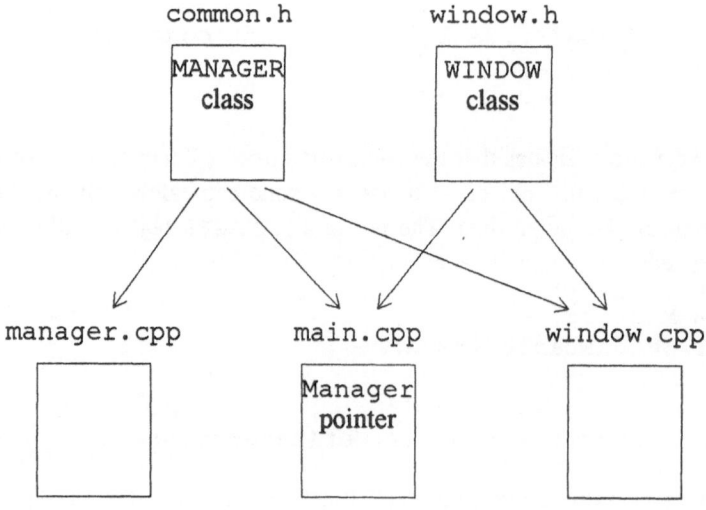

The MANAGER class implementation details are placed in the manager.cpp source file:

```
manager.cpp:

  #include <windows.h>
  #include "common.h"

  void MANAGER::SetInstance(HINSTANCE instance) {
    Instance = instance;
  }

  HINSTANCE MANAGER::GetInstance(void) const {
    return Instance;
  }
```

The Manager object is created in the main.cpp source file — the instance handle (and other global data) is initialized by the WinMain() function within this file:

```
  #include <windows.h>
  #include "common.h"

  MANAGER* Manager;

  int WINAPI
  WinMain(HINSTANCE instance,HINSTANCE,LPSTR,int) {
    Manager = (MANAGER*) new MANAGER;
    Manager->SetInstance(instance);
      .
      .
      .
  }
```

The MANAGER class specification appears in the common.h header — this file is shared throughout the program and will be added to in later chapters.

```
  common.h:

  class MANAGER {
  public:
    void SetInstance(HINSTANCE);
    HINSTANCE GetInstance(void) const;
  private:
    HINSTANCE Instance;
  };

  extern MANAGER* Manager;
```

The **extern** declaration passes the Manager object pointer into any source file that includes the common.h header. For example:

```
window.cpp:

  #include <windows.h>
  #include "common.h"
  #include "window.h"

      .
      .


  HINSTANCE instance = Manager->GetInstance();
```

Hence, global data is passed from the code in main.cpp to other parts of the program.

This section has demonstrated the use of C++ objects — later sections will apply the techniques introduced here to convert the Windows 98 program framework code developed in chapter 2 to an object oriented form.

3.3 Windows and Objects

The next step towards object orientation is the production of a WINDOW class that represents each window with an object. The WINDOW class itself will be identified with a Windows 98 window class — the WINDOW class will provide functions to register and unregister the corresponding window class. Here is a portion of the WINDOW class specification:

```
class WINDOW {
public:
    static int Run(void);
    static void Register(void);
    static void Unregister(void);
       .
       .
};
```

The **static** keyword indicates that the functions belong to the WINDOW class as a whole and not to individual objects. The function definitions are taken directly from the corresponding code in the window.cpp source file of chapter 2. The new window class registration functions are almost identical to the originals — however, there are a couple of modifications:

1. The program instance handle is obtained by calling the Manager object's GetInstance() function

2. Each window has 4 extra bytes of storage allocated to it

The extra storage space is used to hold a pointer to the WINDOW object that corresponds to the window — conversely, each WINDOW object will hold a handle for its window in a Window field. The following figure illustrates the connection between a WINDOW object and the corresponding Windows 98 window:

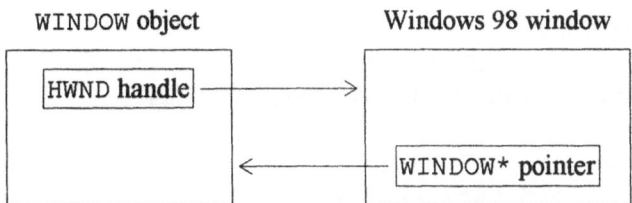

Here are the updated definitions for the class registration functions:

```
void WINDOW::Register(void) {
  WNDCLASS windowclass;
  LPCTSTR icon,cursor;
  HBRUSH brush;
  icon = MAKEINTRESOURCE(IDI_APPLICATION);
  cursor = MAKEINTRESOURCE(IDC_ARROW);
  brush = (HBRUSH) GetStockObject(WHITE_BRUSH);
  windowclass.lpszClassName = "windowclassname";
  windowclass.hInstance = Manager->GetInstance();
  windowclass.lpfnWndProc = WindowProc;
  windowclass.style = CS_HREDRAW|CS_VREDRAW;
  windowclass.lpszMenuName = NULL;
  windowclass.hIcon = LoadIcon(NULL,icon);
  windowclass.hCursor = LoadCursor(NULL,cursor);
  windowclass.hbrBackground = brush;
  windowclass.cbClsExtra = 0;
  windowclass.cbWndExtra = 4;
  RegisterClass(&windowclass);
}

void WINDOW::Unregister(void) {
  UnregisterClass("windowclassname",
    Manager->GetInstance());
}
```

The definition of the Run() function is unchanged from chapter 2 but the function now forms part of the WINDOW class:

```
int WINDOW::Run(void) {
  MSG message;
  while (GetMessage(&message,NULL,0,0))
    DispatchMessage(&message);
  return message.wParam;
}
```

The Run(), Register() and Unregister() functions belong to the WINDOW
class as a whole — the remaining fields and function included in the complete
WINDOW class specification (except the WindowProc() callback function) are
associated with individual WINDOW objects:

```
class WINDOW {
friend LRESULT CALLBACK
   WindowProc(HWND,UINT,WPARAM,LPARAM);
public:
   static int Run(void);
   static void Register(void);
   static void Unregister(void);
   void Create(LPCTSTR);
   void Show(void);
private:
   LRESULT Destroy(HWND,UINT,WPARAM,LPARAM);
       .

       .
   HWND Window;
};
```

The Create() function is invoked to create the object's window and the Show()
function will make this window visible — for example:

```
WINDOW window;
window.Create("Title");
window.Show();
```

The function definitions are taken from chapter 2 but modified as follows:

```
void WINDOW::Create(LPCTSTR title) {
   DWORD style = WS_OVERLAPPEDWINDOW;
   HMENU menu = NULL;
   HWND parent = NULL;
   LPVOID params = this;
   Window =
      CreateWindow(...,Manager->GetInstance(),params);
}

void WINDOW::Show(void) {
   ShowWindow(Window,SW_SHOW);
}
```

The interesting point is that the window handle is now stored in the Window field
of the WINDOW object — the external code no longer needs to worry about
managing this handle. Furthermore, a pointer to the WINDOW object is passed as
the params argument to the CreateWindow() function — the this keyword
supplies a pointer to the current object. The object pointer will be stored in the four

extra bytes allocated for the window — this action occurs in the WM_CREATE handler of the WindowProc() callback function. The callback function is declared as a friend of the WINDOW class to allow it to invoke message handlers such as Destroy() which the WINDOW class provides:

```
LRESULT CALLBACK
WindowProc(HWND window,UINT message,
            WPARAM wparam,LPARAM lparam) {
  if (message == WM_CREATE) {
   CREATESTRUCT* createstruct;
   createstruct = (CREATESTRUCT*)lparam;
   SetWindowLong(window,0,
     (LONG)(createstruct->lpCreateParams));
   return 0;
  }
  WINDOW* object = (WINDOW*)GetWindowLong(window,0);
  if (object) {
   if (message == WM_DESTROY)
    return object->Destroy(window,message,
                                 wparam,lparam);
     .
     .
  }
  return DefWindowProc(window,message,wparam,lparam);
}
```

This function is modelled on the WindowProc() function presented in chapter 2. The type of the message is determined by examining the message parameter and an appropriate message handler is invoked — if the message type is not explicitly handled then the message is passed along to the DefWindowProc() function. However, the message handlers are now provided by the WINDOW object associated with the window. A WINDOW* pointer to this C++ object is stored in the window's extra bytes by calling the SetWindowLong() function — the function GetWindowLong() retrieves the pointer when needed. The pointer arrives with the WM_CREATE message and is held in the lpCreateParams field of a CREATESTRUCT structure — a pointer to this structure is supplied as the lparam parameter of the callback function. Before the WM_CREATE message has been processed the GetWindowLong() function will retrieve a null pointer and so all earlier messages are passed to the DefWindowProc() function. The only other handler mentioned here is for the WM_DESTROY message:

```
LRESULT
WINDOW::Destroy(HWND window,UINT message,
                   WPARAM wparam,LPARAM lparam) {
   PostQuitMessage(0);
   return 0;
}
```

Additional messages can be handled by including new message handler functions in the WINDOW class and adding extra tests to the WindowProc() callback function — section 3.6 describes an alternative approach based on C++ inheritance.

Finally, the WinMain() function is rewritten to use the WINDOW class:

```
int WINAPI
WinMain(HINSTANCE instance,HINSTANCE,LPSTR,int) {
    .
    .
  WINDOW::Register();
  WINDOW window;
  window.Create("Test Program");
  window.Show();
  return WINDOW::Run();
}
```

The Windows 98 program is now fully object oriented — all the implementation details are hidden and the functionality is available through an easy-to-use interface consisting of the Register(), Create(), Show() and Run() functions.

3.4 Message Boxes

The basic WINDOW class will be extended in section 3.6 so that it can handle a wider range of messages. In particular the WM_CLOSE message will be processed — this message is generated when a user requests closure of a window. A common approach is to display a message box that asks the user to confirm the request — the MessageBox() function provides a quick way to communicate with the user. The following figure illustrates a typical message box:

The message box displays the program name in its title bar and also some message text — an optional icon may be added and a selection of buttons provided. Here the following call to the MessageBox() function is made:

```
MessageBox(window,"Ready to Quit?",
  "Test Program",MB_ICONQUESTION|MB_YESNO);
```

The icon and buttons are specified by passing various flags as the final function parameter. The range of available icons (together with the corresponding flags) includes the following:

 MB_ICONINFORMATION   MB_ICONQUESTION

 MB_ICONEXCLAMATION   MB_ICONSTOP

These icons denote various degrees of urgency — the sudden appearance of a message box with a stop icon can be very disconcerting. Similarly the button options include:

```
MB_OK
MB_OKCANCEL
MB_YESNO
MB_YESNOCANCEL
```

The MessageBox() function returns a code that indicates which button was pressed to close the message box — for example:

```
IDOK
IDYES
IDNO
IDCANCEL
```

The return code can be used to modify the subsequent behaviour of the program — for example, the WM_CLOSE message handler may or may not destroy a window depending on the user's response to its prompt for confirmation of the window closure request. Message boxes are not particularly useful in a finished graphics application but they can help out during debugging.

3.5 Popup Menus

A slightly more sophisticated way of communicating with the user is through a menu — many windows provide a menu bar or alternatively a popup menu can be activated by right-clicking in the window area. The processing for both types of menu is similar and only popup menus are discussed here. A menu may be designed graphically and made available as a program resource — the next chapter looks at Windows 98 resources in some detail. However, it is very easy to create a menu programmatically:

```
HMENU Menu = CreatePopupMenu();
AppendMenu(Menu,MF_STRING,IDM_CHECK,"&Check");
AppendMenu(Menu,MF_SEPARATOR,0,NULL);
AppendMenu(Menu,MF_STRING,IDM_QUIT,"&Quit");
```

These lines of code create a popup menu with two items (`Check` and `Quit`) that are separated by a horizontal bar:

In the menu item strings the & symbol causes the following letter to be underlined — this allows the menu items to be selected using the keyboard. The menu ID values `IDM_CHECK` and `IDM_QUIT` are defined in a header file — they will be used to identify the individual menu items within the menu's message handler.

The popup menu is displayed with the `TrackPopupMenu()` function — this function contains all the functionality necessary to track the mouse pointer as it moves over the various menu items. Just as the `MessageBox()` function waits for a button to be pressed so the `TrackPopupMenu()` function waits until a menu item is selected. When this eventually happens a `WM_COMMAND` message is placed in the message queue to indicate which item was selected — the appropriate actions to take in response to the menu selection are coded into the `WM_COMMAND` message handler. The popup menu may be displayed again and again simply by calling the `TrackPopupMenu()` function — whenever the menu is no longer required it should be destroyed using the `DestroyMenu()` function. The following figure illustrates the sequence of events involved:

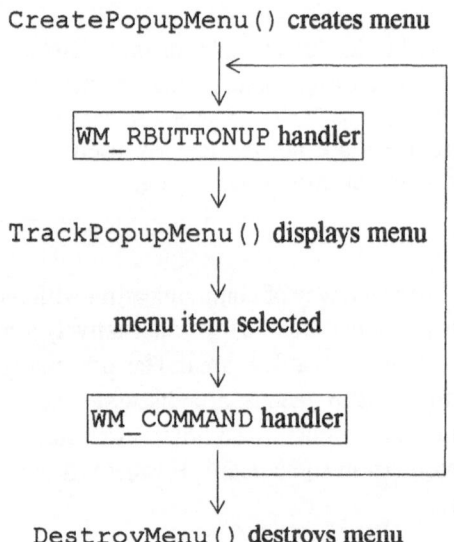

The next section will show how popup menus (and message boxes) are integrated into a Windows 98 application. By way of an introduction the popup menu is packaged into a MENU class. The approach is similar to that adopted for the Microsoft Foundation Class (MFC) library — many of these classes simply package the functionality provided by Windows 98 API functions. The MENU class discussed here is too specific for general use but it illustrates some important ideas about C++ objects — the class has the following specification:

```
class MENU {
public:
  MENU(void);
  ~MENU(void);
  void Show(HWND,int,int);
  void Check(int);
private:
  HMENU Menu;
};
```

The MENU() function is a 'constructor' for the MENU class and the ~MENU() function is the class 'destructor' — these kinds of function play an important role in C++ programming. A constructor is automatically invoked to initialize new objects of a particular class — similarly a destructor is called when an object is destroyed so that it can release any resources which it still holds. The definitions for the MENU class constructor and destructor are straightforward:

```
MENU::MENU(void) {
  Menu = CreatePopupMenu();
  AppendMenu(Menu,MF_STRING, IDM_CHECK,"&Check");
  AppendMenu(Menu,MF_SEPARATOR,0,NULL);
  AppendMenu(Menu,MF_STRING, IDM_QUIT,"&Quit");
}

MENU::~MENU(void) {
  DestroyMenu(Menu);
}
```

The constructor and destructor functions provide an alternative to explicit initialization and finalization. For example, each WINDOW object calls its Create() function to perform initialization rather than relying on a constructor — the next section discusses why this option is chosen. The Show() function is responsible for displaying the popup menu:

```
void MENU::Show(HWND window,int x,int y) {
  POINT point = {x,y};
  ClientToScreen(window,&point);
  UINT flags = TPM_CENTERALIGN|TPM_LEFTBUTTON;
  TrackPopupMenu(Menu,flags,
    point.x,point.y,0,window,NULL);
}
```

The Show() function takes parameters that specify the parent window of the menu and the coordinates within the parent window where the menu should be displayed. Finally, the MENU class Check() function may be called to add or remove a checkmark on the Check menu item — the request is passed along to the Windows 98 CheckMenuItem() function:

```
void MENU::Check(int check) {
if (check)
   CheckMenuItem(Menu,IDM_CHECK,MF_CHECKED);
else
   CheckMenuItem(Menu,IDM_CHECK,MF_UNCHECKED);
}
```

The Show() and Check() functions provide an interface through which the functionality of the MENU object is made available to the rest of the program — the management of the associated popup menu is hidden as implementation detail.

3.6 The VIEW Class

One approach to using the WINDOW class is to modify it for each new project — an alternative is to transform the WINDOW class into a C++ base class. In the latter case a VIEW class can be derived from the WINDOW base class thereby inheriting its basic functionality — any specializations required for a particular application are applied to the VIEW class. The key point is that the WINDOW base class is able to define an interface (see section 3.1) whose implementation is actually provided by the derived VIEW classes — the base class may supply a default implementation for those functions not explicitly defined by a particular derived class. This mechanism is supported in C++ by virtual functions — these are denoted in the class specification using the **virtual** keyword. The C++ language allows virtual functions to be 'overridden' by a derived class under the following circumstances:

— A base class pointer refers to an object from a derived class
— A virtual function is invoked using the base class pointer
— The derived class redefines the virtual function

In this case the derived class version of the virtual function overrides the one supplied by the base class. Here the base and derived classes are the WINDOW and VIEW classes respectively and the object pointer (of WINDOW* type) in the WindowProc() callback function (see section 3.3) will refer to a VIEW object — if the VIEW class redefines any of the virtual functions from the WINDOW class then these new versions will be invoked by the callback function. Hence the VIEW class can modify the basic behaviour of the WINDOW class to suit the individual requirements of the current application.

When derived classes are involved the C++ language provides the **protected** keyword to permit a finer degree of protection control for the fields and functions of a class — whereas the **public** keyword provides no protection and the **private** keyword allows only objects belonging to the class to use its fields and functions, the **protected** keyword treats objects from derived classes much the same as those from the base class. In particular, the new WINDOW class will define its Window and Count fields using the **protected** keyword — these fields can then be manipulated directly within functions of the derived VIEW class. The WINDOW base class will similarly define its Dispatch(), Initialize() and Destroy() functions as protected functions.

The updated specification for the WINDOW class follows:

```
class WINDOW {
friend LRESULT CALLBACK
  WindowProc(HWND,UINT,WPARAM,LPARAM);
public:
  static int Run(void);
  static void Register(void);
  static void Unregister(void);
  void Create(LPCTSTR);
  void Show(void);
protected:
  virtual LRESULT
    Dispatch(HWND,UINT,WPARAM,LPARAM);
  virtual LRESULT
    Initialize(HWND,UINT,WPARAM,LPARAM);
  virtual LRESULT
    Destroy(HWND,UINT,WPARAM,LPARAM);
  HWND Window;
  static int Count;
};
```

The Run(), Register(), Unregister() and Show() functions maintain their previous definitions from section 3.3 but the remaining functions are modified slightly. There are also a couple of other changes:

1. A static Count field holds the number of active windows

2. The Dispatch() and Initialize() message handlers are new

The Count field must be initialized with a global declaration statement:

```
int WINDOW::Count = 0;
```

The value of Count is incremented by each call to the Create() function:

```
void WINDOW::Create(LPCTSTR title) {
   .
   .
   Count++;
}
```

The remainder of the Create() function is unchanged — it creates a new window and stores the window handle in the Window field. The Destroy() handler for the WM_DESTROY message uses the value of Count to determine when to post the WM_QUIT message:

```
LRESULT
WINDOW::Destroy(HWND window,UINT message,
                WPARAM wparam,LPARAM lparam) {
   if (--Count == 0)
     PostQuitMessage(0);
   return 0;
}
```

The program will only exit its message loop whenever the last active window is destroyed.

The callback function WindowProc() is updated to accommodate the new Initialize() and Dispatch() message handlers — the Initialize() handler is called upon receipt of a WM_CREATE message whilst the Dispatch() handler is invoked for all messages except WM_CREATE and WM_DESTROY.

```
LRESULT CALLBACK
WindowProc(HWND window,UINT message,
           WPARAM wparam,LPARAM lparam) {
   .
   .
   if (object) {
     if (message == WM_CREATE)
       return object->Initialize(window,message,
                                 wparam,lparam);
     if (message == WM_DESTROY)
       return object->Destroy(window,message,
                              wparam,lparam);
     return object->Dispatch(window,message,
                             wparam,lparam);
   }
   return
     DefWindowProc(window,message,wparam,lparam);
}
```

The Initialize() and Dispatch() handlers provide default processing:

```
LRESULT
WINDOW::Initialize(HWND window,UINT message,
                   WPARAM wparam,LPARAM lparam) {
  return 0;
}

LRESULT
WINDOW::Dispatch(HWND window,UINT message,
                 WPARAM wparam,LPARAM lparam) {
  return
    DefWindowProc(window,message,wparam,lparam);
}
```

The WINDOW class Initialize(), Dispatch() and Destroy() functions are designed to be overridden by corresponding functions in the VIEW class. The VIEW class can place its own initialization and finalization code in the overriding versions of the Initialize() and Destroy() functions respectively — alternative locations for this code are the VIEW class constructor and destructor functions. Finally, if a VIEW object needs to handle any new message types it should test for them in the VIEW class Dispatch() function — the Dispatch() function will pass the messages along to the corresponding message handler functions supplied by the VIEW class.

The VIEW class is now derived from the WINDOW base class — the example program presented in this section includes both a message box and a popup menu. The popup menu is packaged in the MENU class of section 3.5 whilst the MessageBox() function is called directly and is viewed simply as an implementation detail of the VIEW class.

```
class MENU;

class VIEW : public WINDOW {
public:
  VIEW(LPCTSTR);
  ~VIEW(void);
protected:
  virtual LRESULT
    Dispatch(HWND,UINT,WPARAM,LPARAM);
private:
  LRESULT Paint(HWND,UINT,WPARAM,LPARAM);
  LRESULT ButtonUp(HWND,UINT,WPARAM,LPARAM);
  LRESULT Command(HWND,UINT,WPARAM,LPARAM);
  LRESULT Close(HWND,UINT,WPARAM,LPARAM);
  MENU* Menu;
  int Check;
};
```

Each VIEW object holds a pointer to its associated MENU object. The forward declaration for the MENU class avoids the necessity of including the menu.h header whenever the VIEW class is required — this is not possible if the VIEW class embeds the MENU object directly rather than using a pointer. The Dispatch() message handler is overridden so that the WM_PAINT, WM_RBUTTONUP, WM_COMMAND and WM_CLOSE messages can be handled explicitly:

```
LRESULT
VIEW::Dispatch(HWND window,UINT message,
                    WPARAM wparam,LPARAM lparam) {
  if (message == WM_PAINT)
   return Paint(window,message,wparam,lparam);
  if (message == WM_RBUTTONUP)
   return ButtonUp(window,message,wparam,lparam);
  if (message == WM_COMMAND)
   return Command(window,message,wparam,lparam);
  if (message == WM_CLOSE)
   return Close(window,message,wparam,lparam);
  return
   WINDOW::Dispatch(window,message,wparam,lparam);
}
```

The VIEW class constructor initializes the Check field and creates a new MENU object:

```
VIEW::VIEW(LPCTSTR title) {
  Check = 0;
  Menu = (MENU*) new MENU;
  Create(title);
};
```

The MENU object is destroyed by the VIEW class destructor:

```
VIEW::~VIEW(void) {
  delete Menu;
}
```

The VIEW class constructor also creates a Windows 98 window with a call to the base class Create() function. This method of initialization is preferred to the alternative of creating the window in a WINDOW class constructor because virtual functions are not overridden if invoked whilst a base class constructor is executing — the current approach ensures that the Initialize() function can be overridden successfully by the VIEW class.

The Check field is used to control the action of the WM_PAINT message handler:

```
LRESULT VIEW::Paint(HWND window,UINT message,
                      WPARAM wparam,LPARAM lparam) {
  PAINTSTRUCT paint;
  HDC dc = BeginPaint(window,&paint);
  RECT rect;
  GetClientRect(window,&rect);
  LPCTSTR text = (Check?"Goodbye!":"Hello!");
  UINT flags = DT_CENTER|DT_VCENTER|DT_SINGLELINE;
  DrawText(dc,text,-1,&rect,flags);
  EndPaint(window,&paint);
  return 0;
}
```

The value of Check may be flipped by selecting the Check item from the popup menu. The popup menu is activated by right-clicking — the message handler for the WM_RBUTTONUP message is defined as follows:

```
LRESULT VIEW::ButtonUp(HWND window,UINT message,
                        WPARAM wparam,LPARAM lparam) {
  int x = LOWORD(lparam);
  int y = HIWORD(lparam);
  Menu->Show(window,x,y);
  return 0;
}
```

The current position of the mouse pointer is supplied in the lparam parameter and is decoded with the LOWORD and HIWORD macros. The popup menu is displayed by invoking the Show() function of the Menu object. When the Show() function returns it has already posted a WM_COMMAND message to the message queue and this will indicate which menu item was selected — the VIEW class Command() function will handle the WM_COMMAND message:

```
LRESULT VIEW::Command(HWND window,UINT message,
                       WPARAM wparam,LPARAM lparam) {
  int code = HIWORD(wparam);
  int menuID = LOWORD(wparam);
  if (!code)
    if (menuID == IDM_CHECK) {
      Check = 1-Check;
      Menu->Check(Check);
      InvalidateRect(window,NULL,TRUE);
    }
    else if (menuID == IDM_QUIT)
      PostMessage(window,WM_CLOSE,0,0);
  return 0;
}
```

From an object oriented perspective these actions could be viewed as the VIEW and
MENU objects holding a small conversation — the VIEW object asks the MENU
object to elicit a response from the user and then the MENU object informs the
VIEW object of the user's choice so that it can perform the appropriate processing.
When the Command() function is called the wparam parameter supplies the ID
value of the selected menu item as well as a command code — this code is always
zero for menu commands. If the Check menu item is selected then the Check
field is flipped and the Check() function of the Menu object is invoked to update
the menu item checkmark. The call to the InvalidateRect() function requests
that the window contents be redrawn — the next chapter examines this process in
more detail. Alternatively if the Quit menu item is selected a WM_CLOSE message
is posted to request closure of the window. This message is received by the
WM_CLOSE handler:

```
LRESULT
VIEW::Close(HWND window,UINT message,
            WPARAM wparam,LPARAM lparam) {
  char title[1000];
  GetWindowText(window,title,1000);
  LPCTSTR text = "Ready to Quit?";
  UINT flags = MB_ICONQUESTION|MB_YESNO;
  int code = MessageBox(window,text,title,flags);
  if (code == IDYES)
    DestroyWindow(window);
  return 0;
}
```

The handler displays a message box asking for confirmation of the window closure
request — the window is only destroyed if the Yes button is pressed. The message
box title is copied from the parent window using the GetWindowText()
function.

All the message handlers are now defined and so it just remains to write a suitable
WinMain() function:

```
int WINAPI
WinMain(HINSTANCE instance,HINSTANCE,LPSTR,int) {
    .
    .
  VIEW::Register();
  VIEW view("Test Program");
  view.Show();
  return VIEW::Run();
}
```

The Register(), Show() and Run() functions inherited from the WINDOW
class are available to the VIEW class. When the view object is created its

constructor is automatically invoked and passed the window title string "Test Program" as an argument — the constructor creates a Windows 98 window with a call to the WINDOW class Create() function and passes along this string. The following figure shows the program in action:

3.7 Summary

This chapter has provided an introduction to object oriented programming and its use in writing Windows 98 applications. The essential idea in object oriented programming is to separate the internal implementation of an object from the interface presented to the outside world — a request is made by invoking a function in the object's interface and a reply may be sent back as the function return value. The implementation comprises two elements: the object's personal data structures and code to manipulate this data. The separation of implementation and interface enables both encapsulation and polymorphism — these are key concepts in object oriented programming. Encapsulation refers to the hiding of implementation details within an object — polymorphism occurs when a collection of objects are sent identical messages but they each exhibit their own individual behaviours. In C++ every object belongs to some class — the class provides a blue-print for each of the objects created from the class. Whenever a new object is created the class constructor is automatically invoked to initialize the object — similarly a call is made to the class destructor when the object is eventually destroyed. Object implementation details can be encapsulated by use of the **private** and **protected** keywords in the class specification — the **public** keyword is applied to functions in the object's interface. One C++ class may be derived from another by the mechanism of inheritance — the derived class inherits the characteristcs of the base class but may modify or extend these characteristcs as required. If a base class function is designated as being virtual it can be redefined in a derived class and the new version invoked through a base class pointer that references a derived class object — real (non-virtual) functions from the base class are not overridden in this situation. The MANAGER and MENU classes illustrated many of the basic techniques for programming with C++ objects. Two versions of the WINDOW class have also been defined — this class embodies the code developed in chapter 2 and is designed to provide a Windows 98 program framework. The first version of the WINDOW class is intended to be updated for each new project whereas the second acts as a fixed base class for a range of derived VIEW classes. Finally, the chapter also discussed two ways of using the graphical items provided by Windows 98. The first alternative is to make direct calls to the Windows 98 API functions and treat these calls simply as the implementation detail of some C++ object — for example, the MessageBox() function was called directly by a VIEW class message handler. The second option is to package the API functions within a new C++ class and then associate each C++ object with a Windows 98 graphical item — the WINDOW and MENU classes are two examples of this approach.

4. Pens and Brushes

The previous chapters have laid the foundations for creating a Windows 98 graphics application — the facilities which Windows 98 provides specifically to support such an application now need to be investigated a little more deeply. This chapter introduces the Graphics Device Interface (GDI) and discusses how it may be applied to the creation of graphical images. The following topics are covered in some detail:

— device contexts
— the WM_PAINT message handler
— Windows 98 coordinate systems
— pens and brushes
— drawing lines and filling rectangles
— accepting user input from the mouse

The chapter concludes with a couple of simple graphics applications that are built around two versions of the VIEW class. The additional code required for each application is minimal — this is a good example of software reuse and it demonstrates the power of object oriented programming.

4.1 Graphics Device Interface

The Windows 98 operating system is arranged into a number of component blocks each responsible for some aspect of system management — the component most closely involved with drawing is the Graphics Device Interface (GDI). This chapter shows how to use the functionality provided by the GDI to produce a variety of graphics applications — the WINDOW base class supplies the basic program framework whilst the graphics-related code will be placed in a derived VIEW class. The GDI manages graphical objects such as pens, brushes, bitmaps and palettes — the fundamental operation of the GDI is explained here by considering only pens and brushes whilst the following chapters deal with bitmaps and palettes. Each of the GDI objects in some way controls the action of the drawing routines provided by the GDI. A pen determines the properties of lines drawn by the GDI whilst a brush affects how the GDI fills in various areas of the screen — for example, the WINDOW class uses a WHITE_BRUSH to fill in the entire background of a window when it needs to be repainted.

An important notion to understand is that of a 'device context' — instead of passing lots of parameters to every call to a GDI function, a device context is established which holds the default values for most of the parameters. In particular, each device context holds a pen to control line drawing and a brush for shape-filling operations. Furthermore, the device contexts considered here each refer to a particular window — the next chapter will examine device contexts which draw to an off-screen bitmap rather than to a window. Windows 98 uses handles to identify many items such as windows and menus — each device context is similarly identified by a device context handle (HDC). The BeginPaint() function invoked in a WM_PAINT message handler returns a handle for the device context associated with the window receiving the message — the message handler can then use this device context to redraw the window. For example:

```
LRESULT
VIEW::Paint(HWND window,UINT message,
            WPARAM wparam,LPARAM lparam) {
  PAINTSTRUCT paint;
  HDC dc = BeginPaint(window,&paint);
  // redraw window here
  EndPaint(window,&paint);
  return 0;
}
```

There is a lot of activity concealed here which is worth examining in greater detail — a good place to start is to assume that the WM_PAINT message originated in a call to the InvalidateRect() function:

```
RECT rect;
BOOL erase;
InvalidateRect(window,&rect,erase);
```

The rect parameter defines a rectangular area of the window that should be redrawn — if a NULL pointer is passed instead then the whole window is redrawn. The boolean flag erase indicates whether or not the background of the window is erased before any drawing takes place. Invoking the InvalidateRect() function only requests that the window be updated and does not actually change the window contents — however, the function does ensure that there is a WM_PAINT message in the program's message queue. A number of redraw requests may accumulate before the WM_PAINT message is eventually received by the Paint() message handler function — the rectangles from each of these requests are combined into an 'update region'. Of course, the redraw requests may also originate from user interaction with the window — for example, the user may resize the window or remove another overlapping window. In any case the update region is used by BeginPaint() to set a 'clipping region' for the window's device context — any drawing performed outside the clipping region is invisible. If any of the redraw requests indicate that the window background should be erased, then the BeginPaint() function sends a WM_ERASEBKGND message — by default this erases the update region using the brush specified when the window class was registered. Finally, BeginPaint() validates the update region so that the WM_PAINT message is not returned to the message queue.

The device context supplied by the BeginPaint() function may be used to draw to the update region. Since BeginPaint() has already set the clipping region for this device context, a simple approach is to redraw the entire window and let the GDI take care of clipping to the requested update region. After completion of the redraw operation the device context must be released — the 'acquire-use-release' procedure is common in the sharing world of Windows 98 where limited resources are made available to more than one program. The EndPaint() function is responsible for releasing the device context — it obtains a handle for the device context from the paint structure which BeginPaint() initialized.

There are a few more functions for dealing with device contexts that are useful for a graphics application. The BeginPaint() and EndPaint() functions should only be called within a WM_PAINT message handler — however, a graphics program which performs animation may require a very high frame rate and it is then desirable to place the drawing code outside the WM_PAINT message handler. There are of course alternatives to the BeginPaint() and EndPaint() functions — given a window handle the GetDC() function will retrieve the window's device context and the ReleaseDC() function will release it. In this case the clipping region is not automatically set for the device context but the GetUpdateRect() function will provide an 'update rectangle' — the update rectangle is the smallest rectangle which bounds the window's current update region. Finally, the validation of the update rectangle provided automatically by BeginPaint() can instead be performed by a call to ValidateRect().

To move an image from one place to another often requires two device contexts. The first device context specifies the source of the image whilst the second defines the destination — for example, the contents of one window can be copied to another or an image can be sent to a printer. As discussed in the next chapter, a graphics application often stores images in memory as bitmaps — a 'memory device context' is required here and this can be created with the CreateCompatibleDC() function. The following WM_PAINT handler uses two device contexts:

```
LRESULT VIEW::Paint(HWND window,UINT message,
                    WPARAM wparam,LPARAM lparam) {
    PAINTSTRUCT paint;
    HDC windowdc = BeginPaint(window,&paint);
    HDC memorydc = CreateCompatibleDC(windowdc);
    // transfer bitmap to window
    DeleteDC(memorydc);
    EndPaint(window,&paint);
    return 0;
}
```

The window device context is obtained from BeginPaint() whilst the memory device context is created by calling the function CreateCompatibleDC(). The first device context is released by EndPaint() but the other must be destroyed using the DeleteDC() function. The two device contexts enable a bitmap image to be transferred to the screen.

4.2 GDI Objects

When Windows 98 provides a device context it uses default values to initialize the various objects (pen, brush, font, bitmap, palette, clipping region and so on) which the device context holds. These objects can all be referred to by handles of the appropriate types (HPEN, HBRUSH, HFONT, HBITMAP, HPALETTE, HRGN) or by generic GDI object handles (HGDIOBJ). The procedure for updating the default values is as follows:

1. Select a new object into the device context and save the handle of the old object
2. Perform any necessary processing using the new object
3. Use the saved handle to select the old object back into the device context

A device context should not be released or destroyed until it again holds all its original objects — of course, a whole sequence of new objects may be selected before the device context is eventually restored to its initial state. A program can obtain new GDI objects either by requesting stock objects from Windows 98 or by explicitly creating the objects itself. In the latter case each object must be created before selection into the device context and destroyed only after it is displaced by another object — stock objects supplied by the operating system need not be destroyed by the program. Apart from palettes (which are covered in chapter 6) each of the GDI objects may be selected in and out of a device context using the SelectObject() function — the return value from the function provides a handle for the displaced object. For example:

```
LRESULT VIEW::Paint(HWND window,UINT message,
                    WPARAM wparam,LPARAM lparam) {
  PAINTSTRUCT paint;
  HDC dc = BeginPaint(window,&paint);
  HPEN oldpen = (HPEN)
    SelectObject(dc,GetStockObject(BLACK_PEN));
  HBRUSH brush, oldbrush;
  brush = CreateSolidBrush(RGB(255,0,0));
  oldbrush = (HBRUSH)SelectObject(dc,brush);
  // perform drawing here
  SelectObject(dc,oldpen);
  SelectObject(dc,oldbrush);
  DeleteObject(brush);
  EndPaint(window,&paint);
  return 0;
}
```

Here the `GetStockObject()` function is used to obtain a `HGDIOBJ` handle for the chosen stock object (`BLACK_PEN`) — this handle is not stored as there is no need to destroy the stock object later. By contrast the handle for the explicitly created brush object must be saved so that it can eventually be destroyed by the `DeleteObject()` function. The `RGB()` macro is used to specify the colour of the brush (bright red) — section 5.1 discusses `RGB` colours in more detail.

When a call is made to the `SelectObject()` function it returns a `HGDIOBJ` handle for the displaced GDI object — this generic handle should be cast to a handle of the appropriate type. Here `HGDIOBJ` handles are cast to `HPEN` and `HBRUSH` handles before saving them in the `oldpen` and `oldbrush` variables respectively — the original objects are restored by selecting them back into the device context with the saved handles. When the device context is finally released by the `EndPaint()` function it holds exactly the same objects as it did when supplied by `BeginPaint()`.

4.3 Windows 98 Coordinate Systems

Before actually drawing anything using the GDI it is important to understand the various coordinate systems used by Windows 98. The units involved are usually 'pixels' — one pixel (picture element) corresponds to each dot of colour on the screen. A point is specified by a (x,y) coordinate pair which gives the point's horizontal and vertical offset relative to some origin — the following figure demonstrates the idea:

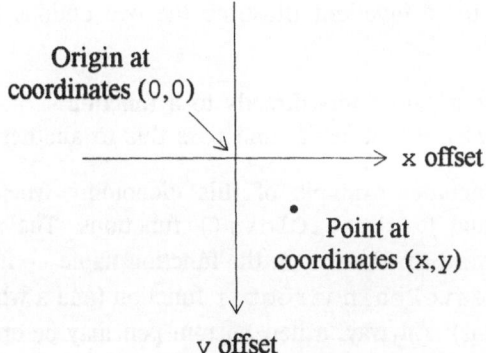

The strange thing about Windows 98 coordinate systems is that the y-axis typically points towards the bottom of the screen — the top left corner of the screen (or a window) acts as the origin of the coordinate system. In fact Windows 98 commonly use three types of coordinates:

— Screen coordinates
— Window coordinates
— Client coordinates

The three types are distinguished by the location of the origin — screen coordinates have their origin fixed at the top left corner of the screen but the other two types define their origin relative to a particular window. The origin of a window coordinate system is positioned at the top left corner of the whole window (including title bar and window frame) whilst a client coordinate system has its origin at the top left corner of the window's drawable area. It is possible to convert from client coordinates to screen coordinates with the ClientToScreen() function — the reverse transformation is performed by the ScreenToClient() function. As an example of the usage of different coordinate systems, messages from the mouse supply position data as client coordinates whilst the GetCursorPos() function retrieves the current location of the mouse pointer in screen coordinates.

Finally, the functions GetWindowRect() and GetClientRect() provide the rectangular extents of a window and its drawable area respectively — the former function specifies the extents in screen coordinates whilst the latter uses client coordinates instead. The GetDesktopWindow() function returns a handle to the desktop window — this can be used to determine the size of the screen.

4.4 GDI Drawing Functions

The GDI provides functions to make drawing with pens and brushes easy — as noted in section 4.2 the GetStockObject() function will supply a number of stock pens and brushes defined by Windows 98. This section will use the CreatePen() and CreateBrushIndirect() functions to create custom pens and brushes — these functions illustrate the two options for creating new objects in Windows 98:

1. Pass a list of creation parameters directly to a function
2. Fill in an object descriptor structure and pass this to another function

Chapter 2 provided another example of this dichotomy when discussing the CreateWindow() and RegisterClass() functions. The second option is often denoted by the word Indirect in the function name — in particular, note that there is also a CreatePenIndirect() function (and a whole host of other brush creation functions). Anyway, a new custom pen may be created as follows:

```
HPEN pen = CreatePen(PS_SOLID,0,RGB(0,0,0));
```

The first parameter specifies the pen style (PS_SOLID) — pens that draw dotted or dashed lines may also be created with an appropriate choice of style (PS_DOT or PS_DASH). The second parameter defines the thickness of the line in logical units — the default logical units for a device context are pixels but this can be changed with the SetMapMode() function. A value of zero for the thickness parameter ensures that the pen draws lines which are always one pixel wide regardless of the current logical units. Finally, the last parameter to the CreatePen() function sets the colour of the pen — here the pen is black. In fact exactly the same type of pen is available as a stock object:

```
HPEN pen = (HPEN)GetStockObject(BLACK_PEN);
```

Similarly, the generic `CreateBrushIndirect()` function provides flexibility not available with the specialized `CreateSolidBrush()` alternative from section 4.2 — for example:

```
LOGBRUSH logicalbrush;
logicalbrush.lbStyle = BS_SOLID;
logicalbrush.lbColor = RGB(255,0,0);
HBRUSH brush;
brush = CreateBrushIndirect(&logicalbrush);
```

A logical brush (LOGBRUSH) structure is used to describe the type of brush to create — there are similar structures (LOGPEN, LOGFONT, LOGPALETTE) for pens, fonts and palettes. Here a brush is created which paints in a solid red colour — other choices for the brush style generate brushes which hatch, cross-hatch or even draw a specific user-defined pattern.

The black pen and red brush created above can now be used to draw a simple design. The `FillRect()` function will fill a rectangle using a brush passed as a parameter — unlike the majority of GDI functions `FillRect()` ignores the brush currently selected into the device context. The position of the rectangle is specified with a RECT structure — as noted in section 2.5 this comprises the four fields left, top, right and bottom. The left and top fields locate the pixel at the top left-hand corner of the rectangle — this pixel is inside the rectangle. However, the pixel at the bottom right-hand corner of the rectangle is positioned at the coordinates (right-1,bottom-1) and the point (right,bottom) falls outside the rectangle. The following figure illustrates this arrangement:

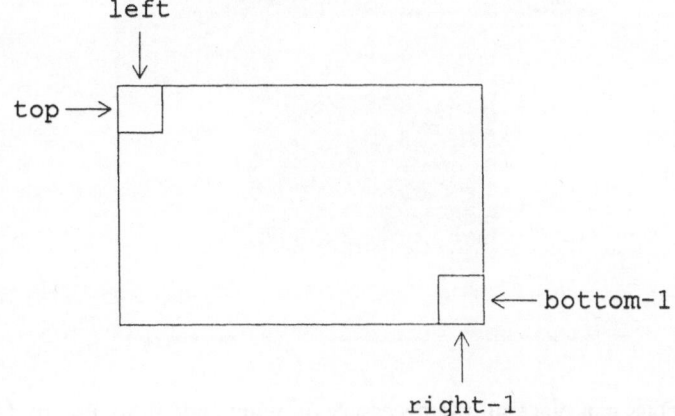

The is the usual convention for representing a rectangle throughout Windows 98 — for example, the update rectangle associated with a WM_PAINT message is represented in this way. The reason for this approach is simple — the width of a rectangle then equals right-left and the height equals bottom-top.

The following code will fill the centre of a window with a red rectangle:

```
RECT rect;
GetClientRect(window,&rect);
InflateRect(&rect,-rect.right/4,-rect.bottom/4);
FillRect(dc,&rect,brush);
```

The call to InflateRect() deflates the area of the drawable area to quarter size. Now the black pen can be used to draw upon the red rectangle by calling the MoveToEx() and LineTo() functions. Both these functions work with a value held by the device context referred to as the 'current point' — the MoveToEx() function moves the current point to a specific location on the screen and the LineTo() function draws a line from the current point to a new point. In fact, the line produced by the LineTo() function stops just short of the new point — this point becomes the current point and the next call to the LineTo() function will update the pixel there. Here is the code to draw diagonals across the red rectangle:

```
MoveToEx(dc,rect.left,rect.top,NULL);
LineTo(dc,rect.right,rect.bottom);
OffsetRect(&rect,0,-1);
MoveToEx(dc,rect.left,rect.bottom,NULL);
LineTo(dc,rect.right,rect.top);
```

The following figure illustrates the completed design:

The VIEW class can place all the necessary drawing code in its Paint() function which then acts as the message handler for the WM_PAINT message:

```
LRESULT
VIEW::Paint(HWND window,UINT message,
            WPARAM wparam,LPARAM lparam) {
  // initialize
  PAINTSTRUCT paint;
  HDC dc = BeginPaint(window,&paint);
  HPEN oldpen = (HPEN)SelectObject(dc,Pen);
  // redraw window
  RECT rect;
  GetClientRect(window,&rect);
  InflateRect(&rect,-rect.right/4,-rect.bottom/4);
  FillRect(dc,&rect,Brush);
  MoveToEx(dc,rect.left,rect.top,NULL);
  LineTo(dc,rect.right,rect.bottom);
  OffsetRect(&rect,0,-1);
  MoveToEx(dc,rect.left,rect.bottom,NULL);
  LineTo(dc,rect.right,rect.top);
  // finalize
  SelectObject(dc,oldpen);
  EndPaint(window,&paint);
  return 0;
}
```

The VIEW object actually defines Pen and Brush fields to hold handles for its two GDI objects and these are available for use in the WM_PAINT handler. The custom pen and brush are created and destroyed in the VIEW class WM_CREATE and WM_DESTROY message handlers respectively:

```
LRESULT
VIEW::Initialize(HWND window,UINT message,
                 WPARAM wparam,LPARAM lparam) {
  Pen = CreatePen(PS_SOLID,0,RGB(0,0,0));
  LOGBRUSH logicalbrush;
  logicalbrush.lbStyle = BS_SOLID;
  logicalbrush.lbColor = RGB(255,0,0);
  Brush = CreateBrushIndirect(&logicalbrush);
  return 0;
}

LRESULT
VIEW::Destroy(HWND window,UINT message,
              WPARAM wparam,LPARAM lparam) {
  DeleteObject(Pen);
  DeleteObject(Brush);
  return
    WINDOW::Destroy(window,message,wparam,lparam);
}
```

The WINDOW class Destroy() function is invoked by the VIEW class version so that a WM_QUIT message is eventually posted to the message queue.

4.5 Tracking the Mouse

The previous program demonstrated the use of the Windows 98 Graphics Device Interface but it is not very interactive. The only feedback provided occurs whenever the window dimensions are changed — the Paint() handler then automatically repositions and resizes its design to fit the window. The next step is to allow the mouse to control the image that will be displayed — as a simple example the mouse coordinates will be constantly reported whilst a geometric pattern is constructed from a series of mouse clicks. A typical run of the program produces the following output:

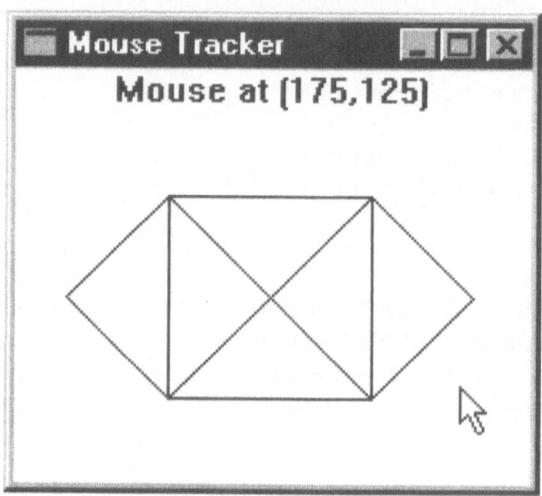

Displaying the mouse coordinates is easy — the simplest approach is to record the mouse position within the WM_MOUSEMOVE message handler then issue a request to redraw the window and wait for the VIEW class Paint() function to display the stored mouse coordinates. The VIEW class uses a Windows 98 POINT structure called Mouse to store the coordinates during execution of the MouseMove() handler function:

```
LRESULT
VIEW::MouseMove(HWND window,UINT message,
                WPARAM wparam,LPARAM lparam) {
  Mouse.x = LOWORD(lparam);
  Mouse.y = HIWORD(lparam);
  InvalidateRect(window,NULL,TRUE);
  return 0;
}
```

As with the WM_RBUTTONUP message previously discussed in section 3.6 the WM_MOUSEMOVE message supplies the mouse coordinates in the lparam parameter — the LOWORD() and HIWORD() macros can be used to extract the x and y values. The Paint() handler includes the following code to output the mouse coordinates with a call to the DrawText() function:

```
RECT rect;
GetClientRect(window,&rect);
char text[1000];
wsprintf(text,"Mouse at (%i,%i)",
            Mouse.x,Mouse.y);
DrawText(dc,text,-1,&rect,DT_CENTER);
```

The output text is formatted with the wsprintf() function using %i to denote an integer value — this function is a version of the C language sprintf() function which is built into Windows 98. The remainder of the Paint() message handler will display the pattern constructed with mouse clicks — the pattern consists of lines drawn between the points where the mouse button is clicked. The series of points is stored as the Dots array — this forms part of the VIEW object just like the Mouse field:

```
class VIEW : public WINDOW {
  .
  .
private:
  POINT Mouse;
  POINT Dots[MAX_DOTS];
  int Length;
};
```

The Length variable will hold the number of points in the pattern — it is initialized to zero in the WM_CREATE message handler Initialize(). Whenever the left mouse button is clicked another point is added to the Dots array:

```
LRESULT
VIEW::ButtonDown(HWND window,UINT message,
                  WPARAM wparam,LPARAM lparam) {
  if (Length < MAX_DOTS) {
    Dots[Length].x = LOWORD(lparam);
    Dots[Length].y = HIWORD(lparam);
    Length++;
    InvalidateRect(window,NULL,TRUE);
  }
  return 0;
}
```

To actually draw the pattern the `Paint()` handler acquires the following code:

```
if (Length)
  MoveToEx(dc,Dots[0].x,Dots[0].y,NULL);
for (int i=1; i<Length; i++)
  LineTo(dc,Dots[0].x,Dots[0].y);
```

This program illustrates two complementary ways of obtaining information in a Windows 98 environment:

— Process window messages
— Call operating system functions

Here the mouse coordinates are stored when `WM_MOUSEMOVE` messages are received but the size of the window's drawable area is retrieved directly through a call to the `GetClientRect()` function. The `GetCursorPos()` function provides an alternative method of determining the cursor position — similarly the information supplied by each `WM_SIZE` message will specify the size of the drawable area. However, there is an essential difference between the two approaches — each message contains information that was accurate when the message was generated whilst the operating system functions typically provide current values. Nonetheless, messages are particularly useful when they notify the program that an event has occurred — continually polling the value of some quantity to determine if it has changed is an inefficient option.

4.6 Summary

The Windows 98 operating system is composed of a number of functional blocks — the block most closely associated with drawing operations is the Graphics Device Interface (GDI). This chapter has described some common GDI drawing functions — to avoid passing a large number of parameters to these functions the GDI uses device contexts. A device context tells the GDI where to draw and also supplies default objects (pen, brush, font and so on) that modify the actions of the drawing operations. Each device context is typically associated with a particular window but a memory device context may be used to draw to an off-screen bitmap. The objects held by a device context can be updated through calls to the `SelectObject()` function — the new objects may be stock objects provided by Windows 98 or they may be explicitly created by the program through calls to functions such as `CreatePen()` or `CreateBrushIndirect()`. The `WM_PAINT` handler can obtain a device context with the `BeginPaint()` function — this function sets the clipping region of the device context using the window's update region and sends a `WM_ERASEBKGND` message to erase the window background. The window's update region is built by Windows 98 from a series of rectangles passed to it in redraw requests — the update region is automatically reset to null by each call to `BeginPaint()`. The window redraw requests may originate in calls to the `InvalidateRect()` function or through user actions. Outside the WM_PAINT handler a window device context should be obtained with the GetDC() function — a memory device context can be created using the CreateCompatibleDC() function. Windows 98 supports a variety of coordinate systems but units are commonly measured in pixels. Screen coordinates specify pixel offsets from the top left-hand corner of the screen whilst client coordinates are measured relative to a window's drawable area — the two functions ClientToScreen() and ScreenToClient() will convert between these coordinate systems. Each device context defines the coordinates of a reference point known as the current point — this point interacts with many GDI drawing functions such as MoveToEx() and LineTo(). Finally, the RECT structure plays an important role in Windows 98 programming — there are a number of rectangle functions including OffsetRect(), IntersectRect() and InflateRect() for manipulating these structures.

5. Bitmaps

The previous chapter introduced the Windows 98 Graphics Device Interface —
to exploit the graphics capabilities of the GDI more fully a good knowledge of
bitmaps is required. A bitmap represents a graphical image — the structure and
colour information for the image are encoded by the bitmap as a collection of bits.
Bitmaps are fundamental to practically all the graphical techniques presented
throughout the remainder of this book (whether they involve the animation of
simple bitmapped graphics or the construction of a complex 3D scene). The
essential bitmap topics include:

— image bits and colour tables
— Windows 98 bitmap resources
— device dependent and device independent bitmaps
— the DIB class
— the .BMP bitmap file format

The chapter develops a series of related bitmap applications which demonstrate the
various options possible with Windows 98 bitmaps.

5.1 Pixels and Colours

A bitmap is a collection of bits used to hold a computerized image. The bitmap
may be stored in a file or in memory and is easily transmitted from one location to
the other — the image which the bitmap represents can be displayed in a window
or even sent to a printer to obtain a hard copy. Windows 98 bitmaps hold
rectangular images with the width and height of the image being measured in pixel
units — each pixel corresponds to one coloured dot within the image. The colour
information for a pixel may be encoded in many ways but a common approach is to
assign a fixed number of image bits per pixel — the bits specify the red, green and
blue (RGB) components of the pixel's colour. There are two basic colour coding
schemes:

— The image bits hold the colour component values directly
— A colour table holds the colour component values and the image bits for each
  pixel point at an entry within this table

In any case the RGB components are sufficient to completely describe the colour of
each pixel — the number of bits per pixel needed to hold this information is known
as the 'colour depth' of an image. Windows 98 stores RGB values in a variety of

ways — the COLORREF data type has already made an appearance and the RGBQUAD structure is common with bitmaps. Both COLORREF and RGBQUAD formats accept RGB colour components in the range 0 to 255 — the higher the value the more intense the colour contribution. The RGB() macro will convert from a triple of RGB component values to a COLORREF variable:

```
COLORREF yellow = RGB(255,255,0);
```

The GetRValue(), GetBValue() and GetGValue() macros extract individual component values from a COLORREF variable. The RGBQUAD structure has the following format:

```
struct RGBQUAD {
   BYTE rgbBlue;
   BYTE rgbGreen;
   BYTE rgbRed;
   BYTE rgbReserved;
};
```

Section 5.4 will discuss how an array of RGBQUAD structures are used to construct the colour table for one type of bitmap. The next chapter on Windows 98 colour palettes introduces the PALETTEENTRY structure — this provides yet another way of storing RGB components.

Each Windows 98 bitmap belongs to one of two broad categories — the bitmap may be a device dependent bitmap (DDB) or a device independent bitmap (DIB). The primary difference is that a DIB exposes its image bits to direct manipulation by the program but for a device dependent bitmap calls to functions such as SetPixel() and GetPixel() are necessary — these functions use a graphics device driver to process the bitmap. A device dependent bitmap can be loaded as a Windows 98 program resource with the LoadBitmap() function — this is the topic of the next two sections. However, a DIB is much more versatile and is recommended for most applications — section 5.4 discusses the creation of a DIB whilst section 5.5 shows how to move a DIB between memory and a .BMP file.

5.2 Windows 98 Resources

One of the wonders of working in a graphical development environment such as Microsoft's Visual C++ is that many elements can be designed graphically on-screen and then made available to the program as resources. All that is necessary is a resource compiler capable of supplying resources to the linker in the proper binary format. The resource compiler also generates a header file which defines integer constants that the program may use to identify the various resources available — the MAKEINTRESOURCE() macro is provided to convert from ID values to the resources themselves. Resources are typically loaded by a program with functions such as LoadIcon(), LoadCursor() and LoadBitmap().

The first pair of functions were used in the definition of the WINDOW class to load icon and cursor resources (see section 3.3) — in this case the initial parameter supplied to the functions was NULL to indicate that standard resources (IDI_APPLICATION and IDC_ARROW) were required. When icon and cursor resources are loaded by a program they are automatically released when the program exits — however, if a bitmap is loaded with the LoadBitmap() function it must eventually be destroyed with a call to the DeleteObject() function. For example:

```
HBITMAP Bitmap =
  LoadBitmap(Manager->GetInstance(),
             MAKEINTRESOURCE(IDB_BITMAP));
        .
        .

DeleteObject(Bitmap);
```

Here the IDB_BITMAP value identifies a particular bitmap resource that is packaged in the program's own executable file — the first parameter to the LoadBitmap() function specifies the program instance handle and this is retrieved from the Manager object as described in section 3.2.

5.3 Displaying a Bitmap Resource

This section details the process of loading a bitmap resource from a .BMP file and displaying the bitmap image in a window — the internal format of the .BMP file is discussed in section 5.5. The first step is to create a resource file that will link the bitmap image into the program's executable file — the details of performing this operation in Visual C++ (version 4.0) are as follows:

1. Import the Bitmap File

— on the Insert menu click the Resource... option
— select Bitmap from the Insert Resource box
— click the Import... button
— select the desired bitmap file and click the Import button

2. Edit the Bitmap Properties
The bitmap ID value needs changing to IDB_BITMAP to work with the code in this section:

— close the bitmap editing window to reveal the resources window
— select the IDB_BITMAP1 item and right click for a popup menu
— click on the Properties option from this menu
— edit the ID field of the Bitmap Properties box
— close the Bitmap Properties box

3. Generate a Resource File
— on the File menu click the Save As... option
— enter the filename `resource.rc` and click the Save button

4. Add the Resource File to the Project
— on the Insert menu click the Files into Project... option
— select the `resource.rc` file and click the Add button

The program resources may later be viewed by selecting the ResourceView tab of the Project Workspace window. When the project is complete it can be built in the usual way and the inclusion of the resource file will ensure that the bitmap resource is placed into the program executable by the linker. However, the compiled resource file `resource.res` must end up in the project directory — one way to achieve this involves the following steps:

— on the Build menu click the Settings... item
— in the Settings For: window select the desired project configuration
— select the Resources tab of the Project Settings box
— edit the Resource file name field so it contains `resource.res`
— click the OK button

Fortunately, all this button clicking activity is much easier to do than to read about — with the bitmap available as a program resource life is now reasonably straightforward. The first question is how to locate the bitmap resource programmatically — the answer is that the `IDB_BITMAP` bitmap ID will identify the bitmap resource in a call to the `LoadBitmap()` function as discussed in the previous section:

```
HBITMAP Bitmap =
   LoadBitmap(Manager->GetInstance(),
              MAKEINTRESOURCE(IDB_BITMAP));
```

The next point to consider is how to display the newly created device dependent bitmap in a window — the easiest way to achieve this is to perform a Bit Block Transfer (blit). The `BitBlt()` function will transfer a rectangular image such as a bitmap — it takes a whole string of parameters to describe which image block to move and where to send the bits. For example:

```
BitBlt(dc,left,top,width,height,
                  source,x,y,SRCCOPY);
```

As noted in section 4.1 it requires both a source device context (`source`) and a destination device context (`dc`) to transfer an image from one place to another. The `left`, `top`, `width` and `height` arguments describe the location of the bit block in the image destination (a window) whilst the `x`, `y`, `width` and `height` arguments are the corresponding values for the image source (the bitmap) — in particular if all units are measured in pixels then the BitBlt() function does not scale the image during the transfer. Finally, the SRCCOPY argument requests a straightforward copy from source to destination without any fancy effects to transform the image.

The one remaining problem is determining the size of the bitmap so that the width and height parameters to BitBlt() can be set properly. Fortunately, the GetObject() function provides information on all sorts of GDI objects — for a device dependent bitmap it fills in a BITMAP structure and the bmWidth and bmHeight fields of this structure contain the relevant values. For example:

```
BITMAP BitmapInfo;
GetObject(Bitmap,sizeof(BitmapInfo),&BitmapInfo);
```

To demonstrate a bitmap resource in action the Mouse Tracker program from chapter 4 will be modified to draw a small bitmap image wherever the left mouse button is clicked. If supplied with a bitmap image that represents a house the program produces a window display such as the following:

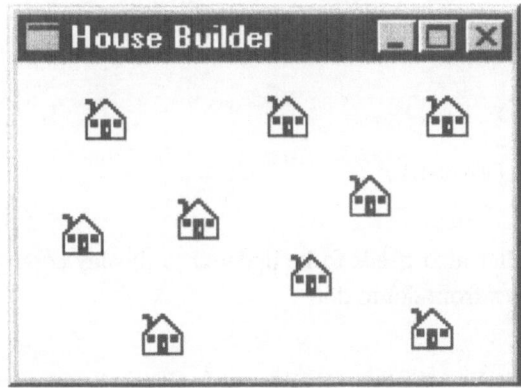

The new version of the VIEW class required to implement this functionality has the following class specification:

```
const int MAX_DOTS = 100;

class VIEW : public WINDOW {
    .
    .
private:
    void SetupBitmap(BOOL);
    HBITMAP Bitmap;
    BITMAP BitmapInfo;
    POINT Dots[MAX_DOTS];
    int Length;
};
```

As before the number of points selected is stored in the Length field whilst the
Dots array holds the coordinates of these points. The Bitmap and BitmapInfo
fields hold the bitmap handle and bitmap information respectively — the
SetupBitmap() helper function manages these fields.

```cpp
void VIEW::SetupBitmap(BOOL init) {
  if (init) {
    Bitmap = LoadBitmap(Manager->GetInstance(),
                        MAKEINTRESOURCE(IDB_BITMAP));
    GetObject(Bitmap,
              sizeof(BitmapInfo),&BitmapInfo);
  }
  else
    DeleteObject(Bitmap);
}
```

The SetupBitmap() function is called in both the VIEW class constructor and
destructor:

```cpp
VIEW::VIEW(LPCTSTR title) {
  SetupBitmap(TRUE);
  Create(title);
}

VIEW::~VIEW(void) {
  SetupBitmap(FALSE);
}
```

The WM_PAINT handler also needs to be updated to display copies of the bitmap
instead of drawing lines from dot to dot:

```cpp
LRESULT
VIEW::Paint(HWND window,UINT message,
            WPARAM wparam,LPARAM lparam) {
  PAINTSTRUCT paint;
  HDC windowdc = BeginPaint(window,&paint);
  HDC memorydc = CreateCompatibleDC(windowdc);
  HBITMAP oldbitmap;
  oldbitmap = (HBITMAP)SelectObject(memorydc,Bitmap);
  for (int i=0; i<Length; i++)
    BitBlt(windowdc,Dots[i].x,Dots[i].y,
           BitmapInfo.bmWidth,BitmapInfo.bmHeight,
           memorydc,0,0,SRCCOPY);
  SelectObject(memorydc,oldbitmap);
  DeleteDC(memorydc);
  EndPaint(window,&paint);
  return 0;
}
```

As described in section 4.1 a memory device context must be created — the bitmap is selected into this device context before the BitBlt() function is called. Whenever GDI functions such as BitBlt() operate on a memory device context they treat the selected bitmap in much the same way as they treat a window associated with a window device context — here the arguments passed to BitBlt() ensure that the whole of the bitmap image is transferred to the screen. It is not necessary to worry about part of the bitmap image overlapping the edges of the destination window — the GDI will take care of clipping the image as the block is transferred.

5.4 The DIB Class

A device dependent bitmap is manipulated by selecting its HBITMAP handle into a memory device context and then making calls to GDI drawing functions with the device context handle as a parameter. The technique also works with device independent bitmaps but in addition to the HBITMAP handle each DIB can also provide a pointer to its image bits — hence it is possible for a graphics program to directly modify a DIB image. The CreateDIBSection() function will create a device independent bitmap and return both the HBITMAP bitmap handle and also the image bits pointer. With these two items available it is possible to rapidly draw an image on the DIB and then blit that image into a window. This process is essential to producing fast bitmap graphics in Windows 98 — it also forms the foundation for many of the graphical techniques described in the rest of the book.

The details of creating a DIB are quite complex so the object oriented model will be applied to hide this complexity and provide the program with a simple interface — just as each WINDOW object wraps a Windows 98 window so the DIB class will be defined to encapsulate device independent bitmaps. A basic version of the DIB class is presented in this section — the next section adds functions to move a DIB between memory and a file whilst chapter 6 updates the DIB class to work with Windows 98 palettes. The basic DIB class specification follows:

```
class DIB {
public:
  DIB(int,int);
  ~DIB(void);
  BYTE* AcquireBits(void);
  void ReleaseBits(void);
  void Blit(HDC,int,int) const;
private:
  HBITMAP Bitmap;
  BYTE* Bits;
  int Width;
  int Height;
};
```

The AcquireBits() function simply returns the image bits pointer (Bits) for the DIB and ReleaseBits() performs no action — in a multi-threaded environment these functions could coordinate the activities of several concurrently executing threads. In addition to the Bits pointer the DIB object also contains fields for the bitmap handle and the bitmap's width and height — the Blit() function uses these fields to blit the bitmap image to a specified destination. The Bits and Bitmap fields are set when the Windows 98 device independent bitmap is created by the DIB object constructor — this constructor accepts parameters to specify the width and height of the bitmap:

```
DIB::DIB(int width,int height) :
  Width(width),Height(height) {
      .
      .
  Bitmap = CreateDIBSection(dc,format,
    DIB_RGB_COLORS,(void**)&Bits,NULL,0);
      .
      .

}
```

The constructor is built around the CreateDIBSection() function — this function creates the Windows 98 device independent bitmap and supplies both a HBITMAP handle for the bitmap and a void* pointer to the start of the bitmap's image bits. The Bitmap field of the DIB object is set using the function's return value and the address of the Bits field is passed as a parameter so that the function can set the image bits pointer itself. The size of the bitmap and its colour encoding scheme is described by the format parameter — the flag DIB_RGB_COLORS indicates that the format structure will contain a colour table of RGB values. The CreateDIBSection() function also requires a device context handle but this is only important when the DIB_PAL_COLORS flag replaces DIB_RGB_COLORS — the next chapter discusses this alternative. The final two parameters to the CreateDIBSection() function relate only to file-based bitmaps and they remain unused until the next section.

The remainder of the DIB class constructor is concerned with initialization to prepare for the call to CreateDIBSection() and finalization to tidy up afterwards. The initialization starts with the creation of the dc and format parameters:

```
HDC dc = CreateCompatibleDC(NULL);
int heapspace = sizeof(BITMAPINFOHEADER);
heapspace += 256*sizeof(RGBQUAD);
HANDLE heap = GetProcessHeap();
BITMAPINFO* format =
  (BITMAPINFO*)HeapAlloc(heap,0,heapspace);
```

The NULL parameter passed to the CreateCompatibleDC() function creates a memory device context that is compatible with the screen. Storage space for the format structure is allocated from the program's main heap with the HeapAlloc() function — the first parameter to this function is the heap handle and the final parameter is the amount of storage space required. The format structure consists of a bitmap information header followed by a colour table comprising 256 RGB values.

The BITMAPINFOHEADER structure has the following layout:

```
struct BITMAPINFOHEADER {
  DWORD biSize;
  LONG biWidth;
  LONG biHeight;
  WORD biPlanes;
  WORD biBitCount;
  DWORD biCompression;
  DWORD biSizeImage;
  LONG biXPelsPerMeter;
  LONG biYPelsPerMeter;
  DWORD biClrUsed;
  DWORD biClrImportant;
};
```

The fields within this header are set in the next part of the initialization process within the DIB constructor:

```
BITMAPINFOHEADER* header =
  (BITMAPINFOHEADER*)format;
header->biSize = sizeof(BITMAPINFOHEADER);
header->biWidth = Width;
header->biHeight = -Height;
header->biPlanes = 1;
header->biBitCount= 8;
header->biCompression = BI_RGB;
header->biSizeImage = 0;
header->biXPelsPerMeter = 0;
header->biYPelsPerMeter = 0;
header->biClrUsed = 0;
header->biClrImportant = 0;
```

The width and height of the DIB are described by the biWidth and biHeight fields whilst the number of image bits per pixel is placed in the biBitCount field. The DIB_RGB_COLORS flag passed to the CreateDIBSection() function indicates that a colour table is used and so the image bits do not contain colour information directly but instead point to entries in the colour table — a common choice is to allocate 8 image bits per pixel and this requires a colour table holding 256==2**8 different colours. The next chapter looks at some alternative

colour encoding schemes. The biHeight field must be negative to provide a
top-down bitmap with its origin in the top left corner — a positive value results in a
bottom-up bitmap with its origin in the bottom left corner. This apparent mix-up
resulted from an IBM-Microsoft collaboration. The biSize field is assigned the
size of the BITMAPINFOHEADER structure — this is a common programming
technique in Windows 98 whereby a structure can be expanded in future versions of
the operating system and the structure size will distinguish old and new formats.
The biPlanes field must equal 1 and a value of BI_RGB for biCompression
means that the bitmap image data is to be stored in uncompressed format — bitmap
compression algorithms attempt to reduce the number of bits per pixel required to
encode any particular image. With the options chosen the remaining fields of the
bitmap header structure can safely be set to zero.

Now the entries in the colour table need to be initialized — the bmiColors array
of the BITMAPINFO structure holds the colour table:

```
struct BITMAPINFO {
  BITMAPINFOHEADER bmiHeader;
  RGBQUAD bmiColors[1];
};
```

Only the first element is explicitly declared but enough storage for 256 entries has
been allocated. Here the entries are filled in using data from the rgb.h header file:

```
rgb.h:
RGBQUAD Colours[256]= {
  {0,0,0,0},
     .
     .
  {255,255,255,0}
};
```

The following code appears in the DIB class constructor:

```
RGBQUAD* colours = (RGBQUAD*)format->bmiColors;
for (int i=0; i<256 ; i++)
  colours[i] = Colours[i];
```

This completes the initialization phase and a call may now be made to the
CreateDIBSection() function to create the device independent bitmap and to
set the Bitmap and Bits fields of the DIB object. There then only remains the
finalization process of releasing resources:

```
HeapFree(heap,0,format);
DeleteDC(dc);
```

The DIB constructor is complete. The AcquireBits() function can now be called to retrieve the Bits pointer that is used to manipulate the underlying Windows 98 bitmap. From an object oriented viewpoint the DIB object may be considered as managing a shared piece of memory — this is a little tenuous but the approach does permit graphics to be drawn efficiently. The alternative is to define a lot of drawing functions for the DIB class but then a DIB object behaves much like a device dependent bitmap — the general functionality of the basic DIB class is much more widely applicable. When a DIB object is no longer required its destructor destroys the associated bitmap:

```
DIB::~DIB(void) {
    DeleteObject(Bitmap);
}
```

Finally the DIB class Blit() function is a wrapper for the Windows 98 BitBlt() function:

```
void DIB::Blit(HDC dc,int x,int y) const {
    HDC memorydc = CreateCompatibleDC(dc);
    HBITMAP oldbitmap;
    oldbitmap = (HBITMAP)SelectObject(memorydc,Bitmap);
    BitBlt(dc,x,y,Width,Height,
            memorydc,0,0,SRCCOPY);
    SelectObject(memorydc,oldbitmap);
    DeleteDC(memorydc);
}
```

As an example of working with the DIB class the program from the previous section will be updated to use a DIB instead of a device dependent bitmap. The bitmap image actually displayed will correspond to the random bit values existing when the DIB is created — the next section shows how to set up the DIB image from the same .BMP file used to generate the device dependent bitmap resource. Here the first modification is to replace the device dependent bitmap with a DIB in the specification of the VIEW class:

```
class DIB;

class VIEW : public WINDOW {
    .
    .
private:
    DIB* Dib;
    POINT Dots[MAX_DOTS];
    int Length;
};
```

The SetupBitmap() function is replaced by implicit calls to the DIB class constructor and destructor:

```
VIEW::VIEW(LPCTSTR title) {
  Dib = (DIB*) new DIB(DIBSIZE,DIBSIZE);
  Create(title);
}

VIEW::~VIEW(void) {
  delete Dib;
}
```

The WM_PAINT handler also needs to be modified:

```
LRESULT
VIEW::Paint(HWND window,UINT message,
            WPARAM wparam,LPARAM lparam) {
  PAINTSTRUCT paint;
  HDC dc = BeginPaint(window,&paint);
  for (int i=0; i<Length; i++)
    Dib->Blit(dc,Dots[i].x,Dots[i].y);
  EndPaint(window,&paint);
  return 0;
}
```

With the help of the DIB class the code is a lot cleaner than in the previous version. The display produced by the program is similar to before but the bitmap images are now a random arrangement of coloured dots — the next section shows how to restore the original image from the .BMP file.

5.5 Storing Images in Files

The image held by a DIB may be transferred between memory and a corresponding .BMP file — this allows the bitmap image to be stored in a standard format and transmitted from program to program or even from computer to computer. The layout of the .BMP file is illustrated in the following figure:

BITMAPFILEHEADER
BITMAPINFOHEADER
Colour Table
Image Bits

The BITMAPINFOHEADER structure, the colour table and the image bits were discussed in the previous section — the BITMAPFILEHEADER structure contains the following fields:

```
struct BITMAPFILEHEADER {
  WORD bfType;
  DWORD bfSize;
  WORD bfReserved1;
  WORD bfReserved2;
  DWORD bfOffBits;
};
```

The important field here is bfOffBits which indicates where the image bits begin — the start of the colour table can be calculated from the biSize field in the BITMAPINFOHEADER structure.

There are two possibilities for transferring an image:

1. Saving an image to a file
2. Loading an image from a file

For the sake of simplicity the DIB class will be provided with a second constructor that generates a new type of DIB object which is file-based — the constructor takes the name of an associated .BMP file and any changes made to the DIB object image are reflected in the contents of the file. The DIB class destructor will break the association between object and file. The object oriented approach ensures that the AcquireBits() and Blit() functions are used in the same way with both memory-based and file-based DIB objects — the actual implementation of the object is hidden. To permit memory-based DIB objects to be stored in a file Save() and Load() functions could be defined or alternatively a memory-based DIB object could be copied to and from a file-based DIB object — these functions are not difficult to implement but the details are omitted. To formalize the distinction between memory-based and file-based DIB objects the C++ inheritance mechanism may be applied to derive two new bitmap classes from a common base class — shared functions such as AcquireBits() and Blit() are placed in the base class whilst other functions (Save() and Load() for example) belong only to one derived class or the other. The 'multiple-constructor' and 'class-hierarchy' techniques provide two routes to polymorphism (see section 3.1) — the former approach is adopted here since it is unnecessary to emphasize the difference between the two types of DIB.

The problem of transferring the bitmap image to a file is solved by using a 'file mapping' — the CreateFileMapping() and MapViewOfFile() functions together request that Windows 98 map a file into a region of memory. This solution forces the operating system to manage the actual transfer of data — the contents of a mapped file can be manipulated directly with ordinary pointers. The DIB class acquires some extra fields to accommodate file-based objects:

```cpp
class DIB {
    .
    .
private:
    BOOL FileBased;
    HANDLE FileHandle;
    HANDLE FileMapping;
    BITMAPFILEHEADER* FileHeader;
};
```

The new constructor initializes these fields as follows:

```cpp
DIB::DIB(LPCTSTR filename) {
    FileBased = TRUE;
    FileHandle = CreateFile(filename,
        GENERIC_READ|GENERIC_WRITE,
        0,NULL,OPEN_EXISTING,0,NULL);
    FileMapping = CreateFileMapping(FileHandle,
        NULL,PAGE_READWRITE,0,0,NULL);
    FileHeader = (BITMAPFILEHEADER*)
        MapViewOfFile(FileMapping,
            FILE_MAP_WRITE,0,0,0);
    DWORD offset = FileHeader->bfOffBits;
    BITMAPINFO* format;
    format = (BITMAPINFO*)(FileHeader+1);
    HDC dc = CreateCompatibleDC(NULL);
    Bitmap = CreateDIBSection(dc,format,
        DIB_RGB_COLORS,(void**)&Bits,
        FileMapping,offset);
    BITMAPINFOHEADER* header;
    header = (BITMAPINFOHEADER*)format;
    Width = header->biWidth;
    Height = header->biHeight;
    DeleteDC(dc);
}
```

The CreateFile() function opens the bitmap file — the functions CreateFileMapping() and MapViewOfFile() together map this file into memory. The MapViewOfFile() function returns a pointer to the start of the file — this pointer is cast to a BITMAPFILEHEADER* pointer to reference the first structure in the file. The bitmap format information is passed directly to the CreateDIBSection() function — the final two parameters to this function specify that the file image bits should be incorporated into the new bitmap. Finally, the Width and Height fields are set from the bitmap information in the file and the FileBased flag is set to denote that the DIB object is file-based — of course, the original constructor must now reset the FileBased flag.

The DIB destructor checks the FileBased flag and releases the file resources if it is set:

```
DIB::~DIB(void) {
  DeleteObject(Bitmap);
  if (FileBased) {
    UnmapViewOfFile(FileHeader);
    CloseHandle(FileMapping);
    CloseHandle(FileHandle);
  }
}
```

To finally restore the correct behaviour for the VIEW class of section 5.3 its constructor should now create a file-based DIB as follows:

```
VIEW::VIEW(LPCTSTR title) {
  Dib = (DIB*) new DIB("C:\\images\\bitmap.bmp");
  Create(title);
}
```

The program will once again produce the display depicted at the end of section 5.3 — however, there are a couple of technicalities relating to the .BMP file which must be attended to. Firstly, the new DIB constructor assumes that the bitmap is stored in bottom-up format with a positive value appearing in the biHeight field — to accommodate top-down bitmaps too the absolute value of the biHeight field should be stored in the Height variable. Secondly, the function CreateDIBSection() requires that the image bits begin on a DWORD boundary (i.e. the offset parameter must be divisible by 4) — it may be necessary to place padding bytes within the .BMP file to meet this requirement.

5.6 Summary

Bitmaps are fundamental to graphics programming in Windows 98 — a bitmap contains a computerized image stored as a collection of bits. The colour of each pixel within the image may be described directly by the image bits or these bits may act as pointers into a colour table associated with the bitmap. In any case the colours are commonly represented as RGB triples which describe the red, green and blue components — the colour depth of the image refers to the number of bits required to specify the colour of each pixel. Windows 98 bitmaps are available in two varieties — a bitmap may be device dependent or device independent. A device dependent bitmap can be loaded as a program resource with the LoadBitmap() function — the resource should eventually be freed by making a call to the DeleteObject() function. A device independent bitmap (DIB) is more flexible and is recommended for most graphics applications — the image bits within a DIB are directly available to the program. Windows 98 provides the CreateDIBSection() function to create either memory-based or file-based device independent bitmaps — a file-based DIB requires the mapping into memory of a file containing the bitmap's image bits. The DIB class has been defined to encapsulate a Windows 98 device independent bitmap — the class provides functions to display the bitmap and to transfer its image between memory and an associated .BMP file. Both device dependent and device independent bitmaps can be displayed with the BitBlt() function — a pair of device contexts are required and the bitmap must be selected into the source device context before the transfer takes place. A common procedure when working with a DIB is to draw an image directly to the bitmap using the image bits pointer and then to display the bitmap with a call to the BitBlt() function.

6. Palettes

A Windows 98 palette is used to hold colour information. However, a palette is typically only required whenever the range of available colours is limited — with enough bits per pixel a computer image can encode its colour information directly into the image bits and no palette is required. Nowadays computer displays provide a variety of colour modes, some that work with a palette and some that do not — to achieve the best performance a graphics application should match the colour format of its bitmaps to that of the display. The following palette-related topics are discussed here:

— computer display modes and colour formats
— logical and system palettes
— handling Windows 98 palette messages
— the PALETTE class
— associating a palette with a bitmap

The chapter concludes by updating the DIB class from the previous chapter so that it will accommodate a range of different colour formats — this will complete the preliminaries necessary to create a Windows 98 graphics application.

6.1 Logical and System Palettes

Just as a DIB can encode its colour information directly into the image bits or instead use a colour table to describe the colours indirectly so a display device such as the computer screen can operate without or with a palette. Some display modes place the colour information directly into video memory whilst other modes use the video memory to hold pointers to colour entries in the display's palette — this palette is known as the 'system palette' and it contains the range of colours which are currently supported by the display. Each application can also define its own palette to hold all the colours that it will require — these are 'logical palettes' and they must be selected into a device context to become effective. The contents of the system palette can be modified by the function RealizePalette() — this function attempts to match the range of colours supported by the system palette as closely as possible to the colours specified in a logical palette. The colour matching process gives preference to the current foreground application with all the background applications competing on a first-come-first-served basis. Palettes are only used when it is necessary to share a limited range of colours — with newer computer displays that support colour depths of 16 bits or more palettes become unnecessary. Nonetheless the VGA display with its palette of 256 colours is still common — furthermore, a palette can reduce the amount of video memory required to display an image by assigning fewer bits to each pixel. This chapter examines the following display modes:

Bits per Pixel	Use System Palette?
8	Yes
16	No
24	No
32	No

However, the principal emphasis is on the first option since this is the only one that uses a system palette. The next section looks in detail at how the colour entries in the system palette are set using a logical palette — sections 6.3 and 6.4 deal with creating a logical palette in the first place. Finally, section 6.5 shows how a DIB can replace its built-in colour table with an associated (but independent) palette — the DIB class is updated to work efficiently with the display modes listed above.

6.2 Palette Messages

Whenever the GDI functions draw to a window they are influenced by the palette currently selected into the window's device context — unlike other GDI objects which are selected by the SelectObject() function, a new logical palette is selected by calling the function SelectPalette(). The contents of the window are actually drawn by placing colour data into video memory — to determine which values to use the GDI must map from colours in the logical palette to colours in the system palette. The RealizePalette() function sets up this mapping after first placing new colours in the system palette to achieve the best possible colour matching — the foreground window realizes its logical palette in the WM_QUERYNEWPALETTE message handler whilst the background windows perform this action in the WM_PALETTECHANGED message handler. A WM_QUERYNEWPALETTE message is sent by Windows 98 whenever a window moves to the foreground — the message handler is typically implemented as follows:

```
LRESULT
VIEW::QueryNewPalette(HWND window,UINT message,
                      WPARAM wparam,LPARAM lparam) {
  HDC dc = GetDC(window);
  HPALETTE oldpalette;
  oldpalette = SelectPalette(dc,Palette,FALSE);
  RealizePalette(dc);
  SelectPalette(dc,oldpalette,FALSE);
  ReleaseDC(window,dc);
  return TRUE;
}
```

Here the `Palette` field of the `VIEW` object holds a `HPALETTE` handle for the application's logical palette — the message handler must return `TRUE` to signal that it has realized this palette. The first call to `SelectPalette()` swaps the new palette into the window device context and then the call to `RealizePalette()` maps the logical palette to the system palette — the actual mapping procedure is considered in greater detail in the next section. The second call to `SelectPalette()` restores the original logical palette but does not affect the system palette.

Whenever a new palette is realized by the foreground window the operating system sends a `WM_PALETTECHANGED` message to each top-level window — this allows all the background windows to remap their colours as best they can by calling `RealizePalette()` themselves. The process will not affect the colours set in the system palette by the foreground window — indeed the foregound window must avoid any action when it receives its `WM_PALETTECHANGED` message.

For example:

```
LRESULT
VIEW::PaletteChanged(HWND window,UINT message,
                     WPARAM wparam,LPARAM lparam)
{
  HWND foregroundwindow = (HWND)wparam;
  if (window != foregroundwindow) {
    HDC dc = GetDC(window);
    HPALETTE oldpalette;
    oldpalette = SelectPalette(dc,Palette,FALSE);
    RealizePalette(dc);
    SelectPalette(dc,oldpalette,FALSE);
    ReleaseDC(window,dc);
  }
  return 0;
}
```

The current foreground window is specified by the `wparam` parameter — the palette realization procedure must be avoided if this handle matches that of the window receiving the message.

6.3 Creating a Palette

A Windows 98 logical palette is created using a technique that will be familiar from experience with other GDI objects (windows, pens, brushes, bitmaps and so on) — a `LOGPALETTE` structure is filled in and then passed to the `CreatePalette()` function. Storage space for the `LOGPALETTE` structure may be allocated on the main process heap and once the logical palette has been created the structure may be discarded — the logical palette itself should eventually be destroyed by passing its `HPALETTE` handle to the `DeleteObject()` function.

The LOGPALETTE structure has the following format:

```
struct LOGPALETTE {
  WORD palVersion;
  WORD palNumEntries;
  PALETTEENTRY palPalEntry[1];
};
```

The palVersion field contains the Windows version number (currently 0x300) whilst the palNumEntries field holds the number of entries in the palPalEntry array — this array consists of PALETTEENTRY structures that contain the RGB components of the colours defined by the palette. Here the RGB colour values will be copied from a header file in much the same way that the DIB colour table was initialized in the previous chapter — the only difference is that PALETTEENTRY structures replace RGBQUAD entries. The layout of each PALETTEENTRY structure is arranged as follows:

```
struct PALETTEENTRY {
  BYTE peRed;
  BYTE peGreen;
  BYTE peBlue;
  BYTE peFlags;
};
```

Assuming that the palettesize variable holds the number of colours in the palette, the essential procedure for creating a new palette is illustrated by the following code:

```
int heapspace = sizeof(LOGPALETTE)+
  (palettesize-1)*sizeof(PALETTEENTRY);
HANDLE heap = GetProcessHeap();
LOGPALETTE* palette =
  (LOGPALETTE*)HeapAlloc(heap,0,heapspace);
palette->palVersion = 0x300;
palette->palNumEntries = palettesize;
PALETTEENTRY* colours = palette->palPalEntry;
for (int i=0 ; i<palettesize; i++)
  colours[i] = Colours[i];
HPALETTE Palette = CreatePalette(palette);
HeapFree(heap,0,palette);
```

Firstly, storage space is allocated for a LOGPALETTE structure that is extended to hold all the colour entries for the palette. Next the various fields of this structure are set — in particular the array of PALETTEENTRY structures is copied from a corresponding Colours array placed in a header file. Finally, the logical palette is created with a call to the CreatePalette() function and the HPALETTE handle returned by the function is stored in the `Palette` variable — the `LOGPALETTE` structure may then be discarded. This procedure will produce a perfectly good logical palette — however, to achieve optimum performance when working with bitmaps it is preferable to create an 'identity palette'. When a logical palette is mapped to the system palette there is obviously some translation involved in converting from the index of a logical palette entry to the equivalent system palette index — an identity palette makes this translation step unnecessary by ensuring that every logical palette index is identical to its corresponding system palette index. The recommended procedure for generating an identity palette is as follows:

1. Initialize the static colour palette entries by calling the function `GetSystemPaletteEntries()`

2. Set the `peFlags` field of the other palette entries with the `PC_NOCOLLAPSE` flag

These two steps clearly require some explanation — in particular, what are 'static colours' and what does the `PC_NOCOLLAPSE` flag do? Well, at either end of the the system palette there are ten static colours which cannot be changed — these twenty colours correspond to the 16-colour palette originally defined for the CGA display plus another four. The static colours provide a modicom of stability in the fast changing world of colour palettes — applications can always rely on these palette entries to provide the colours they expect. The RGB values for the static colours may be retrieved by calling the `GetSystemPaletteEntries()` function to set the appropriate `PALETTEENTRY` structures. In between the static colours a program can map any other colours it requires — for the standard palette of 256 colours this involves the palette entries numbered from 10 to 245 inclusive. The `PC_NOCOLLAPSE` flag should be applied to these entries — normally the `RealizePalette()` function will collapse duplicated colours from the logical palette into the same entry in the system palette but the `PC_NOCOLLAPSE` flag inhibits this behaviour. In summary, when an identity palette is realized the static colours map to the ends of the system palette and the remaining palette entries slot in between — this is exactly the mapping required to make each logical palette index identical to its corresponding system palette index. The `PALETTE` class defined in the following section creates an identity palette and section 6.5 discusses the benefits of using an identity palette with bitmaps.

6.4 The `PALETTE` Class

The `PALETTE` class will package Windows 98 logical palettes. Each `PALETTE` object holds the handle for an associated logical palette in its `Palette` field and a call to the object's `Select()` function will select the palette into a specified device context — the handles for this device context and for the displaced logical palette are stored in the `DeviceContext` and `OldPalette` fields respectively. If Select () is invoked with a NULL parameter the original palette is restored to the device context. The full specification for the PALETTE class is as follows:

```
class PALETTE {
public:
  PALETTE(void);
  ~PALETTE(void);
  void Select(HDC);
  void Realize(void);
private:
  HPALETTE Palette;
  HPALETTE OldPalette;
  HDC DeviceContext;
};
```

Here is the Select () function definition:

```
void PALETTE::Select(HDC dc) {
  if (dc) {
    OldPalette = SelectPalette(dc,Palette,FALSE);
    DeviceContext = dc;
  }
  else
    SelectPalette(DeviceContext,OldPalette,FALSE);
}
```

The PALETTE class also provides a Realize () utility function to map a logical palette to the display's system palette — this is built around the Windows 98 RealizePalette() function but it hides the messy implementation details. The Realize () function is defined as follows:

```
void PALETTE::Realize(void) {
  HWND window = GetDesktopWindow();
  HDC dc = GetDC(window);
  HPALETTE oldpalette;
  oldpalette = SelectPalette(dc,Palette,FALSE);
  RealizePalette(dc);
  SelectPalette(dc,oldpalette,FALSE);
  ReleaseDC(window,dc);
}
```

The RealizePalette() function requires the handle of a device context associated with the screen — one way to obtain a suitable handle is to call the GetDC() function for the desktop window. The PALETTE class Realize () function may be used by the VIEW class palette message handlers — the

WM_QUERYNEWPALETTE handler is defined as follows:

```
LRESULT
VIEW::QueryNewPalette(HWND window,UINT message,
                          WPARAM wparam,LPARAM lparam) {
  Palette->Realize();
  return TRUE;
}
```

Here Palette is a pointer held by the VIEW object which references an object of the newly defined PALETTE class. The handler for the WM_PALETTECHANGED message is similar but it must ensure that the window is in the background:

```
LRESULT
VIEW::PaletteChanged(HWND window,UINT message,
                          WPARAM wparam,LPARAM lparam) {
  HWND foregroundwindow = (HWND)wparam;
  if (window != foregroundwindow)
    Palette->Realize();
  return 0;
}
```

Once the logical palette has been realized it may be selected into a window's device context during execution of the WM_PAINT message handler simply by calling the PALETTE class Select() function. For example:

```
LRESULT
VIEW::Paint(HWND window,UINT message,
              WPARAM wparam,LPARAM lparam) {
  PAINTSTRUCT paint;
  HDC dc = BeginPaint(window,&paint);
  Palette->Select(dc);
  // perform redraw here
  Palette->Select(NULL);
  EndPaint(window,&paint);
  return 0;
}
```

The most complicated part of the PALETTE class is the constructor — like the DIB class constructor this is built around a single Windows 98 function:

```
PALETTE::PALETTE(void) {
    .
    .
  Palette = CreatePalette(palette);
    .
    .
}
```

The initialization and finalization stages before and after this call are also similar to the `DIB` class constructor. The previous section has already outlined the procedure — the first step is to retrieve the size of the system palette and the number of static colours:

```
HDC dc = CreateCompatibleDC(NULL);
int palettesize,staticcolours;
palettesize = GetDeviceCaps(dc,SIZEPALETTE);
staticcolours = GetDeviceCaps(dc,NUMCOLORS)/2;
```

Next, sufficient storage space is allocated from the program's main heap to hold an extended `LOGPALETTE` structure:

```
int heapspace = sizeof(LOGPALETTE)+
   (palettesize-1)*sizeof(PALETTEENTRY);
HANDLE heap = GetProcessHeap();
LOGPALETTE* palette =
   (LOGPALETTE*)HeapAlloc(heap,0,heapspace);
```

The `palVersion` and `palNumEntries` fields of this structure are set:

```
palette->palVersion = 0x300;
palette->palNumEntries = palettesize;
```

Then the colour information is copied from the system palette and from the `Colours` array located in a header file:

```
PALETTEENTRY* colours = palette->palPalEntry;
GetSystemPaletteEntries(dc,
                0,palettesize,colours);
DeleteDC(dc);
for (int i=staticcolours;
              i<palettesize-staticcolours; i++)
  colours[i] = Colours[i];
```

The `peFlags` field of each `PALETTEENTRY` structure is set appropriately:

```
for (i=0; i<palettesize; i++)
  if (i<staticcolours ||
                  i>=palettesize-staticcolours)
    colours[i].peFlags = 0;
  else
    colours[i].peFlags = PC_NOCOLLAPSE;
```

These last two steps are designed to create an identity palette. The function `CreatePalette()` may now be called and afterwards the storage space allocated to the `LOGPALETTE` structure is released:

```
HeapFree(heap,0,palette);
```

Whenever the `PALETTE` object is destroyed its destructor deletes the associated logical palette:

```
PALETTE::~PALETTE(void) {
   DeleteObject(Palette);
}
```

As a demonstration of the `PALETTE` class the `VIEW` class will be modified to draw a grid of squares each containing one colour from the palette. The output from the program is illustrated by the following grey-scale figure — with a full-colour display the individual squares will be coloured according to the contents of the newly created palette:

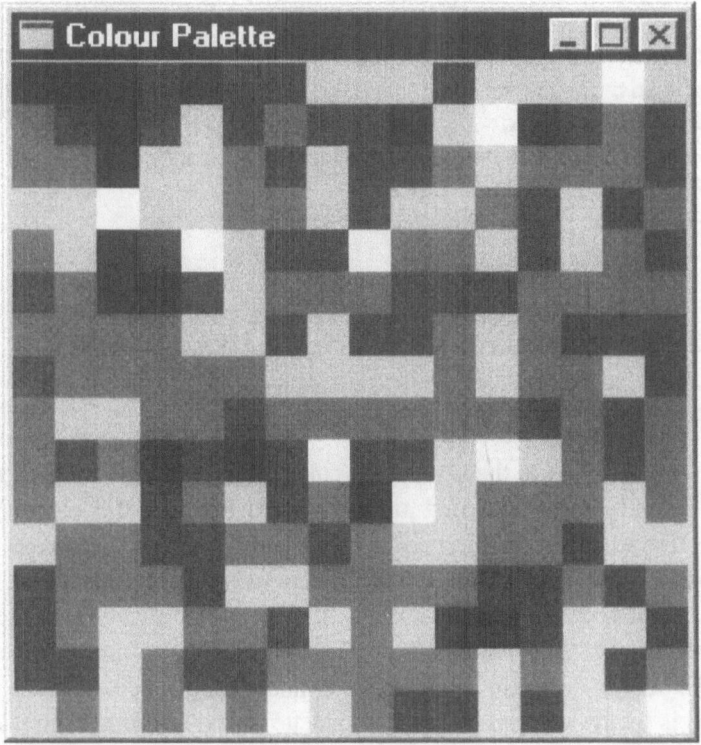

Each square in the grid is painted with a brush created by the function `CreateSolidBrush()` first introduced in chapter 4 — the `PALETTEINDEX()` macro is used to specify a colour by its position in the logical palette rather than by its RGB colour components:

```
void VIEW::PaintSquare(HDC dc,int x,int y) {
  COLORREF colour = PALETTEINDEX(x/16+y);
  HBRUSH brush = CreateSolidBrush(colour);
  RECT rect;
  rect.right = 16+(rect.left=x);
  rect.bottom = 16+(rect.top=y);
  FillRect(dc,&rect,brush);
  DeleteObject(brush);
}
```

The PaintSquare() helper function is called by the VIEW class Paint()
function which serves as the main WM_PAINT handler:

```
LRESULT
VIEW::Paint(HWND window,UINT message,
            WPARAM wparam,LPARAM lparam) {
  PAINTSTRUCT paint;
  HDC dc = BeginPaint(window,&paint);
  Palette->Select(dc);
  for (int y=0; y<256; y+=16)
    for (int x=0; x<256; x+=16)
      PaintSquare(dc,x,y);
  Palette->Select(NULL);
  EndPaint(window,&paint);
  return 0;
}
```

The PaintSquare() function consequently displays the 256 palette colours in
order arranging them as a series of 16 rows each containing 16 colours.

6.5 Updating the DIB Class

When a DIB is blitted to the screen, the colour information it contains may be
transformed several times. The first transformation involves the bitmap's own
colour table, the second uses the logical palette for the device context of the
destination window and the last maps to the system palette — curiously, the logical
palette for the device context actually holding the DIB is not involved. Each byte in
the DIB image is used as a pointer into the DIB colour table and this colour is
matched to the nearest available colour in the window's logical palette. The palette
index selected is finally mapped to a system palette index — this is the data value
that is stored in video memory to display the pixel on the screen. The PALETTE
class creates an identity palette so that these transformations of the bitmap colour
information can be avoided — the efficiency of bitmap graphics applications is
consequently increased.

The following figure illustrates the flow of colour information when BitBlt() is called:

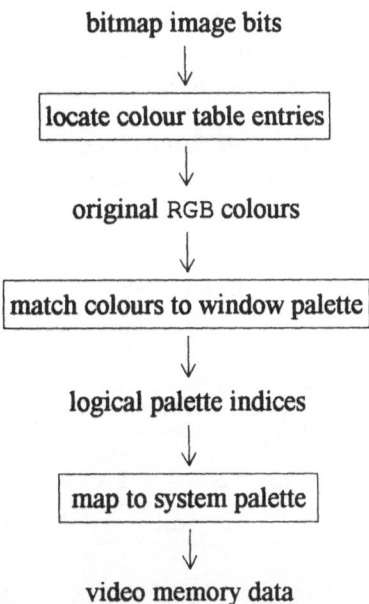

The identity palette provided by the PALETTE class removes the final transformation — the other necessity for efficient bitmap processing is to abandon the DIB colour table and use logical palette indices directly in the image bits of the bitmap. The colour matching process is then removed entirely — in fact with an identity palette the bitmap image bits are valid video memory data and so the BitBlt() function can transfer the image bits to the window with a simple memory-to-memory copy.

Of course, when the image bits of a bitmap contain RGB colour information directly this data can also be transferred straight to video memory by the BitBlt() function. The only catch is that the colour format of the bitmap must match that of the display — if the formats differ then a transformation is once more required. Section 6.1 listed the range of display modes which are commonly available — the various modes differ in the number of bits per pixel required and whether or not a system palette is involved. The number of bits per pixel supported by the display can be determined by calling the GetDeviceCaps() function with the BITSPIXEL flag as a parameter — the GetDeviceCaps() function will also determine if the device is palettized or not. For example:

```
BOOL systempalette =
  RC_PALETTE&GetDeviceCaps(dc,RASTERCAPS);
BitsPerPixel = GetDeviceCaps(dc,BITSPIXEL);
```

Here the `systempalette` variable is `TRUE` if there is a system palette and `FALSE` if the display does not use a palette. In either case the `BitsPerPixel` variable holds the number of bits needed in video memory to display each pixel — this is not necessarily the same value as the colour depth of the display. For example, a palettized device may have a colour depth which exceeds the `BitsPerPixel` value but not all colours are available simultaneously.

The following figure illustrates the four formats supported by Windows 98 for directly incorporating the colour information into the image bits:

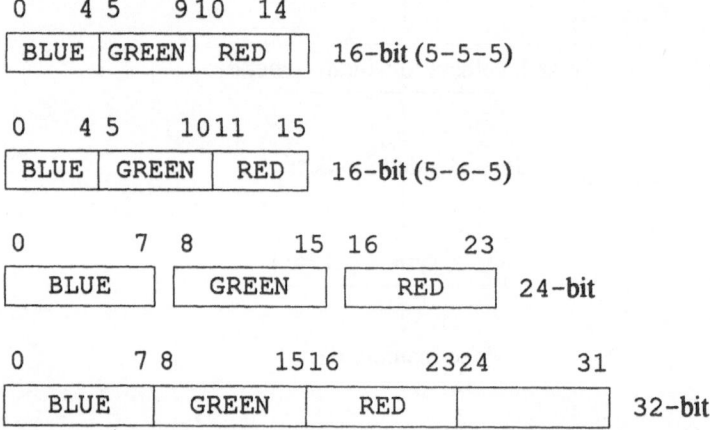

The 16-bit formats store the RGB values in a WORD whilst the 32-bit format uses a DWORD instead — the 24-bit format arranges its RGB colour information in three consecutive bytes. There are a number of unused bits — bit 15 in the first 16-bit format and also bits 24 to 31 in the 32-bit format. In general the `GetDeviceCaps()` function can be called to determine the current display mode. However, distinguishing between the two 16-bit formats is a little more complicated because the basic Windows 98 API does not provide a function to retrieve this information — one approach involves the following steps:

1. create a DIB with a known 16-bit format
2. select the bitmap into a display-compatible device context
3. create an icon using the `CreateIcon()` function
4. draw the icon to the bitmap with the `DrawIcon()` function
5. delete the icon by calling the `DestroyIcon()` function
6. examine the bitmap image bits directly

By choosing appropriate colours for the icon it is possible to establish if the DIB format matches the display format — the key is to test if the drawing operation modified the colour information transferred from the icon to the bitmap.

Once the display format is known a DIB can be created with a compatible format — for the sake of simplicity the DIB class will assume that only the first 16-bit format is available. The choice of colour format selects the layout of image bits for each individual pixel but it is also necessary to understand how the collection of pixels are arranged within the completed image. In fact, the pixels will be stored line-by-line from the top of the image to the bottom and each line in turn is scanned from left to right — an alternative is to scan the lines in bottom-up order but this option is not discussed here. Consequently when the DIB is displayed, the first pixel described by the bitmap image bits appears at the top left of the image and the last pixel appears at the bottom right. The following figure illustrates the arrangement for a 4-by-4 bitmap image:

Top Scanline	0	1	2	3
	4	5	6	7
	8	9	10	11
Bottom Scanline	12	13	14	15

The numbers in the image grid refer to the ordering of pixels within the image bits of the bitmap. The dimensions of the DIB passed to the CreateDIBSection() function are in pixel units and for each pixel there are 1, 2, 3 or 4 bytes of colour data depending on the format used — however, each scanline must contain a multiple of four bytes so the end of each line is padded with extra bytes if necessary. Apart from any padding bytes the colour data for the pixel at the end of one line is directly followed by that for the pixel at the start of the next line — the image bits data may therefore be treated as a continuous single-dimension array if suitable indexing is used. For a bitmap with 8 bits per pixel the following code to set a pixel at coordinates (x,y) within the image is typical:

```
int pitch = Dib->GetPitch();
BYTE* bits = Dib->AcquireBits();
bits[x+y*pitch] = colour;
Dib->ReleaseBits();
```

The next chapter discusses the procedure in more detail and the remainder of the book is devoted to implementing various algorithms for drawing an image in a bitmap. Note here that the DIB object provides the GetPitch() function to return the padded width of the bitmap — this value is pre-calculated in the DIB constructor as follows:

```
Pitch = (Width*BitsPerPixel/8+3)&~3;
```

The Width field of the DIB object holds the width of the bitmap in pixel units and the BitsPerPixel field takes one of the values 8, 16, 24 or 32 depending on the colour format. The new DIB class will handle a variety of colour formats:

```
class PALETTE;

class DIB {
public:
  DIB(int,int,int,PALETTE* = NULL);
  ~DIB(void);
  BYTE* AcquireBits(void);
  void ReleaseBits(void);
  void Blit(HDC,int,int) const;
  int GetPitch(void) const;
private:
  PALETTE* Palette;
  HBITMAP Bitmap;
  BYTE* Bits;
  int Width;
  int Height;
  int Pitch;
  int BitsPerPixel;
};
```

When BitsPerPixel equals 8 the Palette field holds a handle to the logical palette associated with the bitmap — the bitmap no longer stores colour information directly in its colour table. The DIB class constructor is again built around the CreateDIBSection() function:

```
DIB::DIB(int width,int height,
         int bits,PALETTE* palette) :
  Width(width), Height(height) {
     .
     .
  flag = (Palette?DIB_PAL_COLORS:DIB_RGB_COLORS);
  if (Palette)
    Palette->Select(dc);
  Bitmap = CreateDIBSection(dc,format,flag,
                            (void**)&Bits,NULL,0);
  if (Palette)
    Palette->Select(NULL);
     .
     .
}
```

However, the DIB_RGB_COLORS flag is now replaced by the DIB_PAL_COLORS flag whenever the colour information for the bitmap is supplied by a palette — the palette must be selected into the device context which is passed to the CreateDIBSection() function. The initialization procedure prior to creating the bitmap begins in a similar manner to before:

```
HDC dc = CreateCompatibleDC(NULL);
int heapspace = sizeof(BITMAPINFOHEADER);
if ((BitsPerPixel=bits) == 8) {
  Palette = palette;
  heapspace += 256*sizeof(WORD);
}
HANDLE heap = GetProcessHeap();
BITMAPINFO* format =
  (BITMAPINFO*)HeapAlloc(heap,0,heapspace);
```

However, for a colour format with 8 bits per pixel the DIB object now expects to receive an associated palette — furthermore, the array of RGBQUAD colour descriptors within the BITMAPINFO structure is replaced with an array of WORD entries that will hold logical palette indices. For the other colour formats neither a colour table nor an associated palette are required — in this case the colour information appears directly in the image bits. The header portion of the format structure is filled in using similar values to the original DIB class:

```
BITMAPINFOHEADER* header =
  (BITMAPINFOHEADER*)format;
header->biSize = sizeof(BITMAPINFOHEADER);
header->biWidth = Width;
header->biHeight = -Height;
header->biPlanes = 1;
header->biBitCount = BitsPerPixel;
header->biCompression = BI_RGB;
header->biSizeImage = 0;
header->biXPelsPerMeter = 0;
header->biYPelsPerMeter = 0;
header->biClrUsed = 0;
header->biClrImportant = 0;
```

The only change is that the biBitCount field now holds the appropriate number of bits per pixel. If BitsPerPixel holds the value 8 then the array of logical palette indices needs to be initialized:

```
if (BitsPerPixel == 8) {
  WORD* indices = (WORD*)format->bmiColors;
  for (WORD i=0; i<256; i++)
    indices[i] = i;
}
```

The values are assigned in such a way that the image bits directly correspond to logical palette indices — this cuts out any unnecessary transformation of the colour information whenever the BitBlt() function is invoked to blit the bitmap to a window. The CreateDIBSection() function can now be called to create a device independent bitmap with or without an associated palette — afterwards the clean-up procedure is straightforward:

```
HeapFree(heap,0,format);
DeleteDC(dc);
```

Whenever the DIB object is destroyed the destructor deletes the object's bitmap as before — if there is an associated palette its destruction is left to the PALETTE object which created it. However, the DIB class Blit() function is updated to select a bitmap's palette in and out of a device context:

```
void DIB::Blit(HDC dc,int x,int y) const {
  HDC memorydc = CreateCompatibleDC(dc);
  HBITMAP oldbitmap;
  oldbitmap = (HBITMAP)SelectObject(memorydc,Bitmap);
  if (Palette)
    Palette->Select(dc);
  BitBlt(dc,x,y,Width,Height,
          memorydc,0,0,SRCCOPY);
  if (Palette)
    Palette->Select(NULL);
  SelectObject(memorydc,oldbitmap);
  DeleteDC(memorydc);
}
```

This considerably simplies the VIEW class WM_PAINT handler — for example, the House Builder program from chapter 5 is implemented as follows:

```
LRESULT
VIEW::Paint(HWND window,UINT message,
            WPARAM wparam,LPARAM lparam) {
  PAINTSTRUCT paint;
  HDC dc = BeginPaint(window,&paint);
  for (int i=0; i<Length; i++)
    Dib->Blit(dc,Dots[i].x,Dots[i].y);
  EndPaint(window,&paint);
  return 0;
}
```

Of course, the VIEW class must initialize the PALETTE and DIB objects:

```
VIEW::VIEW(LPCTSTR title) {
  SetupPalette();
  SetupDib();
  Create(title);
}
```

The helper functions SetupPalette() and SetupDib() actually do the work:

```
void VIEW::SetupPalette(void) {
  HDC dc = CreateCompatibleDC(NULL);
  BOOL systempalette =
    RC_PALETTE&GetDeviceCaps(dc,RASTERCAPS);
  BitsPerPixel = GetDeviceCaps(dc,BITSPIXEL);
  DeleteDC(dc);
  Palette = (PALETTE*)
    (systempalette?new PALETTE():NULL);
}

void VIEW::SetupDib(void) {
  Dib = (DIB*) new
    DIB(DIBSIZE,DIBSIZE,BitsPerPixel,Palette);
}
```

Similarly the VIEW class destructor deletes the DIB and PALETTE objects and so releases the underlying Windows 98 resources:

```
VIEW::~VIEW(void) {
  delete Dib;
  if (Palette)
    delete Palette;
}
```

The VIEW class must also handle the palette messages introduced in section 6.2 using the PALETTE class Realize() function (see section 6.4 for details).

6.6 Summary

Windows 98 palettes are used to hold RGB colour information for bitmaps, windows or the computer display. A logical palette is associated with a window or bitmap by selecting it into a device context — the system palette applies to the computer display and is used whenever a limited range of colours must be shared amongst a number of different applications. The only common display mode to need a system palette assigns 8 bits per pixel and so provides a range of 256 colours — display modes with 16 or more bits per pixel do not require a system palette. A logical palette is created by placing its description in a LOGPALETTE structure and then passing this structure to the CreatePalette() function. The logical palette can influence the colours held by the system palette through the RealizePalette() function — this function attempts to match the system palette colours as closely as possible to the colours specified in the logical palette. The window message WM_QUERYNEWPALETTE is sent to a window whenever it moves to the foreground — the window should realize its palette in the handler for this message. Once the system palette is changed background windows receive the WM_PALETTECHANGED message to notify them that they should do their best to remap their colours. The PALETTE class has been defined to embody an identity palette — such a palette is required to deal with bitmaps efficiently. The PALETTE class provides utility functions to select its logical palette into a device context and to realize the logical palette. The DIB class has also been updated to accommodate a variety of colour formats — the DIB colour format should match that of the display if the best performance is to be achieved by a graphics application. The DIB class can now work with an associated PALETTE object — the DIB class Blit() function takes care of selecting the bitmap's palette before transferring the bitmap image to a window.

7. Sprite Animation

All the Windows 98 facilities needed to produce a graphics application have now been discussed — this chapter starts to look at methods of utilizing these building blocks. In particular the chapter discusses the 2D images known as 'sprites' which move independently about the screen — later chapters will develop techniques for generating the computer representation of an entire 3D virtual world. Nonetheless, the essential animation techniques covered here are common to both 2D and 3D applications. The main topics include:

— the SPRITE class
— basic computer animation
— avoiding flicker with a back buffer
— transparent pixels
— manipulating bitmap image bits directly
— driving an animation with a timer
— accepting user input from the keyboard
— thread synchronization techniques

The chapter also derives a couple of sprite classes (SPACECRAFT and BOUNCER) from the SPRITE base class to illustrate the power of object oriented programming.

7.1 The SPRITE Class

A bounded graphical image which can be moved from one position on the screen to another is known as a sprite. The sprite image may remain constant or alternatively it can change as the sprite moves — for example, a collection of related images could be used to simulate the motion of a creature walking or a spacecraft firing booster rockets. The following figure illustrates a typical image loop:

The SPRITE class will be defined to implement a sprite — each SPRITE object must contain the current state of the sprite (position, velocity, image and so on) along with functions to update this state. The class also needs a Draw() function to display the sprite image at the correct location on the screen.

Here is the SPRITE class specification:

```
class DIB;

class SPRITE {
public:
    SPRITE(DIB**);
    virtual ~SPRITE(void);
    virtual void Move(void);
    virtual void Animate(DIB* = NULL);
    virtual void Update(void);
    virtual void Draw(HDC);
    virtual void SetScale(int);
    virtual POINT SetPosition(const POINT*);
    virtual POINT SetVelocity(const POINT*);
    virtual POINT SetAcceleration(const POINT*);
protected:
    POINT Position;
    POINT Velocity;
    POINT Acceleration;
    DIB* Images[MAX_IMAGES];
    DIB** Image;
    int Scale;
};
```

The class is designed as a base class that will be extended by other derived classes — the protected keyword allows the derived classes to directly manipulate the internal state of the SPRITE object whilst the virtual functions can be overridden by the derived classes to provide specific behaviours. The constructor initializes the Images array with a sequence of DIB* pointers terminated by a NULL pointer value:

```
SPRITE::SPRITE(DIB** images) {
    int i = 0;
    while (Images[i++] = *images++);
    Image = Images;
    Position.x = Position.y = 0;
    Velocity.x = Velocity.y = 0;
    Acceleration.x = Acceleration.y = 0;
    Scale = 1;
}
```

The constructor also zeroes the Position, Velocity and Acceleration fields. The SetPosition() function may be called to set the Position field to some other value — the current position can be retrieved by passing a NULL pointer as a parameter. The SetVelocity() and SetAcceleration() functions have similar capabilities to the SetPosition() function. A common alternative is simply to define three `Get` functions to complement the `Set` functions. Here is the definition of the `SetPosition()` function:

```
POINT
SPRITE::SetPosition(const POINT* position) {
  if (position)
    Position = *position;
  return Position;
}
```

The `SetVelocity()` and `SetAcceleration()` functions are similarly defined. The `Move()` function updates the `Position` and `Velocity` fields:

```
void SPRITE::Move(void) {
  Position.x += Velocity.x;
  Position.y += Velocity.y;
  Velocity.x += Acceleration.x;
  Velocity.y += Acceleration.y;
}
```

A steady sprite motion may be achieved by setting the acceleration to zero. Alternatively, the `Scale` field permits the gentle application of a non-zero acceleration by allowing the sprite position to be measured in fractions of a pixel.

The `Animate()` function can select a particular image from the `Images` array but by default it simply cycles through array entries:

```
void SPRITE::Animate(DIB* image) {
  if (image) {
    Image = Images;
    while (*Image != image)
      Image++;
  }
  else {
    Image++;
    if (!*Image)
      Image = Images;
  }
}
```

The `Update()` function combines the `Move()` and `Animate()` functions — the `Update()` function is intended to update the overall state of a sprite and should be overridden in derived sprite classes to implement specific behaviours.

```
void SPRITE::Update(void) {
  Move();
  Animate();
}
```

Finally the Draw() function draws the current image at the correct position:

```
void SPRITE::Draw(HDC dc) {
  POINT pixel;
  pixel.x = Position.x/Scale;
  pixel.y = Position.y/Scale;
  (*Image)->Blit(dc,pixel.x,pixel.y);
}
```

In the following sections the general-purpose SPRITE class will be extended by the derivation of specific sprite classes — this is exactly the same technique as used with the WINDOW and VIEW classes.

7.2 Animation

An important characteristic of a sprite is that its state evolves over time — the sprite moves and changes its image. This section describes the process of computer animation and its application to sprites. The basic animation procedure involves the following three steps repeated over and over:

1. Erase the original image of the sprite
2. Update the sprite with Move() and Animate() functions
3. Draw the new image of the sprite

The following figure illustrates the sequence of events:

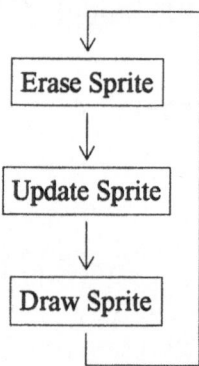

To produce a smooth animation this loop must be synchronized so that each iteration takes approximately the same amount of time. The approach adopted here is to generate a stream of WM_TIMER messages — the message handler updates the sprite and posts a WM_PAINT message to redraw the sprite. Chapter 10 discusses an alternative technique that separates the animation loop from any message handlers — this option typically allows a higher iteration rate by synchronizing the loop directly to the system clock with the GetTickCount() function.

Here are the VIEW class message handlers:

```
LRESULT
VIEW::Timer(HWND window,UINT message,
            WPARAM wparam,LPARAM lparam) {
  Sprite->Update();
  InvalidateRect(window,NULL,TRUE);
  return 0;
}

LRESULT
VIEW::Paint(HWND window,UINT message,
            WPARAM wparam,LPARAM lparam) {
  PAINTSTRUCT paint;
  HDC dc = BeginPaint(window,&paint);
  Sprite->Draw(dc);
  EndPaint(window,&paint);
  return 0;
}
```

The Sprite pointer which references the sprite object is a base class pointer of SPRITE* type — this permits the VIEW class code to handle all types of sprite in a uniform manner. If the derived sprite classes override the virtual functions provided by the SPRITE class then these new versions are invoked by the VIEW object — this is an example of the object oriented mechanism of polymorphism previously discussed in section 3.1.

The SPACECRAFT class is now derived from the SPRITE class to implement a spacecraft that drifts to the surface of a planet under the influence of gravity — the spacecraft is also provided with booster rockets that are ignited by calling the object's Burn() function. The following figure shows the completed program in action:

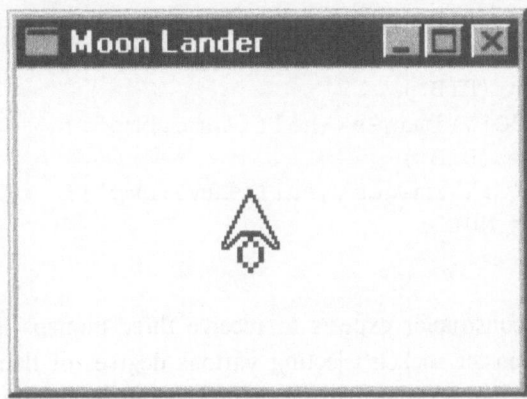

Here is the SPACECRAFT class specification:

```
class DIB;

class SPACECRAFT : public SPRITE {
public:
  SPACECRAFT(DIB**);
  virtual void Update(void);
  void Burn(BOOL);
  void SetGravity(int);
  void SetThrust(int);
private:
  int Gravity;
  int Thrust;
  BOOL Booster;
  int Ignition;
};
```

The SPACECRAFT object is created when the VIEW class constructor calls the SetupSprite() helper function:

```
void VIEW::SetupSprite(void) {
  Sprite = (SPRITE*) new SPACECRAFT(Images);
  POINT velocity = {SPEED_X,SPEED_Y};
  Sprite->SetVelocity(&velocity);
  Sprite->SetScale(VIEW_SCALE);
}
```

The VIEW class has previously created the bitmaps in its Images array with the SetupImages() function:

```
void VIEW::SetupImages(void) {
  Images[0] = (DIB*)
    new DIB("C:\\images\\noflame.bmp");
  Images[1] = (DIB*)
    new DIB("C:\\images\\halfflame.bmp");
  Images[2] = (DIB*)
    new DIB("C:\\images\\fullflame.bmp");
  Images[3] = NULL;
}
```

The SPACECRAFT constructor expects to receive three bitmaps that depict the spacecraft with its booster rockets ejecting various degrees of flame — suitable bitmaps are illustrated in section 7.1. The DIB* pointers are stored by passing them to the SPRITE class constructor as follows:

```
SPACECRAFT::SPACECRAFT(DIB** images) :
  SPRITE(images) {
  Gravity = GRAVITY;
  Thrust = THRUST;
  Booster = FALSE;
  Ignition = MIN_IGNITION;
}
```

The SPACECRAFT constructor also initializes the Gravity, Thrust, Booster and Ignition fields with default values from a header file. These fields are used to control the actions of the overriding Update() function defined by the SPACECRAFT class. This function is concerned with managing the spacecraft's booster rockets — it omits calling the SPRITE class Animate() function and instead updates the Image field directly. The Booster field indicates if the booster rockets are currently being fired and causes the value of the Ignition field to fluctuate between the MIN_IGNITION and MAX_IGNITION limits — when the Ignition value is sufficiently high the booster rockets are ignited by selecting a new bitmap image. Here is the implementation of the SPACECRAFT class Update() function:

```
void SPACECRAFT::Update(void) {
  Image = &Images[NO_FLAME];
  Acceleration.y = Gravity;
  if (Booster && Ignition<MAX_IGNITION)
    Ignition++;
  else if (!Booster && Ignition>MIN_IGNITION)
    Ignition--;
  if (Ignition>=MAX_FLAME_LEVEL) {
    Image = &Images[FULL_FLAME];
    Acceleration.y -= Thrust;
  }
  else if (Ignition>=HALF_FLAME_LEVEL) {
    Image = &Images[HALF_FLAME];
    Acceleration.y -= Thrust/2;
  }
  Move();
}
```

The Burn() function controls the value of the Booster field:

```
void SPACECRAFT::Burn(BOOL booster) {
  Booster = booster;
}
```

The VIEW class should call the Burn() function upon receipt of some user input such as pressing or releasing a key:

```
LRESULT
VIEW::KeyMovement(HWND window,UINT message,
                  WPARAM wparam,LPARAM lparam) {
  SPACECRAFT* spacecraft = (SPACECRAFT*)Sprite;
  BOOL pressed = !(lparam&0x80000000);
  spacecraft->Burn(pressed);
  return 0;
}
```

Here the KeyMovement() handler is called for both WM_KEYDOWN and WM_KEYUP messages — bit 31 of the lparam parameter indicates the type of message received.

The final problem is to generate the WM_TIMER messages to drive the animation along — a timer which will provide these messages is created and destroyed in the VIEW class Initialize() and Destroy() message handlers respectively:

```
LRESULT
VIEW::Initialize(HWND window,UINT message,
                 WPARAM wparam,LPARAM lparam) {
  SetTimer(window,0,TIMER_PERIOD,NULL);
  return 0;
}

LRESULT
VIEW::Destroy(HWND window,UINT message,
             WPARAM wparam,LPARAM lparam) {
  KillTimer(window,0);
  return
    WINDOW::Destroy(window,message,wparam,lparam);
}
```

The timer is identified in the SetTimer() and KillTimer() calls by the window to which it belongs and a timer ID (0). The third parameter to the SetTimer() function fixes the interval between timer messages — the value is specified in milliseconds.

7.3 Flicker

One problem with the program developed in the previous section is that the display flickers quite noticeably — this spoils the illusion of smooth motion. The problem is that the window background is erased before each redraw operation — the solution is to modify the animation loop so that it uses an off-screen buffer to prepare each new image. The off-screen buffer holds a copy of the window contents — it is often referred to as a 'back buffer'. The image of the sprite now moves in the buffer — firstly the old image is erased, then the sprite is updated and finally the new image is drawn. At the end of each iteration the updated buffer is copied to the screen — the result is that the sprite appears to move smoothly from one position to the next without flickering on and off. The following figure depicts the processing performed by the animation loop:

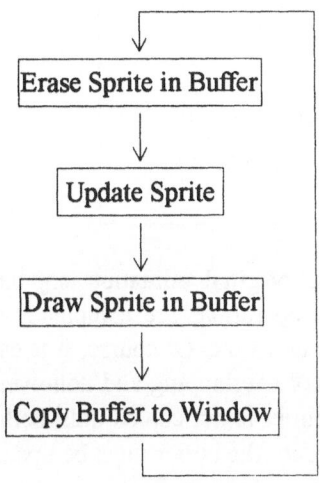

The back buffer is typically implemented as a DIB — the bitmap may hold the entire window contents or alternatively it may be just large enough to contain both old and new sprite images. The following figure demonstrates the latter possibility:

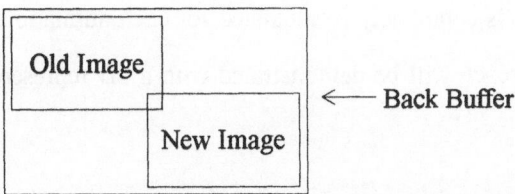

The old sprite image is erased by copying a background image to the back buffer and then the new sprite image can be drawn over the background — the newly composed result is then transferred to the window at the appropriate location. For the next iteration through the animation loop the back buffer will update a different portion of the window but it always contains the old and new sprite images. Unfortunately this means that the back buffer must be large if the sprite moves very rapidly. The solution is to separate the two cases where the old and new images overlap and where they do not — the back buffer is made just large enough to handle the first case. In the second case the animation loop is modified again:

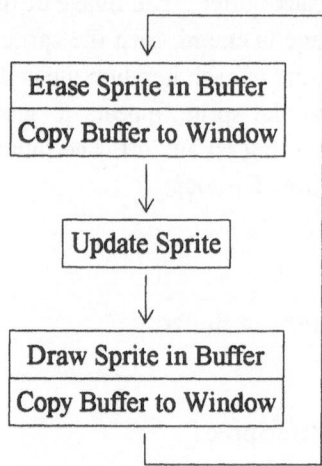

This is essentially the same as the original animation loop but now a back buffer is involved — the erase and draw operations are completely separate so the buffer need only hold one sprite image at a time. Of course, it is easy to merge the loops required to handle the two cases of overlapping and non-overlapping sprite images — in the former case the back buffer is not copied until both erase and draw steps are complete whilst in the latter case the buffer must be updated to represent a new window location before the sprite is redrawn.

A common theme throughout is how to erase the sprite and replace the original background image — there are basically three solutions to this problem:

1. The sprite saves the background which it obscures and later restores it
2. The entire background is stored separately in yet another bitmap
3. The background is completely recalculated for each animation frame

Here the third approach will be demonstrated with a 2D representation of a moon landscape:

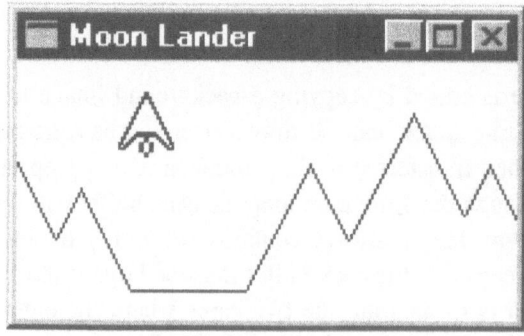

Later chapters will deal with the production of a much more complicated background image that represents a 3D virtual world. In any case the back buffer is implemented using the `DIB` class — to permit maximum flexibility in applying GDI functions to the background bitmap the `DIB` class needs a `Select()` function that selects its bitmap (and associated palette) into a device context:

```
void DIB::Select(HDC dc,HDC palettedc) {
  if (dc) {
    AcquireBits();
    OldBitmap = SelectObject(dc,Bitmap);
    DeviceContext = dc;
    if (Palette)
      Palette->Select(palettedc?palettedc:dc);
  }
  else {
    ReleaseBits();
    SelectObject(DeviceContext,OldBitmap);
    if (Palette)
      Palette->Select(NULL);
  }
}
```

This function is modelled on the `PALETTE` class `Select()` function. However, it also calls `AcquireBits()` to indicate that the bitmap is currently being drawn — a matching call to `ReleaseBits()` is made when drawing is complete. This procedure is intended to coordinate the actions of several concurrent threads which all attempt to manipulate the bitmap simultaneously — section 7.5 discusses this point in more detail. The `DIB` class `Blit()` function can be modified to call the `Select()` function internally:

```
void DIB::Blit(HDC dc,int x,int y) const {
  HDC memorydc = CreateCompatibleDC(dc);
  DIB* dib = (DIB*)this;
  dib->Select(memorydc,dc);
  BitBlt(dc,x,y,Width,Height,
         memorydc,0,0,SRCCOPY);
  dib->Select(NULL);
  DeleteDC(memorydc);
}
```

With the proper code in the `AcquireBits()` and `ReleaseBits()` functions the `DIB` object is able to ensure that its bitmap cannot be blitted by one thread whilst it is being redrawn by another.

Meanwhile, the VIEW class Paint() handler takes care of managing the back buffer:

```
LRESULT
VIEW::Paint(HWND window,UINT message,
            WPARAM wparam,LPARAM lparam) {
  PAINTSTRUCT paint;
  HDC windowdc = BeginPaint(window,&paint);
  HDC memorydc = CreateCompatibleDC(windowdc);
  Background->Select(memorydc);
  Draw(memorydc);
  Sprite->Draw(memorydc);
  Background->Select(NULL);
  DeleteDC(memorydc);
  Background->Blit(windowdc,0,0);
  EndPaint(window,&paint);
  return 0;
}
```

The background bitmap is selected into a memory device context and the sprite now draws itself onto this bitmap — the composite image is finally blitted to a window. The VIEW class Draw() function is called to erase the old sprite image by completely redrawing the background image:

```
void VIEW::Draw(HDC dc) {
  RECT rect;
  rect.left = rect.top = 0;
  rect.right = Terrain[LENGTH].x;
  rect.bottom = Terrain[LENGTH].y;
  FillRect(dc,&rect,GetStockObject(WHITE_BRUSH));
  MoveToEx(dc,Terrain[0].x,Terrain[0].y,NULL);
  for (int i=1; i<LENGTH; i++)
    LineTo(dc,Terrain[i].x,Terrain[i].y);
}
```

The Terrain array is defined in a header file and contains a number of POINT structures that specify the moon landscape to be drawn — the point held in Terrain[LENGTH] gives the dimensions of the image.

The final step in eliminating flicker from the animation is to update the WM_TIMER message handler:

```
LRESULT
VIEW::Timer(HWND window,UINT message,
            WPARAM wparam,LPARAM lparam) {
  Sprite->Update();
  InvalidateRect(window,NULL,FALSE);
  return 0;
}
```

The only modification is to change the final parameter of the function
InvalidateRect() from TRUE to FALSE — this prevents Windows 98 from
automatically erasing the window background whenever the BeginPaint()
function is invoked. The call to blit the back buffer to the window is now the only
operation which updates the window contents and so there is no flicker.

The back buffer technique for removing flicker is applied in most animation
programs — however, there is an alternative to blitting as the means of transferring
the back buffer to the screen. The process is known as 'flipping' and it requires
specialized video hardware — the video memory holding the current screen image
is instantaneously switched with the back buffer. To perform animation a pair of
video buffers are flipped back and forth — whilst one buffer is displaying the
current animation frame the other buffer is being used to construct the next frame.
Flipping is faster than blitting and can be synchronized with the display hardware
to avoid the problem of 'tear' — this occurs when the top of one frame is
simultaneously displayed with the bottom of another frame. Fortunately, tear is
much less noticeable than flicker and so blitting is usually quite acceptable. The
DirectX software development kit from Microsoft provides a hardware-independent
interface to the video buffer flipping mechanism.

7.4 Transparency

A close inspection of the output produced by the Moon Lander program
shows that the displayed sprite image actually includes the whole of the sprite's
bitmap — the rectangular bitmap will obscure parts of the background image even
when the sprite outline itself does not. This is hardly realistic behaviour but the
problem is easily solved by using transparent pixels for that portion of the sprite
bitmap which surrounds the sprite outline. Whenever the sprite is displayed the
transparent pixels allow the background image to show through — furthermore,
with a collection of sprites it is possible for a nearby sprite to apparently pass in
front of another more distant sprite. To illustrate the transparency mechanism the
VIEW class will now animate a host of sprites that bounce around the screen — the
background will be drawn as a checkerboard pattern. Firstly the SPRITE class is
modified to overload the Draw() function with a version that will handle
transparent pixels:

```
class DIB;

class SPRITE {
public:
  virtual void Draw(DIB*);
    .
    .
};
```

The new `Draw()` function is passed a `DIB` object pointer — the sprite image should overlay the bitmap held by this object:

```
void SPRITE::Draw(DIB* dib) {
  POINT pixel;
  pixel.x = Position.x/Scale;
  pixel.y = Position.y/Scale;
  (*Image)->Overlay(dib,pixel.x,pixel.y);
}
```

This function is simply a wrapper for a new `DIB` class `Overlay()` function — the initialization for the `Overlay()` function obtains parameters from the back buffer bitmap:

```
void DIB::Overlay(DIB* dib,int x_origin,
                            int y_origin) const {
  BYTE pixel;
  int x,y,x_buffer,y_buffer;
  int width = dib->Width;
  int height = dib->Height;
  int pitch = dib->Pitch;
  int bits = dib->AcquireBits();
  ((DIB*)this)->AcquireBits();
  BYTE transparent = Bits[0];
  RECT overlay = {0,0,Width,Height};
  RECT buffer = {0,0,width,height};
```

The `AcquireBits()` function is called both for the buffer bitmap and also for the overlay bitmap — as noted in the previous section this is intended to prevent simultaneous manipulation of the bitmaps by more than one thread. The transparent pixel colour is taken from the first pixel in the image bits array of the overlay bitmap — for the sake of simplicity the code assumes that the colour format is 8 bits per pixel. Whenever bitmaps are manipulated directly the program cannot rely on the GDI to perform clipping operations — instead the `overlay` and `buffer` rectangles are used here to clip the region of pixels actually transferred. In particular, the `IntersectRect()` function clips the `overlay` rectangle to the bounds of the `buffer` rectangle — the function returns TRUE only if the two rectangles intersect.

```
OffsetRect(&overlay,x_origin,y_origin);
if (IntersectRect(&overlay,&overlay,&buffer)) {
  buffer = overlay;
  OffsetRect(&overlay,-x_origin,-y_origin);
     .
     .
```

The pixels are now transferred from the `overlay` rectangle (in the sprite) to the `buffer` rectangle (in the background bitmap):

```
        .
        .
    y = overlay.top;
    y_buffer = buffer.top;
    while (y < overlay.bottom) {
      x = overlay.left;
      x_buffer = buffer.left;
      while (x < overlay.right) {
        pixel = Bits[x+y*Pitch];
        if (pixel != transparent)
          bits[x_buffer+y_buffer*pitch] = pixel;
        x++, x_buffer++;
      }
      y++, y_buffer++;
    }
  }
```

Each pixel in the `Bits` array is tested against the transparent pixel colour — no transparent pixels are transferred to the buffer bitmap. The final action of the `Overlay()` function is to release the buffer and overlay image bits:

```
    dib->ReleaseBits();
    ((DIB*)this)->ReleaseBits();
  }
```

The latest `VIEW` class can now display an array of bouncing sprites:

The background pattern is clearly visible through the transparent portions of the sprites.

The VIEW class Paint() function has the following definition:

```
LRESULT VIEW::Paint(HWND window,UINT message,
                    WPARAM wparam,LPARAM lparam) {
  PAINTSTRUCT paint;
  HDC windowdc = BeginPaint(window,&paint);
  Draw();
  for (int i=0; i<MAX_SPRITES; i++)
    Sprites[i]->Draw(Background);
  Background->Blit(windowdc,0,0);
  EndPaint(window,&paint);
  return 0;
}
```

The VIEW class Draw() function is responsible for producing the checkerboard pattern that forms the background image:

```
void VIEW::Draw(void) {
  int x,y;
  BOOL colour;
  int pitch = Background->GetPitch();
  BYTE* bits = Background->AcquireBits();
  for (y=0; y<HEIGHT; y++)
    for (x=0; x<WIDTH; x++) {
      colour = ((x/16)+(y/16))%2;
      bits[x+y*pitch] = (colour?WHITE:BLACK);
    }
  Background->ReleaseBits();
}
```

The BOUNCER class is derived from the SPRITE class — it overrides the Update() function to change the velocity of the sprite if it reaches a boundary:

```
void BOUNCER::Update(void) {
  Move();
  Animate();
  POINT pixel;
  pixel.x = Position.x/Scale;
  pixel.y = Position.y/Scale;
  if (pixel.x<Boundary.left ||
                     pixel.x>=Boundary.right)
    Velocity.x = -Velocity.x;
  if (pixel.y<Boundary.top ||
                     pixel.y>=Boundary.bottom)
    Velocity.y = -Velocity.y;
}
```

The Boundary rectangle is passed to the BOUNCER sprite object as a parameter to its constructor and is then adjusted to account for the sprite dimensions.

7.5 Threads

A Windows 98 program can have several threads of execution all running concurrently. Whenever a program starts there is a single thread — new threads may be created with the `CreateThread()` function. Windows 98 passes control to the original thread by invoking the `WinMain()` function — for new threads an analogous 'thread function' is specified as a parameter of the `CreateThread()` function. Just like `WinMain()` the thread function encompasses all processing performed by a thread — each new thread is started when `CreateThread()` invokes its thread function and it can exit by returning from the thread function. The important point is that all threads belonging to the program share their resources — a possible application here is to distribute the processing for a collection of sprites amongst a number of threads and allow the threads to share the back buffer bitmap. Most of the code in this book assumes a single-thread program but the `DIB` class `AcquireBits()` and `ReleaseBits()` functions illustrate multi-threaded programming — to avoid corruption when several threads attempt to manipulate the same bitmap simultaneously this pair of functions synchronize the activities of the threads. The technique uses a Windows 98 'mutex' object — this object is designed to enforce mutual exclusion since only one thread can acquire the mutex at a time. Each `DIB` object creates its own mutex with a call to `CreateMutex()` in the `DIB` constructor — similarly the mutex is destroyed with the `CloseHandle()` function in the `DIB` destructor. The `DIB` class function `AcquireBits()` waits until the `DIB` object's mutex becomes free before releasing control of the image bits:

```
BYTE* DIB::AcquireBits(void) {
  WaitForSingleObject(Mutex,INFINITE);
  return Bits;
}
```

Similarly, the `ReleaseBits()` function releases the mutex to allow other threads to manipulate the bitmap's image bits:

```
void ReleaseBits(void) {
  ReleaseMutex(Mutex);
}
```

The following three activities for processing the bitmap should be considered as indivisible:

— `AcquireBits()`, update image bits directly, `ReleaseBits()`
— `Select(dc)`, call GDI drawing functions, `Select(NULL)`
— `Blit(dc,x,y)` or `Overlay(dib,x,y)`

A pair of functions such as `LockBits()` and `UnlockBits()` could be defined to bracket a sequence of steps which must not be interleaved with processing by another thread.

A final word on the sharing of resources — the `AcquireBits()` and `ReleaseBits()` functions defined above do not prevent one thread from selecting a bitmap into several different device contexts. If this is attempted the current implementation will corrupt the `OldBitmap` and `DeviceContext` fields of the `DIB` object — a similar problem arises with `PALETTE` objects and is particularly likely to occur if several bitmaps attempt to share a common `PALETTE` object. A possible solution for palettes is to enforce the rule that a `PALETTE` object may only be selected into a single device context but to allow several `PALETTE` objects to share an underlying Windows 98 palette.

7.6 Summary

A sprite is a computer image which moves about the screen — the sprite may also change its image as it moves. The `SPRITE` class has been defined to provide the basic functionality required by a sprite — the class is intended to serve as a base class from which other sprite classes may be derived. The derived classes (such as `SPACECRAFT` and `BOUNCER`) implement more complex sprite behaviours. A sprite is animated using an erase-update-redraw loop — here the loop is driven by the regular arrival of `WM_TIMER` pulses. A straightforward approach to animation is to draw each image frame directly to the window — however, the continual erase-redraw sequence for sprites is clearly visible as flicker. To overcome this problem an off-screen buffer may be used to compose the next animation frame — once the image is complete it can be transferred to the window in a single operation (blitting or flipping). There are several alternatives for mapping a back buffer to the screen but one possibility is to hold the entire window contents in the buffer — this approach is particularly appropriate for animating 3D scenes. The `Overlay()` function has been added to the `DIB` class to accommodate transparent pixels — wherever the sprite image has a transparent pixel the background image is allowed to show through. Transparency permits sprites to have irregular outlines and hence enables one sprite to pass in front of another in a realistic manner — direct manipulation of the sprite image bits is necessary to implement transparency efficiently. Finally, a Windows 98 program may operate with multiple execution threads — the thread synchronization mechanisms needed to avoid corruption of a shared bitmap (or other shared data) were outlined by discussing the `AcquireBits()` and `ReleaseBits()` functions.

8. Wire-Frame Graphics

The last chapter showed how the graphics facilities provided by Windows 98 can be applied to generate 2D bitmap graphics — this chapter continues the exploration of new graphical algorithms by creating wire-frame images of 3D objects. Indeed this is the first step in producing a graphical representation of an entire virtual world — the remaining chapters in the book continue to develop this idea. The key topics covered here include:

— polygon representation of 3D objects
— the OBJECT and POLYGON classes
— capturing a 3D image with a SCENE object
— line-drawing and line-clipping algorithms
— managing a virtual world with a WORLD object

The chapter also develops a couple of graphics applications to demonstrate the generation of wire-frame images and to illustrate the line-clipping algorithms.

8.1 Polygon Worlds

The first step in creating a virtual 3D world is to represent each object within the world as a collection of polygons — each polygon can itself be described by a set of vertices. For example, a cube consists of six four-sided polygons that correspond to the faces of the cube — each face is defined by four cube corners and these corners are the vertices belonging to the polygon for that face. The following figure illustrates the terminology:

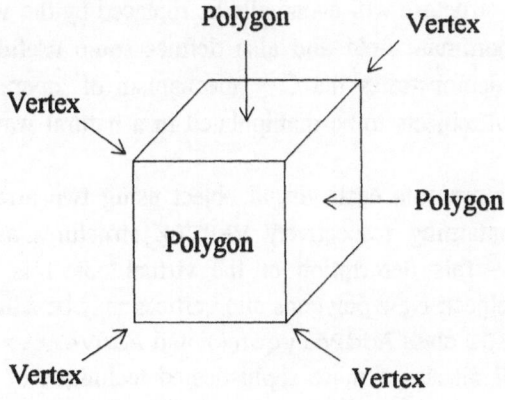

Of course, more complex shapes can be modelled in this way and the polygons can
be triangles, quadrilaterals, pentagons and so on. The only restriction is that objects
in the virtual world cannot have curved surfaces but must be approximated using a
collection of polygons. The results are often close to reality but perhaps more
importantly a computer-generated image of the polygon world can be drawn at
reasonable speed.

The first question to resolve is how to store the objects, polygons and vertices that
make up the virtual world. An important consideration is that each vertex is
typically shared by several of an object's polygons — for example, each vertex of
the cube is shared by three different polygons. This means that storing objects as
collections of polygons and polygons as collections of vertices is rather wasteful —
a good compromise is to store the object's vertices directly in a list and to represent
the associated polygons using pointers into this list. The C++ classes OBJECT and
POLYGON will be defined to realize objects and polygons from the virtual world —
each OBJECT object maintains the list which describes all the vertices for the
corresponding virtual world object whilst each POLYGON object selects from the
list only those vertices belonging to a particular virtual world polygon.

In chapters 8 to 10 an object's vertices are represented using VERTEX structures —
each VERTEX structure has the following layout:

```
struct VERTEX {
    int x;
    int y;
};
```

The x and y fields of the VERTEX structure specify the 2D coordinates of a vertex
in the final computer image — chapter 12 describes the process of deriving the 2D
display coordinates from the original location of the vertex within the 3D virtual
world. The VERTEX structure will eventually be replaced by the VECTOR class —
this adds a third coordinate field and also defines some useful functions. The
VECTOR class also demonstrates the C++ mechanism of 'operator overloading'
which allows VECTOR objects to be manipulated in a natural way.

The OBJECT class represents each virtual object using two arrays (Vertices
and Polygons) containing respectively VERTEX structures and (pointers to)
POLYGON objects — this description of the virtual object is held within an
associated OBJECT object. New polygons and vertices may be added to the virtual
object with the OBJECT class AddPolygon() and AddVertex() functions —
the next chapter will discuss a more sophisticated technique of creating virtual
objects from a file containing a complete description of the virtual world.

Here is the OBJECT class specification:

```
class POLYGON;

class OBJECT {
public:
  OBJECT(void);
  ~OBJECT(void);
  void AddPolygon(POLYGON*);
  void AddVertex(const VERTEX&);
    .

    .
private:
  int PolygonCount;
  POLYGON* Polygons[MAX_POLYGONS];
  int VertexCount;
  VERTEX Vertices[MAX_VERTICES];
};
```

The OBJECT class constructor sets the VertexCount and PolygonCount fields to zero. The AddVertex() and AddPolygon() functions may then be called to add vertices and polygons to the object:

```
void OBJECT::AddVertex(const VERTEX& vertex) {
  Vertices[VertexCount++] = vertex;
}

void OBJECT::AddPolygon(POLYGON* polygon) {
  Polygons[PolygonCount++] = polygon;
}
```

When the OBJECT object is eventually destroyed its destructor also removes any associated POLYGON objects:

```
OBJECT::~OBJECT(void) {
  for (int i=0; i<PolygonCount; i++)
    delete Polygons[i];
}
```

Each POLYGON object contains an array of vertex indices that reference the Vertices array in the OBJECT object to which the POLYGON object belongs.

Here is the POLYGON class specification:

```
class OBJECT;

class POLYGON {
public:
  POLYGON(OBJECT*);
  void AddVertex(int);

    .

    .
private:
  OBJECT* Object;
  int VertexCount;
  int Vertices[MAX_VERTICES_PER_POLYGON];
};
```

The POLYGON class constructor sets the Object field to create the association between POLYGON and OBJECT objects — it also calls the OBJECT class AddPolygon() function to update its owner object:

```
POLYGON::POLYGON(OBJECT* object) {
  VertexCount = 0;
  Object = object;
  Object->AddPolygon(this);
}
```

The following code demonstrates the construction of a virtual cube similar to the one illustrated at the start of the section — the first step is the creation of an OBJECT object to represent the cube:

```
OBJECT* object = (OBJECT*) new OBJECT;
for (i=0; i<CUBE_VERTICES; i++)
  object->AddVertex(CubeVertices[i]);
```

Then a series of POLYGON objects are created and added to the virtual cube:

```
POLYGON* polygon;
for (n=0; n<CUBE_POLYGONS; n++) {
  polygon = (POLYGON*) new POLYGON(object);
  for (i=0; i<FACE_VERTICES; i++)
    polygon->AddVertex(FaceVertices[n][i]);
}
```

The CubeVertices and FaceVertices arrays are defined in a header file.

The CubeVertices array contains the actual positions of the vertices on the screen:

```
VERTEX CubeVertices[CUBE_VERTICES] = {
   {-45,-30},
   {15,-30},
   {-45,30},
   {15,30},
   {-15,-60},
   {45,-60},
   {-15,0},
   {45,0}
};
```

The FaceVertices array describes the cube faces by referencing entries in the CubeVertices array:

```
int
FaceVertices[CUBE_POLYGONS][FACE_VERTICES] = {
   {0,2,3,1}, // front
   {7,6,4,5}, // back
   {0,1,5,4}, // top
   {7,3,2,6}, // bottom
   {0,4,6,2}, // left
   {7,5,1,3}  // right
};
```

8.2 The WORLD and SCENE Objects

There are two more objects that are important in representing a virtual world — these are the WORLD and SCENE objects. The WORLD object is responsible for coordinating all the activities within the virtual world whilst the SCENE object is concerned only with generating a graphical image of the world to display on the screen. The following figure illustrates how the various objects will talk to one another:

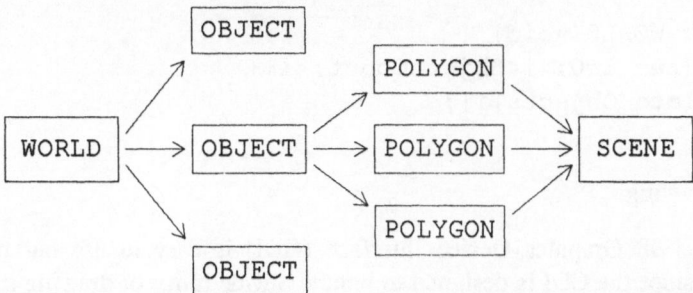

In particular the WORLD object can request each OBJECT object to draw itself — the OBJECT object asks each of its POLYGON objects to draw themselves and they pass information to the SCENE object to tell it how to construct an image. It is possible to generate several different images of the same virtual world by using more than one SCENE object but that possibility is not considered further here. The SCENE object is the only one principally involved with drawing — the next section begins the long process of defining the SCENE object. The POLYGON objects provide little functionality and are basically containers of information about the polygons they describe. The WORLD and OBJECT classes are more concerned with simulating the activities which occur within the virtual world but they do contain some high-level code that manages the image production process — the WORLD class has the following specification:

```cpp
class SCENE;
class OBJECT;

class WORLD {
public:
  WORLD(void);
  ~WORLD(void);
  void AddObject(OBJECT*);
    .
    .
private:
  int ObjectCount;
  OBJECT* Objects[MAX_OBJECTS];
};
```

The operation of the WORLD class is similar to that of the OBJECT class but instead of managing POLYGON objects it manages OBJECT objects — the AddObject() function and the WORLD class destructor mirror the corresponding functions in the OBJECT class:

```cpp
void WORLD::AddObject(OBJECT* object) {
  Objects[ObjectCount++] = object;
}

WORLD::~WORLD(void) {
  for (int i=0; i<ObjectCount; i++)
    delete Objects[i];
}
```

8.3 Line Drawing

Windows 98 Graphics Device Interface (GDI) is easy to use but not very efficient — since the GDI is designed to handle a wide range of drawing scenarios there is not much room for optimization. For example, whenever an image is drawn in a window or bitmap using GDI functions the operating system must ensure that no portions of the image overlap the destination drawable by appropriate clipping.

However, by directly manipulating the image bits of a DIB object it is possible to avoid unnecessary clipping checks. The simplest case is drawing a pixel to the bitmap — as discussed previously (see sections 6.5 and 7.4) the following function can be applied to a bitmap having a colour format with 8 bits per pixel:

```
void
DrawPixel(DIB* dib,POINT pixel,BYTE colour) {
   int pitch = dib->GetPitch();
   BYTE* bits = dib->AcquireBits();
   bits[pixel.x+pixel.y*pitch] = colour;
   dib->ReleaseBits();
}
```

The corresponding DrawLine() function is more interesting. The line to be drawn will be specified by its endpoints and so the intermediate pixels must be determined — since the computer display comprises a matrix of discrete pixels and the line is continuous it is necessary to adopt some scheme for approximating the line with a series of pixels. For example, the line connecting the endpoints (0,0) and (5,2) may be drawn as follows:

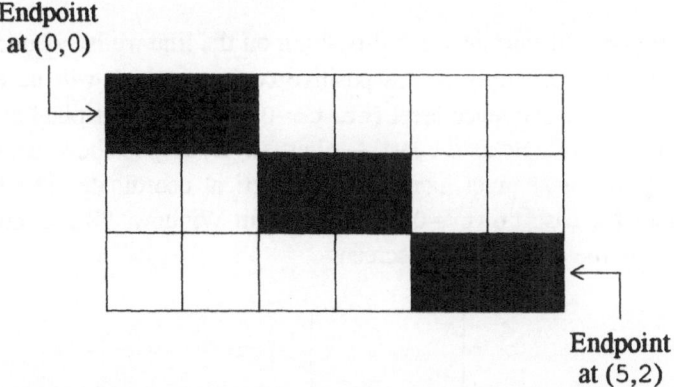

Here the points (1,0), (2,1), (3,1) and (4,2) are selected for the intermediate pixels — the coordinates relate to the centres of each pixel. The selection procedure described in this section is based upon Bresenham's algorithm — this provides an efficient means of selecting the line's pixels in a stepwise manner using only integer arithmetic. At each step the x-coordinate is incremented and a decision is made whether or not to increment the y-coordinate. Hence starting from the endpoint (0,0) the next point in the line could be (1,0) or (1,1) — the point (1,0) is actually chosen so the next point after that is either (2,0) or (2,1) and so on. The decision at each step is made according to the relative vertical offset from the line of the two pixels concerned. For example, with x==1 the corresponding value on the line for y is 0.4 — the two possible pixels are centred at (1,0) and (1,1) so the

two vertical offsets are 0.4 and 0.6 respectively — the following figure illustrates
the situation:

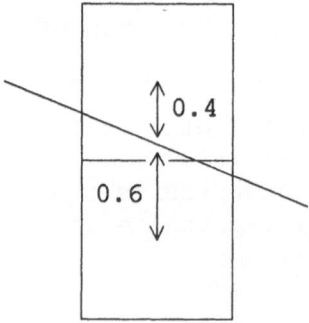

Consequently the pixel at (1,0) is chosen and the process is repeated until the
endpoint at (5,2) is reached. This example uses decimal values in the decision
making process but the calculations can be performed more quickly if only integers
are required. To permit this the first step is the definition of a decision variable
test whose value will indicate which pixel to select next:

```
test = K*(y-y_ref);
```

The value of y gives the current vertical position on the line whilst y_ref is some
reference level — the quantity K is a positive constant which will be explained
later. If y is below the reference level (test<=0) then the next pixel chosen has
the same vertical coordinate as the last — alternatively if y is above the reference
level (test>0) the next pixel increments its vertical coordinate. The following
figure illustrates the case test<=0 — note that in Windows 98 programming y
increases towards the bottom of the screen:

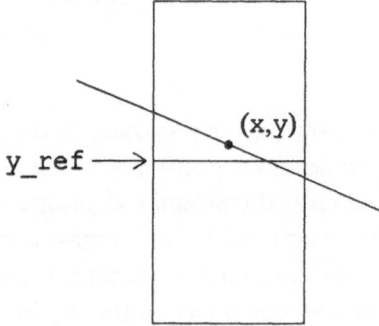

At each step the decision variable must be updated — the y-coordinate of the line
will change with every step and for the case test>0 the reference level y_ref
must also be incremented. To determine the step change in y as x is incremented it
is necessary to obtain the equation of the line — suppose that in the general case

the endpoints are (x0,y0) and (x1,y1) as illustrated in the following figure:

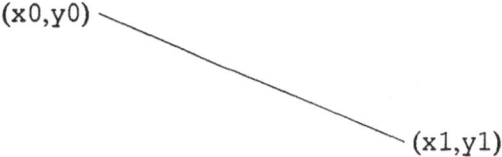

The changes in the values of x and y along the line are referred to as 'delta' (or difference) values and they may be calculated as follows:

```
delta_x = x1-x0;
delta_y = y1-y0;
```

By moving along the line the x and y values change in proportion to the values `delta_x` and `delta_y` respectively — if x increases from x0 by `t*delta_x` then y increases from y0 by `t*delta_y`. The value of the multiplier t changes from 0 to 1 as the point (x,y) moves along the line from one endpoint at (x0,y0) to the other endpoint at (x1,y1). Hence the coordinates of a general point on the line are:

```
x = x0+t*delta_x;
y = y0+t*delta_y;
```

Chapter 11 discusses the vector equivalent of this result for lines in both 2D and 3D. Here a little algebra yields the equation of the line:

$$(y-y0) = \frac{delta\_y}{delta\_x} * (x-x0);$$

This is simply a restatement of the fact that the x- and y-coordinates on the line change in proportion to the values `delta_x` and `delta_y` respectively — in particular if x changes by 1 then y changes by `delta_y/delta_x`. The ratio `delta_y/delta_x` is known as the 'slope' or 'gradient' of the line. To ensure that only integers are needed to compute the decision variable `test` the constant K is defined as `2*delta_x` and then:

```
test = 2*delta_x*(y-y_ref);
```

Now if `test<=0` the next pixel chosen keeps the same vertical coordinate as the last pixel and `y_ref` is unaltered — however, y is increased by `delta_y/delta_x` so test is changed by `2*delta_y`. Alternatively, if `test>0` then not only is y increased but `y_ref` is also incremented — in this case test changes by `2*(delta_y-delta_x)`.

In summary:

```
if (test <= 0)
  test += 2*delta_y;
else if (test > 0)
  test += 2*(delta_y-delta_x);
```

The only detail remaining is the initial value of the decision variable — for the first endpoint y==y0 and the reference level is taken as y_ref==y0+0.5 so that:

```
test = -delta_x;
```

The SCENE class DrawLine() function will implement this algorithm — firstly the variables are initialized:

```
void
SCENE::DrawLine(const POINT* ends,BYTE colour) {
  POINT pixels[2];
  TransformToPixels(ends[0],pixels[0]);
  TransformToPixels(ends[1],pixels[1]);
  POINT pixel = pixels[0];
  int delta_x = pixels[1].x-pixels[0].x;
  int delta_y = pixels[1].y-pixels[0].y;
  int test = -delta_x;
  int length = delta_x;
  int noupdate = 2*delta_y;
  int update = 2*(delta_y-delta_x);
        .
        .
```

Then a for loop steps along the line to draw the individual pixels:

```
        .
        .
  BYTE* bits = Dib->AcquireBits();
  for (int i=0; i<=length; i++) {
    if (test<=0)
      test += noupdate;
    else {
      test += update;
      pixel.y++;
    }
    bits[pixel.x+pixel.y*Pitch] = colour;
    pixel.x++;
  }
  Dib->ReleaseBits()
}
```

The SCENE object draws the line using a DIB object that it holds internally — here (and in later chapters) the colour format of the DIB object bitmap is assumed to be 8 bits per pixel. To improve efficiency the SCENE object sets Width, Height and Pitch fields for its bitmap during construction — the value for the Pitch field is obtained from the DIB object:

```
SCENE::SCENE(int width, int height,
                            PALETTE* palette) {
  Palette = palette;
  Dib = (DIB*) new DIB(width, height, 8, Palette);
  Width = width;
  Height = height;
  Pitch = Dib->GetPitch();
  Scale = 1;
  Origin.x = Width/2;
  Origin.y = Height/2;
}
```

The SCENE class constructor also sets default values for the Scale and Origin fields — these can be modified by calling the SetScale() and SetOrigin() functions. As with the SPRITE class a value of Scale greater than 1 allows units to be measured in fractions of a pixel — the Origin field specifies which pixel corresponds to the point (0,0) and this defaults to the middle of the bitmap.

The actions of the TransformToPixels() helper function called by DrawLine() are controlled by the Scale and Origin fields in the following manner:

```
void
SCENE::TransformToPixels(const POINT& point,
                            POINT& pixels) {
  pixels.x = Origin.x+point.x/Scale;
  pixels.y = Origin.y+point.y/Scale;
}
```

Unfortunately, the code in the DrawLine() function only works for line gradients in the range 0<=delta_y/delta_x<=1 — however, the generalization to all values of the slope is straightforward. Firstly, delta_x and delta_y must be calculated as the absolute change between endpoints:

```
int delta_x = pixels[1].x-pixels[0].x;
int step_x = (delta_x>0?1:-1);
delta_x *= step_x;
```

The delta_y and step_y variables are similarly defined. Then pixel.x and pixel.y are incremented or decremented as appropriate — for example:

```
pixel.x += step_x;
```

Finally, if delta_y>delta_x the roles of x and y in the algorithm are reversed and the following initializations are required:

```
test = -delta_y;
length = delta_y;
noupdate = 2*delta_x;
update = 2*(delta_x-delta_y);
```

To handle the two cases delta_y<=delta_x and delta_y>delta_x together it is possible to modify the line-drawing **for** loop as follows:

```
for (int i=0; i<=length; i++) {
  if (test<=0)
    test += noupdate;
  else {
    test += update;
    pixel.x += jump_x;
    pixel.y += jump_y;
  }
  bits[pixel.x+pixel.y*Pitch] = colour;
  pixel.x += step_x;
  pixel.y += step_y;
}
```

Of the two step variables only step_x is non-zero in the former case whilst only step_y is non-zero in the latter case — the converse is true for the jump_x and jump_y variables. The advantage of this approach is that the code for actually drawing pixels is kept in one place — here the drawing code consists of a single assignment to the image bits array but it can be more complicated if additional colour formats are allowed. The revised algorithm correctly handles horizontal and vertical lines but it may be more efficient to deal with these possibilities separately.

The SCENE class DrawLine() function is not generally available to other objects but is invoked indirectly through the Draw() function — this interface function is passed a series of connected lines by a POLYGON object during a drawing request:

```
void SCENE::Draw(int count,const int* vertices,
                           BYTE colour) {
  POINT ends[2];
  VERTEX vertex = ObjectVertices[vertices[count-1]];
  ends[1] = *(POINT*)&vertex;
  for (int i=0; i<count; i++) {
    vertex = ObjectVertices[vertices[i]];
    ends[0] = ends[1];
    ends[1] = *(POINT*)&vertex;
    DrawLine(ends,colour);
  }
}
```

Each POLYGON object draws itself by calling the SCENE object's Draw() function:

```
void POLYGON::Draw(SCENE* scene) {
  scene->Draw(VertexCount,Vertices,Colour);
}
```

Similarly, an OBJECT object draws itself by passing its vertex coordinates to the SCENE object and then making calls to its POLYGON objects:

```
void OBJECT::Draw(SCENE* scene) {
  scene->SetVertices(Vertices);
  for (int i=0; i<PolygonCount; i++)
    Polygons[i]->Draw(scene);
}
```

The SetVertices() function call initializes the SCENE object's pointer ObjectVertices which references an array of vertices for the object currently being drawn — since a vertex may be shared by several of the object's polygons this approach is better than passing the vertices directly to the SCENE object in each call to its Draw() function.

```
void SCENE::SetVertices(const VERTEX* vertices) {
  ObjectVertices = vertices;
}
```

The WORLD object starts the whole drawing process off by telling each of the virtual world objects to draw themselves:

```
void WORLD::Draw(HDC dc) {
  Scene->BeginFrame();
  for (int i=0; i<ObjectCount; i++)
    Objects[i]->Draw(Scene);
  Scene->EndFrame();
  Scene->Display(dc);
}
```

The calls to the BeginFrame() and EndFrame() functions allow the SCENE object to perform any initialization or finalization procedures required to draw a single image frame — for example, the BeginFrame() function may erase the contents of the SCENE object's bitmap. Finally, the SCENE class Display() function is called to transfer the newly constructed image to the computer display — this is implemented here by blitting the back buffer bitmap to the screen.

The following figure shows the wire-frame image of a virtual world containing a single cube:

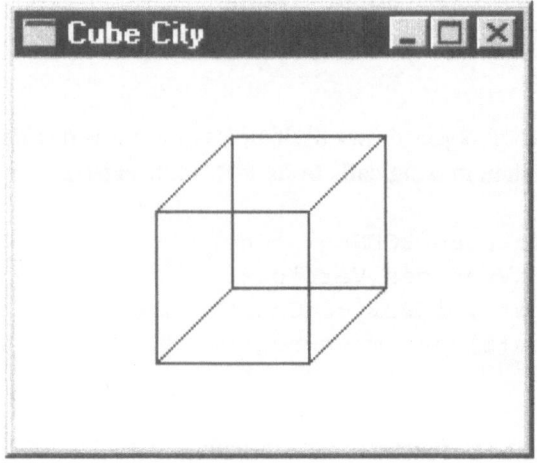

8.4 Line Clipping

As long as the lines drawn by the SCENE object are completely contained within its back buffer bitmap then all is well — however, if the lines extend beyond the limits of the bitmap then they must be clipped. This section will consider two possible line clipping techniques. The first method simply clips each pixel individually by comparing its position against the boundaries of the bitmap. The SCENE class DrawLine() function modifies its line-drawing loop as follows:

```
for (int i=0; i<=length; i++) {
        .
        .
    if (pixel.y>=0 && pixel.y<Height)
      if (pixel.x>=0 && pixel.x<Width)
        bits[pixel.x+pixel.y*Pitch] = colour;
        .
        .
}
```

This method has the advantage of being very easy to implement. Furthermore, it extends nicely to a raster-scan clipping algorithm applicable to the polygon-fill graphics discussed in the next chapter — there the line-drawing process will be used to calculate the outline of the polygon to be filled. The overhead required to clip every pixel in the outline can then easily be outweighed by the processing needed to fill this outline with solid colour.

The second clipping method discussed here is based on the Sutherland-Cohen clipping algorithm that divides the plane into a 3-by-3 grid of rectangular regions. The method just clips line endpoints rather than each and every pixel — however, the trade-off is that it involves multiplication and division operations which are typically very slow. Floating-point calculations will be avoided by measuring units in fractions of a pixel — this is essentially a fixed-point technique where the lower order bits of an integer represent fractional quantities. The nine-region clipping algorithm places the visible region at the centre of its 3-by-3 grid:

Top Left	Top	Top Right
Left	Visible Region	Right
Bottom Left	Bottom	Bottom Right

The regions are separated horizontally by the clipping boundaries at x==ClipRect.left and x==ClipRect.right and separated vertically by the clipping boundaries at y==ClipRect.top and y==ClipRect.bottom. These boundaries are included in the visible region. The algorithm first determines which of the nine regions hold the endpoints of the line — there are several possibilities:

— both endpoints are in the central visible region
— both endpoints lie above/below/left of/right of the visible region
— neither of the above conditions holds

In the first case the line is passed along unchanged whilst in the second case the line does not cross the visible region and so it can be discarded. The third case is the most complicated and requires that at least one endpoint must be clipped — the sub-cases are as follows:

— one endpoint lies in the central region
— at least one endpoint lies in the Left, Right, Top or Bottom regions
— the endpoints lie in regions at opposite corners of the grid

In the first case the other endpoint is clipped and the line accepted as visible. In the second case the specified endpoint need only be clipped against one boundary — this is sufficient to determine whether or not the line is visible and the other endpoint should be clipped (Left-Right and Top-Bottom combinations will always be accepted). The third case is similar to the second but depending on the order chosen for endpoints and clipping boundaries it may require up to four clipping operations.

The SCENE class Clip() function implements this algorithm — the first step is to test the two endpoints against each of the clipping boundaries held by the ClipRect structure:

```
BOOL SCENE::Clip(POINT* ends) {
  int i;
  DWORD codes[2];
  while (TRUE) {
    codes[0] = codes[1] = 0;
    for (i=0; i<2; i++) {
      if (ends[i].x < ClipRect.left)
        codes[i] |= CLIP_LEFT;
      else if (ends[i].x > ClipRect.right)
        codes[i] |= CLIP_RIGHT;
      if (ends[i].y < ClipRect.top)
        codes[i] |= CLIP_TOP;
      else if (ends[i].y > ClipRect.bottom)
        codes[i] |= CLIP_BOTTOM;
    }
           .
           .
```

The codes array is set to indicate how the endpoints should be clipped by using the flags CLIP_LEFT, CLIP_RIGHT, CLIP_TOP and CLIP_BOTTOM — each of these flags sets a different bit in the DWORD values held by the codes array. If no flags are set the line is accepted unclipped by returning TRUE — if both endpoints set the same flag then the line does not cross the visible region and so it is rejected by returning FALSE. The following code tests for these two cases:

```
           .
           .
    if (!codes[0] && !codes[1])
      return TRUE;
    if (codes[0] & codes[1])
      return FALSE;
           .
           .
```

This leaves the final three sub-cases discussed previously — all three possibilities

are handled by performing one clipping operation and repeating the enclosing
while loop:

```
      .
      .
  for (i=0; i<2; i++)
    if (!codes[i]) {
      ClipEnd(ends[1-i],ends[i],codes[1-i]);
      break;
    }
  if (i==2) {
    for (i=0; i<2; i++)
      if (IsSingleClip(codes[i])) {
        ClipEnd(ends[i],ends[1-i],codes[i]);
        break;
      }
  }
  if (i==2)
    ClipEnd(ends[0],ends[1],codes[0]);
  }
}
```

First, a check is made for one endpoint visible. If this check is unsuccessful then
the code looks for an endpoint in the Left, Right, Top or Bottom regions —
the IsSingleClip() function returns TRUE only if the code value equals one of
the CLIP_LEFT, CLIP_RIGHT, CLIP_TOP or CLIP_BOTTOM flags:

```
BOOL SCENE::IsSingleClip(DWORD code) {
  return (code==CLIP_LEFT || code==CLIP_RIGHT
          || code==CLIP_TOP || code==CLIP_BOTTOM);
}
```

Finally, if the endpoints lie in opposite corners of the clipping grid then one is
chosen at random to clip.

The various region tests are fairly fast but the clipping operations can be
computationally expensive to perform since they involve multiplication and
division operations. As an example suppose that the line with endpoints (x0,y0)
and (x1,y1) is to be clipped against the boundary x==ClipRect.right then
the actual clipping procedure is as follows:

```
x = ClipRect.right;
```

$$y = y0 + \frac{(y1-y0)}{(x1-x0)} * (ClipRect.right-x0);$$

In the next iteration of the **while** loop the new y value can be tested against `ClipRect.top` and `ClipRect.bottom` to see if the clipped endpoint is now visible — depending on the situation it may be necessary to clip the point again using one of the boundaries y==`ClipRect.top` or y==`ClipRect.bottom`. In any case the clipping procedure is implemented with the SCENE class `ClipEnd()` function — firstly, the appropriate clipping boundary is selected:

```
void SCENE::ClipEnd(POINT& end,
          const POINT& other_end,DWORD code) {
  int boundary;
  if (code & CLIP_LEFT)
    boundary = ClipRect.left;
  else if (code & CLIP_RIGHT)
    boundary = ClipRect.right;
  else if (code & CLIP_TOP)
    boundary = ClipRect.top;
  else
    boundary = ClipRect.bottom;
      .
      .
```

Then the endpoint is clipped to this boundary:

```
      .
      .
  int delta;
  int delta_x = other_end.x-end.x;
  int delta_y = other_end.y-end.y;
  if (code&CLIP_LEFT || code&CLIP_RIGHT) {
    delta = boundary-end.x;
    end.x = boundary;
    end.y += MulDiv(delta,delta_y,delta_x);
  }
  else {
    delta = boundary-end.y;
    end.y = boundary;
    end.x += MulDiv(delta,delta_x,delta_y);
  }
}
```

The `MulDiv()` function is provided by the Windows 98 operating system — it allows two integers to be multiplied together and then divided by a third integer without causing an overflow in the intermediate result.

To illustrate the clipping process the latest VIEW class sets three BOUNCER sprites in motion and uses their positions to update a three-sided POLYGON object held by an OBJECT object — the following figure illustrates the program in action:

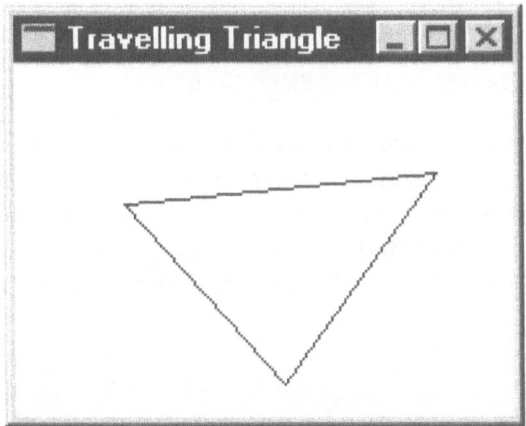

In particular, if the sprites move a little past the edges of the bitmap before bouncing back then the corners of the triangle are safely clipped.

The VIEW class Paint() function is defined as follows:

```
LRESULT
VIEW::Paint(HWND window,UINT message,
            WPARAM wparam,LPARAM lparam) {
  PAINTSTRUCT paint;
  HDC dc = BeginPaint(window,&paint);
  VERTEX vertex;
  for (int i=0; i<3; i++) {
    vertex = *(VERTEX*)
       &(Sprites[i]->SetPosition(NULL));
    Object->SetVertex(i,vertex);
  }
  World->Draw(dc);
  EndPaint(window,&paint);
  return 0;
}
```

The Paint() handler retrieves the current positions of the BOUNCER sprites and passes them to an OBJECT object that has a single triangular face. A call to the SetOrigin() function during initialization moves the origin of the SCENE object to the top left-hand corner of its bitmap — calls are also made to the

SetScale() functions of the SCENE and SPRITE objects as follows:

```
const int VIEW_SCALE = 1000;

POINT origin = {0,0};
Scene->SetOrigin(origin);
Scene->SetScale(VIEW_SCALE);
for (int i=0; i<3; i++)
  Sprites[i]->SetScale(VIEW_SCALE);
```

The sprite Position coordinates thus match the image coordinates and the three sprites are located at the corners of the triangle (although they are not actually displayed). The edges of the triangle are drawn by asking the WORLD object to produce an image of its virtual world — this is not a typical way to move OBJECT objects in a virtual world and is only intended to demonstrate the line clipping process.

8.5 Summary

This chapter begins the development of graphics software which can generate images of a 3D virtual world. For these images to be generated in real-time the current technology available to personal computers imposes some limits on the construction of such a world — in particular, complex geometries must be avoided and the objects within the world should be built from collections of polygons. The OBJECT and POLYGON classes have been defined to embody the concepts of virtual object and polygons. Each OBJECT object represents the state of a virtual object and simulates the activities of the object within the virtual world — from a graphics viewpoint the most important information provided by an OBJECT object is the position of the object's vertices. Each POLYGON object holds the information relating to an individual polygon — the polygon is the basic unit from which a SCENE object may compose an image frame of the virtual world. The overall control of the 3D world is assigned to a WORLD object — its most important function here is to manage the generation of images by sending draw requests to each of the world's objects and to coordinate this process with the workings of the SCENE object. The VIEW class acts as an intermediary between the user and the WORLD object. The chapter has also discussed some techniques for drawing wire-frame images — both line-drawing and line-clipping algorithms have been discussed and typical implementations provided for the SCENE class. The next chapter enhances this code so that polygon-fill graphics are possible — this will greatly increase the realism of the virtual world images which can be created.

9. Polygon-Fill Techniques

The previous chapter introduced the concept of a virtual 3D world and showed how to generate wire-frame images of this world — the present chapter will build on this foundation to create images which contain polygons filled with solid colour. The line-drawing code of the previous chapter is used here to calculate the outline of a polygon — this outline can be filled with coloured pixels in an efficient manner. The essential topics include:

— GDI polygon-fill functions
— calculating a polygon outline
— optimizing the colour-fill process
— hidden polygon removal
— storing a virtual world in a file

The chapter also updates the Cube City program so that it draws a realistic 3D image of a cube.

9.1 The GDI Approach

Chapter 4 showed how the GDI function FillRect() can be used to render the image of a colour-filled rectangular polygon — filled polygons of more general shapes can be produced by invoking other GDI functions. The first step is to create a path associated with a device context — the path represents the outline of the polygon to be filled. The path is created by bracketing a series of requests to GDI drawing functions with calls to BeginPath() and EndPath() — in this case the drawing functions do not produce any output but simply define the points in the path. For example:

```
POINT corners[3] = {
  {50,0},
  {0,100},
  {100,100}
};

BeginPath(dc);
MoveToEx(dc,corners[0].x,corners[0].y,NULL);
for (int i=0; i<3; i++)
  LineTo(dc,corners[i].x,corners[i].y);
EndPath(dc);
```

Here a path is defined in the shape of a triangle but the code readily extends to more complicated polygons. The polygon can now be filled with a call to a GDI function such as FillPath() — if necessary this function will also close the path by adding a line from the last point back to the first point. The GDI drawing procedure is easy to follow but the speed is not sufficiently good for 3D animation applications — with a view to improving efficiency the remainder of this chapter examines another polygon-fill technique based upon the SCENE class introduced in the previous chapter.

9.2 Polygon Outlines

The SCENE class DrawLine() function can be modified to generate polygon outlines from the edges which connect the polygon's vertices. If a polygon is visible in an image generated by the SCENE object it will appear on a number of consecutive 'scanlines' of the SCENE object's internal bitmap — for each scanline where the polygon is drawn the polygon's pixels lie in a continuous strip between start and stop pixels on the scanline. The following figure illustrates the situation:

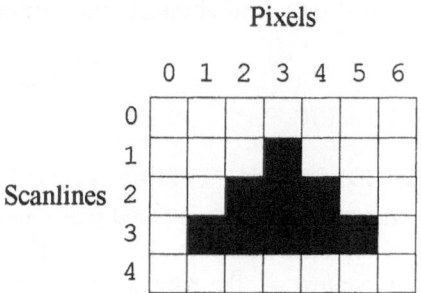

For example on scanline 2 the start pixel is pixel 2 and the stop pixel is pixel 4 — the positions of the start and stop pixels are stored in a SCANLINE structure:

```
struct SCANLINE {
  int Start;
  int Stop;
};
```

This description is only guaranteed to work for 'convex' polygons — a convex polygon has the property that if any two points within the polygon are taken as the endpoints of a line, then all points on the line falling between these endpoints also belong to the polygon. Polygons which do not possess this property are known as 'concave' polygons — the scanline description in terms of start and stop pixels may fail for concave polygons.

The following figure illustrates the differences between convex and concave polygons:

Convex Polygon   Concave Polygon

In particular triangles are always convex — furthermore, a concave polygon can be split into a number of convex polygons (for example triangles). It is assumed here that all images constructed by the SCENE object contain only convex polygons. A collection of SCANLINE structures is stored in the ScanLines array to describe the whole of the SCENE object bitmap — this arrangement of data will prove to be particularly easy to manipulate if the code is rewritten in assembly language as described in the next chapter.

Meanwhile the first task to accomplish is to find upper and lower bounds for the x-coordinates of a polygon's vertices — this is easy to achieve by iterating through the vertices. An alternative approach is to first clip the polygon to fit within a bounding rectangle — this process may alter the number of vertices in the polygon as shown in the following figure:

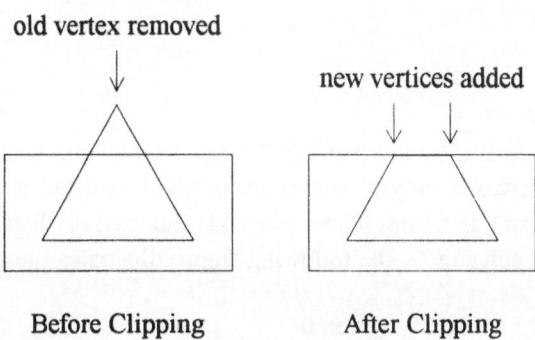

Before Clipping   After Clipping

The bounding rectangle can match the extents of the SCENE object bitmap or it may be larger and so act as a preliminary clipping region — in the latter case the purpose of the clipping is to reduce the dimensions of very large polygons to a more manageable size. In any case the bounding values of the vertex x-coordinates are placed in the SCANLINE structure bounds and this is then copied to all elements in the ScanLines array:

```
for (int y=0; y<Height; y++)
    ScanLines[y] = bounds;
```

The value of bounds.Start is greater than the x-coordinate of every pixel in the polygon outline — similarly the value of bounds.Stop is less than the x-coordinate of every such pixel. The Start and Stop fields in the ScanLines array are subsequently updated by comparing the initial array values with each pixel in the polygon outline. When the outline is complete only those scanlines that cross the polygon have their SCANLINE array elements set with the Start field less than or equal to the Stop field — scanlines that do not contain polygon pixels leave the ScanLines array untouched.

The ScanLines array is initialized by the SCENE class DrawOutline() function which then calls DrawLine() for each of the polygon's edges. Within the DrawLine() function the line-drawing loop from the previous chapter is modified as follows:

```
for (int i=0; i<=length; i++) {
    .
    .

  if (pixel.y>=0 && pixel.y<Height) {
    if (initial &&
          pixel.x<ScanLines[pixel.y].Start)
      ScanLines[pixel.y].Start = pixel.x;
    if (final &&
          pixel.x>ScanLines[pixel.y].Stop)
      ScanLines[pixel.y].Stop = pixel.x;
  }
    .
    .

}
```

The procedure is controlled by the two BOOL flags final and initial — the Start fields are decreased only if initial is TRUE and the Stop fields are increased only if final is TRUE. The initial and final flags indicate how each line bounds the polygon — the following figure illustrates the idea:

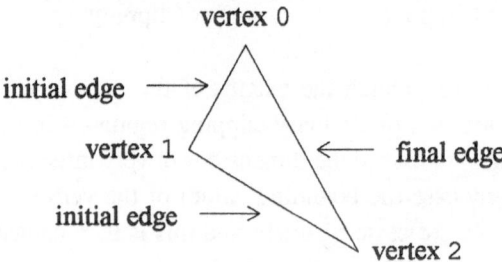

In particular a horizontal line is regarded as both an initial and final edge — the code to set the initial and final flags appears just before the line-drawing loop in the DrawLine() function:

```
BOOL initial = FALSE;
BOOL final = FALSE;
if (delta_y >= 0)
  initial = TRUE;
if (delta_y <= 0)
  final = TRUE;
```

To work properly this code assumes that the polygon vertices are arranged in an anti-clockwise order — the previous figure demonstrates this ordering for a triangle. Section 9.4 discusses the use of vertex ordering to remove the hidden faces from the polygon-filled image of a cube.

Apart from the modifications detailed here the DrawLine() code is basically unchanged — however, it no longer draws any pixels and instead sets the entries in the ScanLines array. The next section shows how the Draw() function can use the information contained in the ScanLines array to construct an image.

9.3 Filling with a Solid Colour

The new SCENE class Draw() function will fill a polygon with a solid colour — chapter 14 covers more sophisticated effects such as colour shading and texture mapping. After asking DrawOutline() to invoke the DrawLine() function for each of the polygon edges, the Draw() function completes its work with a call to the ColourFill() helper function — this fills the polygon scanline by scanline. Pixels are only drawn on a particular scanline if the Start and Stop fields for the corresponding SCANLINE structure have been set by the preceding calls to DrawLine() — the relevant test is simply that the value of the Start field is less than or equal to that of the Stop field. Here is the code to actually draw pixels in the SCENE object bitmap:

```
BYTE* bits = Dib->AcquireBits();
for (int y=0; y<Height; y++) {
  start=ScanLines[y].Start;
  stop=ScanLines[y].Stop;
  if (start < 0)
    start = 0;
  if (stop >= Width)
    stop = Width-1;
  for (int x=start; x<=stop; x++)
    bits[x+y*Pitch] = colour;
}
Dib->ReleaseBits();
```

The only other point of interest is that the start and stop variables must be clipped to the width of the bitmap — chapter 12 extends this clipping process to correctly handle overlapping polygons in a 3D scene. There are a couple of optimizations that are easy to implement — the first is to eliminate the repeated multiplication of y by the Pitch field and the second involves the way colour information is placed in the bitmap. Data transfers are typically more efficient if they use the native data format of the host computer and Windows 98 runs on machines with 32-bit architectures. Hence instead of filling the polygon byte-by-byte the colour information should be transferred in 32-bit blocks — this is easily achieved by replacing the image bits BYTE* pointer with a DWORD* equivalent but the transfers must be aligned to DWORD address boundaries (i.e. the addresses should be divisible by 4). Consequently, there may be 1, 2 or 3 bytes left at the either end of a scanline which must be transferred individually. The first step towards more efficient code is straightforward — the multiplications involving the Pitch field are replaced by a series of additions:

```
BYTE* pixel;
BYTE* line = Dib->AcquireBits();
for (int y=0; y<Height; y++) {
    .
    .
    pixel = line+start;
    .
    .
  line += Pitch;
}
Dib->ReleaseBits();
```

Here the line pointer references the start of each scanline within the image bits of the SCENE object bitmap — the position of the first polygon pixel on a scanline is calculated relative to the start of that scanline. The other optimization requires the definition of a few more variables:

```
DWORD* pixel_block;
DWORD colour_block;
int length,start_bytes,stop_bytes;
```

The pixel pointer will update single pixels whilst the pixel_block pointer will update blocks of 4 pixels — the colour_block variable is set by replicating the BYTE value of the colour parameter:

```
colour_block = (DWORD)colour;
colour_block |= colour_block<<8;
colour_block |= colour_block<<16;
```

The start_bytes and stop_bytes variables count the number of extra bytes at each end of a polygon scanline.

The first possibility is that 3 or less pixels need to be drawn:

```
if (start <= stop) {
  pixel = line+start;
  length = stop+1-start;
  if (length <= 3)
    for (i=0; i<length; i++)
      *pixel++ = colour;
```

In this case the pixels are set directly as before — however, the multiplications involving Pitch are now unnecessary and the pixel pointer is simply incremented to draw each new pixel. For 4 or more pixels the processing is more involved — first, the number of extra bytes at either end of the scanline are calculated along with the number of intermediate DWORD blocks:

```
else {
  start_bytes = (-start)&3;
  stop_bytes = (stop+1)&3;
  length = (length-start_bytes-stop_bytes)/4;
      .
      .
```

The following figure illustrates how the start_bytes and stop_bytes values relate to DWORD address boundaries:

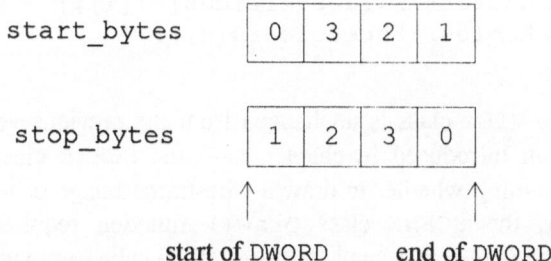

Finally, the colour information is transferred using three **for** loops:

```
      .
      .
  for (i=0; i<start_bytes; i++)
    *pixel++ = colour;
  pixel_block = (DWORD*)pixel;
  for (i=0; i<length; i++)
    *pixel_block++ = colour_block;
  pixel = (BYTE*)pixel_block;
  for (i=0; i<stop_bytes; i++)
    *pixel++ = colour;
}

}
```

This procedure readily converts to an assembly language implementation and the result is very fast indeed — the next chapter provides the details.

9.4 Drawing 3D Images

Chapters 11 to 13 are devoted to describing the process of generating 3D images but this section will introduce some of the essential ideas by creating a realistic image of a cube. To allow different polygons to be filled with different colours the SCENE class Draw() function accepts a colour parameter — whenever a POLYGON object sends a drawing request to the SCENE object it also passes along its colour. The POLYGON object stores the colour of its polygon in the Colour field — this value may be set by the POLYGON class SetColour() function:

```
void POLYGON::SetColour(BYTE colour) {
  Colour = colour;
}
```

The VIEW class sets the colours of the cube faces during initialization:

```
POLYGON* polygon;
for (n=0; n<CUBE_POLYGONS; n++) {
  polygon = (POLYGON*) new POLYGON(object);
  for (i=0; i<FACE_VERTICES; i++)
    polygon->AddVertex(FaceVertices[n][i]);
  polygon->SetColour(FaceColours[n]);
}
```

The remainder of the VIEW class is unchanged from the previous version of the Cube City program introduced in chapter 8 — the SCENE class is entirely responsible for determining whether to draw a wire-frame image or a polygon-fill equivalent. However, the SCENE class Draw() function requires one final modification — for the wire-frame image all faces of the cube were visible but now the SCENE object must only draw the top, front and right faces. To determine if a polygon is visible or hidden the SCENE object uses the ordering of the polygon's vertices — the polygon is visible if the vertex ordering is anti-clockwise and hidden if the ordering is clockwise. The CubeVertices and FaceVertices arrays appearing in section 8.1 must be properly defined to make this work — a portion of the FaceVertices array is repeated below for reference:

```
int
FaceVertices[CUBE_POLYGONS][FACE_VERTICES] = {
  {0,2,3,1}, // front
  {7,6,4,5}, // back
    .
    .
};
```

The following figure depicts the front and back faces of the cube and illustrates the vertex labelling scheme:

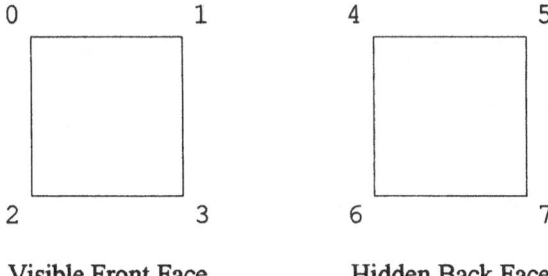

Visible Front Face   Hidden Back Face

According to the vertex ordering in the `FaceVertices` array, the front face vertices are ordered anti-clockwise whilst those of the back face are ordered clockwise — of course, if the cube is viewed from behind these vertex orderings are reversed but then the 'back' face becomes visible and the 'front' face is hidden instead.

The `SCENE` class includes a new `IsPolygonVisible()` function to determine whether a polygon is visible or not:

```
BOOL SCENE::IsPolygonVisible(void) {
   int delta_x[2];
   int delta_y[2];
   VERTEX ends[2];
   ends[0] = ObjectVertices[PolygonVertices[0]];
   int n = PolygonVertices[VertexCount-1];
   for (int i=0; i<2; i++) {
      ends[1] = ObjectVertices[n];
      delta_x[i] = ends[1].x-ends[0].x;
      delta_y[i] = ends[1].y-ends[0].y;
      n = PolygonVertices[1];
   }
   __int64 test
   test  = Int32x32To64(delta_x[0],delta_y[1]);
   test -= Int32x32To64(delta_x[1],delta_y[0]);
   return (test > 0);
}
```

Chapter 11 discusses the logic behind this function — it works by comparing the slopes of two polygon edges which share a common vertex. However, note here the use of the 64-bit integer quantity `test` and the function `Int32x32To64()` which multiplies two 32-bit integers to yield a 64-bit result — like the `MulDiv()` function introduced in section 8.4 the data type `__int64` and the function `Int32x32To64()` are provided by Windows 98 to help avoid overflow problems.

The IsPolygonVisible() function is called as the first processing step in the SCENE class Draw() function:

```
void
SCENE::Draw(int count, const int* vertices,
                               BYTE colour) {
  VertexCount = count;
  PolygonVertices = vertices;
  if (IsPolygonVisible()) {
    // draw polygon image
  }
}
```

Hidden polygons cause an immediate return from the Draw() function so that only visible polygons are drawn. The following figure illustrates the image generated by the new SCENE class object:

It is worthwhile summarizing the steps taken in constructing this image — for each polygon in the virtual world the SCENE object performs the following processing:

1. check for visibility of the polygon
2. clip the polygon and transform the vertices to pixel units
3. initialize the ScanLines array with the bounds structure
4. update the ScanLines array by calling DrawLine() for each polygon edge
5. fill the polygon outline with solid colour

Later chapters will enhance the operation of the SCENE object. Chapter 12 describes the process of mapping 3D vertices to pixel values and chapter 15 allows this mapping to be dynamically controlled by the user. Chapter 13 shows how to clip polygons that are obscured by other polygons in the scene and chapter 14 replaces the solid-colour filling routine with an algorithm to handle colour shading and texture mapping.

9.5 Virtual World Chunks

This chapter and the last have provided many of the ingredients necessary to draw an image of a virtual 3D world — however, the construction of this world using functions such as `AddVertex()`, `AddPolygon()` and `AddObject()` is tiresome. To simplify the procedure the POLYGON, OBJECT and WORLD classes provide `Save()` and `Load()` functions for transferring objects to and from a file — in object oriented language the file storage process is known as 'serializing' the objects. The POLYGON, OBJECT and WORLD objects can all hold varying amounts of data so a flexible file format is required — a common programming technique is to define a file format using 'chunks'. A chunk typically consists of a header to identify the type of chunk followed by the chunk data — each chunk may contain sub-chunks and the file consists of a series of chunks packed one after the other. The following figure illustrates the layout of a single chunk within a file:

```
        .
        .

   ┌─────────────┐
   │   Chunk     │
   │   Header    │
   ├─────────────┤
   │   Chunk     │
   │   Data      │
   ├─────────────┤
   │  Sub-Chunk  │
   │   Header    │
   ├─────────────┤
   │  Sub-Chunk  │
   │   Data      │
   └─────────────┘

        .
        .
```

Here the virtual world will be saved as a WORLD class chunk — this will contain a number of OBJECT class sub-chunks. Similarly within each OBJECT class chunk will be a series of POLYGON class sub-chunks. Each of these chunk types is derived from the common CHUNK structure:

```
const int CHUNK_WORLD = -1;
const int CHUNK_OBJECT = -2;
const int CHUNK_POLYGON = -3;

struct CHUNK {
  int Type;
};
```

The Type field specifies the type of chunk and may be assigned any of the values CHUNK_WORLD, CHUNK_OBJECT or CHUNK_POLYGON. The definitions of the OBJECT class chunk structure is representative of the others:

```
struct OBJECT_CHUNK : public CHUNK {
  int PolygonCount;
  int VertexCount;
  VERTEX Vertices[1];
};
```

The OBJECT_CHUNK structure is extended as the Vertices array grows — sub-chunks for the associated POLYGON objects follow this array.

All of the chunk types are variable in size so the WORLD, OBJECT and POLYGON classes each define a GetChunkSize() function — again the OBJECT class version serves as a typical example:

```
int OBJECT::GetChunkSize(void) const {
  int size = sizeof(OBJECT_CHUNK)+
    (VertexCount-1)*sizeof(VERTEX);
  for (int i=0; i<PolygonCount; i++)
    size += Polygons[i]->GetChunkSize();
  return size;
}
```

The transfer of the virtual world data to and from a file is initiated by calling the WORLD class Save() and Load() functions — these functions manage the file-related processing, transfer the WORLD object and invoke the corresponding functions in the OBJECT class. Similarly the OBJECT class functions transfer the OBJECT objects and call the POLYGON class functions — finally the POLYGON class Save() and Load() functions transfer the POLYGON objects to and from the file. The WORLD class functions are distinctive — the Save() function firstly determines the size of the WORLD class chunk with a call to GetChunkSize() and then creates a file of exactly the right length:

```
void WORLD::Save(LPCTSTR filename) {
  HANDLE file = CreateFile(filename,
    GENERIC_READ|GENERIC_WRITE,
    0,NULL,CREATE_ALWAYS,
    FILE_ATTRIBUTE_NORMAL,NULL);
  SetFilePointer(file,
    GetChunkSize(),NULL,FILE_BEGIN);
  SetEndOfFile(file);
    .
    .
```

The file is mapped into memory so that the virtual world data can be transferred easily using pointers to chunk structures:

```
        .
        .
HANDLE mapping = CreateFileMapping(file,
  NULL,PAGE_READWRITE,0,0,NULL);
void* pointer =
 MapViewOfFile(mapping,FILE_MAP_WRITE,0,0,0);
WORLD_CHUNK* world = (WORLD_CHUNK*)pointer;
world->Type = CHUNK_WORLD;
world->ObjectCount = ObjectCount;
        .
        .
```

After the WORLD object has saved its own data, it calls the OBJECT class Save()
function for each of the OBJECT objects in the world — the OBJECT class
Save() function updates the chunk pointer ready for the following chunk to be
written. Eventually, the WORLD class Save() function unmaps and closes its data
file:

```
        .
        .
CHUNK* chunk = (CHUNK*)++world;
for (int i=0; i<ObjectCount; i++)
  Objects[i]->Save(chunk);
UnmapViewOfFile(pointer);
CloseHandle(mapping);
CloseHandle(file);
}
```

The WORLD class Load() function is similar but it must create new OBJECT
objects as OBJECT class chunks are read from the file. The OBJECT and
POLYGON class transfer functions are similar to those of the WORLD class but they
omit the file handling code — for example, the OBJECT class Load() function
starts by transferring the object's own PolygonCount, VertexCount and
Vertices fields:

```
void OBJECT::Load(CHUNK*& chunk) {
  OBJECT_CHUNK* object = (OBJECT_CHUNK*)chunk;
  PolygonCount = object->PolygonCount;
  VertexCount = object->VertexCount;
  VERTEX* vertices = object->Vertices;
  for (int i=0; i<VertexCount; i++)
    Vertices[i] = vertices[i];
        .
        .
```

Then the Load() function loops through each of the POLYGON class sub-chunks and creates a new POLYGON object to read in each one:

```
        .
        .
    chunk = (CHUNK*)&vertices[VertexCount];
    for (i=0; i<PolygonCount; i++)
      Polygons[i] = (POLYGON*)
        new POLYGON(this,chunk);
  }
```

The POLYGON constructor internally calls the POLYGON class Load() function:

```
POLYGON::POLYGON(OBJECT* object,CHUNK*& chunk) {
  Object = object;
  Load(chunk);
}
```

The following listing is for the virtual world file from the Travelling Triangle program of section 8.4:

WORLD_CHUNK

FF	FF	FF	FF	01	00	00	00
FE	FF	FF	FF	01	00	00	00
03	00	00	00	00	00	00	00
00	00	00	00	00	00	00	00
00	00	00	00	00	00	00	00
00	00	00	00	FD	FF	FF	FF
00	00	00	00	03	00	00	00
00	00	00	00	01	00	00	00
02	00	00	00				

extended
OBJECT_CHUNK

extended
POLYGON_CHUNK

The file contains a WORLD_CHUNK structure followed by extended OBJECT_CHUNK and POLYGON_CHUNK structures.

9.6 Summary

The Windows 98 GDI provides some support for creating images with colour-filled polygons — however, the implementation is too slow to be used by graphics application which will perform 3D animation. This chapter has taken the first step in producing routines that improve on the efficiency of the GDI functions. The line-drawing code from the previous chapter was modified to calculate a polygon outline — the edges which connect the vertices of a polygon define its outline and this information is stored in the `ScanLines` array to provide a scanline description of the polygon. It is then easy to fill in the polygon with solid colour on a line-by-line basis — the approach will extend to handle colour shading and texture mapping. The basic polygon filling code has also been optimized to render the polygon image more quickly — the next chapter discusses how assembly language programming can further increase the speed. To create realistic images of a virtual world the `SCENE` object must only draw polygons which are visible — those polygons which are hidden at the back of an object must be eliminated from the colour-fill process. The ordering of a polygon's vertices is important in deciding whether the polygon is visible or not — an anti-clockwise ordering indicates that the virtual polygon faces towards the viewer. The `SCENE` object calls its `IsPolygonVisible()` function to help determine which polygons are visible within a particular view of the virtual world. Finally, the entire state of the virtual world can easily be captured and stored in a file using a chunk file format — chunks are nestable structures of variable length and so provide a flexible storage mechanism which is well suited to 3D graphics applications.

10. Assembly Language Programming

The last couple of chapters have shown how to produce wire-frame and polygon-fill graphics with software written in C++ — for the generation of complex images which must be updated in real-time it may be necessary to replace some of the C++ code with an assembly language equivalent. The assembly language instruction set is closely connected to the actual machine code executed by the computer — it is therefore possible to approach the optimum utilization of processor resources by rewriting selected sections of a graphics application in asssembly language. The main topics covered by this chapter include:

— microcomputer architecture
— data and address registers
— the 80x86 assembly language instruction set
— operation of the program stack
— working with inline assembly code
— modifying the program message loop

The chapter also provides a number of examples of translating C++ code fragments into their assembly language equivalent — this should provide a good basis for adapting other computationally intensive graphics routines (such as texture mapping) into assembly language.

10.1 Computer Basics

A C++ compiler converts the source code into instructions which the computer can execute directly — the resultant object code can be optimized but it is rarely as fast as hand-crafted code written directly in assembly language. Nonetheless, it is time-consuming to produce assembly language code and so effort should be directed at sections of the program where the pay-off will be greatest — in graphics applications this typically means optimizing the pixel-drawing code since the images created will often contain hundreds of thousands of pixels. Code written in assembly language can be very fast but the level of processing performed by each instruction is low — hence several assembly language instructions may need to be substituted for a single C++ program statement. The following sections discuss in detail the various categories of assembly language instruction:

— data transfer instructions
— arithmetic and logical operations
— flow control instructions
— stack management instructions

However, it is useful to first understand the context in which the instructions are executed — this section provides a review of computer basics as they relate to assembly language programming.

A computer system consists of three fundamental blocks — the central processing unit (CPU), memory and input/output devices. These are illustrated in the following figure:

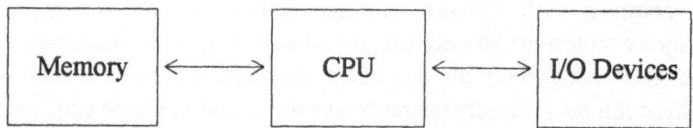

The CPU communicates with the memory and input/output devices by means of data and address connections called 'buses' — the data bus and the address bus respectively carry the data and address values needed to execute the assembly language instructions. The computer memory consists of an array of cells each containing one byte of information — the cell addresses begin with 0 at the start of memory and increase by 1 for each cell until the end of memory is reached. The memory is typically divided into a number of distinct memory ranges that each perform a different function. For example, one section may contain program data whilst another provides storage space for the program stack — the operation of the program stack is considered in section 10.8. In fact the program instructions are also stored in memory — this storage is achieved by encoding the assembly language instructions as bit patterns known as 'machine code'. The CPU holds the memory address of the currently executing instruction so that it can step through the instructions that make up the program. The data and addresses processed by the CPU are stored in internal memory cells known as 'registers' — section 10.3 describes the layout of these registers within the processor. Much of assembly language programming is concerned with shuffling data between the computer memory and the CPU registers.

This chapter concentrates on inline assembly language programming — this technique allows a short section of assembly language code to be inserted into a C++ program. The examples will deal with the construction of an image in the bitmap array provided by a DIB object — the image will be transferred to video memory by a blit operation. This approach avoids the technicalities associated with video memory programming — the DirectX software development kit from Microsoft permits the direct manipulation of video memory in a device-independent manner. The code developed here is specific to Microsoft's Visual C++ but it should work with other assemblers after minimal modification.

10.2 Updating the Message Loop

The first step towards achieving a higher frame rate for image generation does not involve assembly language programming at all — instead the drawing code is moved out of the WM_PAINT message handler and called directly from the VIEW class Run() function. The VIEW class inherits the Run() function from the WINDOW base class — the function implements the program's message loop and was originally defined in chapter 3 but it is now modified as follows:

```
int WINDOW::Run(WINDOW* window) {
  MSG message;
  while (TRUE)
    if (PeekMessage(&message,NULL,0,0,PM_NOREMOVE))
      if (GetMessage(&message,NULL,0,0))
        DispatchMessage(&message);
      else
        break;
    else if (window)
      window->Idle();
  return message.wParam;
}
```

When Run() is invoked (by the WinMain() function) it will accept an optional WINDOW* pointer — the Idle() function of the referenced object will be called when no messages appear in the program's message queue. The PeekMessage() function is used to determine if any messages are currently available — the PM_NOREMOVE flag stops the PeekMessage() function from actually removing the messages from the queue. The WINDOW class Idle() function does nothing — it is declared as a virtual function and should be overridden by a derived VIEW class function which performs the necessary drawing operations. For example:

```
void VIEW::Idle(void) {
  Update();
  Draw();
}

void VIEW::Draw(void) {
  HDC dc = GetDC(Window);
  World->Draw(dc);
  ReleaseDC(Window,dc);
}
```

The Update() and Draw() functions respectively replace the WM_TIMER and WM_PAINT message handlers. In particular the animation is no longer driven by WM_TIMER messages and instead steps forwards as fast as the while loop within the Run() function will allow. To regulate the number of images produced every second it may be necessary to add some kind of synchronization — the GetTickCount() function is useful here since it will return the current time as measured by the tick count of the system clock. The Idle() function can be modified to wait until the clock has ticked on by so many milliseconds before drawing the next image frame.

The updated Idle() function has the following definition:

```
void VIEW::Idle(void) {
  while (NextFrame > GetTickCount());
  NextFrame += FrameInterval;
  Update();
  Draw();
}
```

Here the NextFrame field contains the tick count at which the next frame should be redrawn and the FrameInterval field specifies the gap between frames — for example, setting FrameInterval==50 gives a frame rate of 20 frames per second.

With just the modifications detailed here a polygon-fill version of the Travelling Triangle program from section 8.4 will easily produce 100 animation frames per second — however, for a more complex 3D scene the added efficiency provided by assembly language programming is really necessary.

10.3 The 80x86 Registers

Like other computer processor chips the 80x86 family of Intel processors contain a collection of internal memory cells called registers — in the Pentium processor these registers are each 32 bits in length. In assembly language programs the most commonly used registers are probably the eax, ebx, ecx and edx registers but these are closely followed by the esi, edi, ebp and esp registers. The first set of registers are primarily used to manipulate data whilst the second set deal with memory addresses — however, there is some blurring of this distinction. The e- prefix applied to each of the registers stands for 'extended' — earlier processors in the 80x86 family had registers which could hold only 16 bits of data instead of the current 32-bit capacity. Indeed the lower 16 bits of the data registers eax, ebx, ecx and edx can be treated as two separate 8-bit quantities — the following figure illustrates the layout of the four data registers:

	31	16 15	8 7	0
eax			ah	al
ebx			bh	bl
ecx			ch	cl
edx			dh	dl

The bytes occupying bits 0 to 7 are referred to using an -1 (low) suffix (al, bl, cl and dl) whilst the bytes occupying bits 8 to 15 are referred to using an -h (high) suffix (ah, bh, ch, dh). The individual registers are fairly general purpose but they do have some specific uses. The eax register (accumulator) is the principal register for data processing whilst edx also serves in this role — the ebx register has traditionally been associated with memory addressing operations and ecx is often treated as a counter.

The four address registers may be divided into two sets — the esi and edi registers typically refer to addresses in memory regions containing program data whilst the ebp and esp registers refer to memory addresses in the stack region. The -i suffix for the edi and esi registers denotes them as indexing registers since they are often used to manipulate individual data elements within blocks of memory — the esi register holds source addresses whilst the edi register holds destination addresses. The esp register is known as the 'stack pointer' and holds the address of the current stack top — the ebp register is the 'base pointer' and references a base address within the stack. Section 10.8 provides a more detailed discussion of the operation of the stack and the esp and ebp registers. The esi, edi, ebp and esp registers may be explicitly altered by assembly language instructions — there is also a fifth address register which is implicitly updated as the program executes. This is the eip register or 'instruction pointer' — it contains the address of the currently executing instruction and this address moves sequentially through the assembly language program.

Finally, the 80x86 processors also contain six segment registers (cs, ds, es, fs, gs and ss) which needed to be understood when a segmented memory model was prevalent — fortunately Windows 98 uses a flat 32-bit addressing scheme and so the segment registers play a less important role in applications programming.

10.4 Data Transfer

A large proportion of an assembly language program is spent moving data between memory and the processor's registers or alternatively from register to register — some instructions even move data directly from one location in memory to another. There are a correspondingly large collection of assembly language instructions concerned with data transfers — most of these instructions include the abbreviation mov (move) as part of their mnemonic. This section provides a sample of the 80x86 mov instructions currently available but the list is by no means comprehensive. One of the simplest mov instructions just moves data between a fixed memory location and a particular register — for example:

```
mov eax,[0x3E96DC84]
         .
         .
mov [0x3E96DC84],eax
```

The first instruction moves 32 bits of data from the four consecutive addresses 0x3E96DC84 to 0x3E96DC87 into the eax register whilst the second instruction moves the data back to memory — the square brackets [ ] are used to denote the contents of memory storage. The 80x86 family of processors stores its data in little-endian format so that here bits 0 to 7 of the eax register correspond to the byte at address 0x3E96DC84, bits 8 to 15 come from address 0x3E96DC85 and so on — the start address (0x3E96DC84) need not be a multiple of 4 but the process is more efficient if the condition holds. Alternatively, the sub-registers (al, ah, bl etc.) may be used in 8–bit transfers — then only one memory cell is involved. Yet another way to place data into the processor's registers is to specify the data value directly in a mov instruction:

```
mov ecx,0x00001000
```

Here the 32–bit constant 0x00001000 is stored in the ecx register. In any case, once the registers hold data their contents may be moved from register to register:

```
mov eax,edx
xchg eax,ecx
```

The first of these instruction copies the contents of edx to eax — the second instruction exchanges the contents of eax and ecx.

The next set of data transfer instructions use the contents of one or two registers to calculate a variable memory address — for example:

```
mov [ebx],eax
```

This instruction stores the data from the eax register into the four memory cells whose start address is specified by the ebx register. A more complicated example combines the value of two registers with a constant offset to calculate the memory address:

```
mov eax,[esi+8*edx+0x20]
```

In this type of mov instruction both the scale factor (2, 4 or 8) and the offset are optional. The choice of registers to use in memory address calculations is quite broad but not unlimited.

For the inline assembler packaged with Microsoft's Visual C++ the following short-hand notation is supported to refer to the value of a C++ variable:

```
mov eax,[asm_step_x]
```

Here the value of the C++ variable asm_step_x is loaded into the eax register — as discussed in section 10.8 the instruction actually uses the ebp register to calculate the memory address. The prefix asm_ is not required but is used here to avoid possible conflicts with predefined assembler names.

The final data transfer instructions also use registers to calculate the memory addresses involved — however, the instructions implicitly specify the esi and edi registers.

These instructions include:

```
lodsd
stosd
movsd
```

The first instruction loads the contents of the `eax` register from the memory start address held by the `esi` register whilst the second stores the `eax` contents at the memory location specified by the `edi` register — the third instruction performs a direct memory-to-memory copy of 32 bits of data from the `esi` source address to the `edi` destination address. The `-d` suffix stands for DWORD and after the data transfer the indexing registers involved (`esi` and/or `edi`) are incremented by 4 to point at the next DWORD. There are also `lodsb`, `stosb` and `movsb` equivalents which transfer a single byte of data and cause increments by 1 instead of 4. The `-s-` infix denotes these as string instructions meaning that they are typically used to transfer a whole block of data — the `rep` (repeat) prefix may be added to perform the data block transfer in a single operation:

```
rep stosd
rep movsd
```

The first instruction fills a block of memory with copies of the `eax` register — the second instruction copies a memory block to a new location. In both cases the size of the block (in DWORD units) must be stored in the `ecx` register before the transfer — after the transfer `ecx` will contain a zero value.

As an example of using the data transfer instructions the SCENE class `BeginFrame()` function will be coded in assembly language — the function is used to fill the SCENE object's bitmap with a background colour:

```
void SCENE::BeginFrame(void) {
  DWORD* bits = (DWORD*)Dib->AcquireBits();
  int size = (Height*Pitch)/4;
  for (int i=0; i<size; i++)
    *bits++ = BackgroundColour;
  Dib->ReleaseBits();
}
```

As discussed in section 9.3 the `BackgroundColour` value is obtained by replicating 8-bit colour data in each of the four byte positions within the variable.

The first step in converting to assembly language is to provide variables which can be passed directly to the inline assembly code — these variables should be local and hold 32-bit quantities.

The BeginFrame() function is consequently modified as follows:

```
void SCENE::BeginFrame(void) {
  DWORD* asm_bits = (DWORD*)Dib->AcquireBits();
  DWORD asm_colour = BackgroundColour;
  int asm_size = (Height*Pitch)/4;
  __asm {
    .
    .
  }
  Dib->ReleaseBits();
}
```

In particular, the SCENE object field BackgroundColour needs to be copied to a local variable asm_colour. The inline assembly code is contained within the __asm block as follows:

```
__asm {
  push edi
  mov edi,[asm_bits]
  mov eax,[asm_colour]
  mov ecx,[asm_size]
  rep stosd
  pop edi
}
```

The **for** loop from the C++ version of the BeginFrame() function is replaced by the rep stosd instruction — this fills the bitmap with the background colour held in the eax register and the ecx register acts as a loop counter (instead of the original i variable). Finally, the edi register substitutes for the bits pointer — it is automatically updated by the rep stosd instruction.

The eax, ebx, ecx and edx registers may be used freely within an __asm block — however, the esi and edi registers should be saved and restored using the push and pop instructions respectively. The push instruction copies data to the stack whilst the pop instruction retrieves it — more details on the stack appear in section 10.8.

10.5 Arithmetic and Logical Operations

Another important category of assembly language instructions perform arithmetic and logical operations on the program's data. The simplest arithmetic instructions are probably the inc and dec instructions which respectively increment and decrement the contents of a register:

```
inc edx
dec ecx
```

Next are instructions to add or subtract two 32-bit values — for example:

```
add eax,edx
sub eax,ebx
```

There is also a neg instruction which negates a single operand:

```
neg ebx
```

The assembly language instructions to perform logical operations include and, or and xor — these act in a bitwise-manner like the C++ operators &, | and ^ respectively. For example, the and instruction can be used to mask out everything in the edx register except the lower two bits:

```
and edx,3
```

Finally, there are instructions to perform bit shift operations analogous to those provided by the C++ << and >> operators. However, there are two variants of the right-shift operation which propagate either a zero bit or the sign bit — the sar (shift arithmetic right) instruction is an example of the latter type:

```
sar eax,2
```

Here the eax register is shifted by two bit places and the sign bit (number 31) is replicated in bit positions 31, 30 and 29.

Finally, most of the arithmetic and logical instructions permit a register value to be replaced with the contents of a memory location — for example, the following instruction adds the value of the asm_step_x variable to the eax register:

```
add eax,[asm_step_x]
```

10.6 Flow Control

In C++ code the flow of program control is determined by the **if-else, for, while** statements and so on. With assembly language programming flow control is achieved with jump instructions — the jmp instruction performs an unconditional jump whilst other instructions with a j- prefix perform conditional jumps. Normally the instructions in an assembly language program are executed in order one after the other with the eip register (instruction pointer) keeping track of the current instruction — however, the jump instructions modify the contents of the eip register so that the next instruction to be executed is located at the destination of the jump.

For example:

```
        .
        .
    jmp finish
        .
        .
    finish:
        .
        .
        .
```

Here the `jmp` instruction transfers control to the instruction following the `finish` label and the intermediate instructions are not executed — this is very similar to the action of the C++ **goto** statement.

The conditional jump instructions base their decision of whether or nor to jump upon the contents of a specialized processor register — the bits within this register act as flags and are maintained automatically by the processor. In particular, the contents of the 'flags register' are updated according to the results obtained when arithmetic or logical instructions are executed. For example, the following `xor` instruction zeroes the `eax` register:

```
xor eax,eax
```

The zero result causes the 'zero flag' within the flags register to be set. There are also `cmp` (compare) and `test` instructions which will update the flags register without altering the contents of a data register. The `cmp` instruction performs a subtraction operation whilst the `test` instruction performs a bitwise and operation — however, the results of these operations are simply discarded. For example:

```
cmp eax,3
```

This compares the contents of the `eax` register against the value 3 and sets the flags register accordingly.

Examples of conditional jump instructions include the following:

```
je check   // jump if equal to
jl step    // jump if less than
jg start   // jump if greater than
jne check  // jump if not equal to
jle step   // jump if less than or equal to
jge start  // jump if greater than or equal to
```

Here `check`, `step` and `start` are labels that specify the destination address if the jump is made. This set of jump mnemonics is used when testing signed quantities — `jng` and `jnl` are alternatives for `jle` and `jge` respectively. There are also corresponding mnemonics for unsigned quantities — for example, `jz` (jump if zero) is the unsigned equivalent of `je` (jump if equal) and produces identical machine code.

The instructions to set the flags register are typically paired with a conditional jump instruction as follows:

```
    cmp eax,3
    jg start
        .
        .
start:
        .
        .
```

Here the code immediately following the conditional jump instruction is executed only if `eax` contains a value of 3 or less — if the `eax` register value is greater than 3 then a jump is made to the `start` label.

Finally, there are a couple of specialized control transfer instructions which interact with the `ecx` register. The first is the `jecxz` instruction which makes a jump conditionally on the contents of the `ecx` register being zero — the second is the `loop` instruction which acts similarly but first decrements the value of the `ecx` register. The `loop` instruction can be used to create looping code as follows:

```
    mov ecx,[asm_count]
start:
        .
        .
    loop start
```

Here the assembly language code between the `start` label and the `loop` instruction are repeated — the number of iterations is specified by the value of the `asm_count` variable. However, the range of the `loop` instruction is restricted and care must be taken to ensure than the jump offset it requires can be represented by a signed 8-bit value — an alternative to the `loop` instruction which works with large loops is provided by the following combination:

```
    dec ecx
    jnz start
```

10.7 Faster Polygon-Fill Routines

This section provides two more examples of assembly language programming — the first example replaces a section of code in the SCENE class `ColourFill()` function whilst the second recodes the line-drawing loop from the `DrawLine()` function. The code fragment from the `ColourFill()` function is responsible for drawing a single scanline of a filled polygon — this code was first described in section 9.3 but it is reproduced here for easy reference:

```
start = ScanLines[y].Start;
stop = ScanLines[y].Stop;
        .
        .
if (start <= stop) {
   pixel = line+start;
   length = stop+1-start;
   if (length <= 3)
      for (i=0; i<length; i++)
         *pixel++ = colour;
   else {
      start_bytes = (-start)&3;
      stop_bytes = (stop+1)&3;
      length = (length-start_bytes-stop_bytes)/4;
      for (i=0; i<start_bytes; i++)
         *pixel++ = colour;
      pixel_block = (DWORD*)pixel;
      for (i=0; i<length; i++)
         *pixel_block++ = colour_block;
      pixel = (BYTE*)pixel_block;
      for (i=0; i<stop_bytes; i++)
         *pixel++ = colour;
   }
}
```

Comments in the assembly code will indicate the approximate equivalents to this C++ code — in fact the assembly language version follows the original fairly closely. Nonetheless, a few modifications to the initialization procedure are required:

```
asm_start = ScanLines[y].Start;
asm_stop = ScanLines[y].Stop;
        .
        .
if (asm_start <= asm_stop) {
   asm_colour = ColourBuffer+asm_start;
   asm_pixel = line+asm_start;
```

The asm_colour variable is assigned a pointer to the start pixel within the ColorBuffer array — the array is filled with colour information at the beginning of the ColourFill() function:

```
for (i=0; i<Width; i++)
   ColourBuffer[i] = colour;
```

This approach enables the code to be adapted easily to handle textures and other advanced colour effects — chapter 14 describes how the ColourBuffer array can be filled with colour values that are not all identical.

Anyway, the first part of the __asm block saves the esi and edi registers then loads the initial values into the appropriate registers:

```
__asm {
  push esi
  push edi
  mov esi,[asm_colour]
  mov edi,[asm_pixel]
  mov ebx,[asm_start]
  mov edx,[asm_stop]
     .
     .
```

The esi and edi registers will serve to transfer pixels from the ColourBuffer array to the SCENE object bitmap.

Next the length of the polygon image within the scanline is calculated — the neg ebx and inc edx instructions place the values -start and stop+1 in the ebx and edx registers respectively:

```
     .
     .
  neg ebx        // length = stop+1-start;
  inc edx
  mov eax,ebx
  add eax,edx
     .
     .
```

If there are three pixels or less these are copied individually and this concludes the processing for the current scanline:

```
     .
     .
  cmp eax,3      // if (length <= 3)
  jg start
  xchg eax,ecx   // for (i=0; i<length; i++)
  rep movsb      //   *pixel++ = colour;
  jmp finish
     .
     .
```

Alternatively, if there are 4 or more pixels then the code proceeds to check for any start bytes that cannot be transferred as a DWORD block:

```
        .
        .
start:              // else
    and ebx,3       // start_bytes = (-start)&3;
    sub eax,ebx     // length -= start_bytes;
    mov ecx,ebx     // for (i=0; i<start_bytes; i++)
    jecxz middle
    rep movsb       //   *pixel++ = colour;
        .
        .
```

Next the middle section of the polygon is transferred in DWORD blocks:

```
        .
        .
middle:
    and edx,3       // stop_bytes = (stop+1)&3;
    sub eax,edx     // length = (length-stop_bytes)/4;
    sar eax,2
    xchg eax,ecx    // for (i=0; i<length; i++)
    jecxz stop
    rep movsd       //   *pixel_block++ = colour_block;
        .
        .
```

And lastly any extra bytes at the right-hand side of the polygon are transferred:

```
        .
        .
stop:
    mov ecx,edx     // for (i=0; i<stop_bytes; i++)
    jecxz finish
    rep movsb       //   *pixel++ = colour;
        .
        .
```

Note that the explicit casting between BYTE* and DWORD* pointers required in the C++ code is not necessary here. The assembly language code ends by restoring the edi and esi registers from the stack:

```
        .
        .
finish:
    pop edi
    pop esi
}
```

This first example has replaced three C++ **for** loops with single instructions (rep movsb and rep movsd) making the code very fast indeed. The next example shows how to recode a more complicated loop using assembly language instructions — the original C++ code in this case is the line-drawing loop from the SCENE class DrawLine() function. The C++ version of this loop is replicated here for easy reference:

```cpp
for (int i=0; i<=length; i++) {
  if (test<=0)
    test += noupdate;
  else {
    test += update;
    pixel.x += jump_x;
    pixel.y += jump_y;
  }
  if (pixel.y>=0 && pixel.y<Height) {
    if (initial &&
          pixel.x<ScanLines[pixel.y].Start)
      ScanLines[pixel.y].Start = pixel.x;
    if (final &&
          pixel.x>ScanLines[pixel.y].Stop)
      ScanLines[pixel.y].Stop = pixel.x;
  }
  pixel.x += step_x;
  pixel.y += step_y;
}
```

The important variables are again replaced by equivalents having an asm_ prefix. The __asm block starts by saving the esi register and storing the initial data values into registers:

```asm
__asm {
  push esi
  mov esi,[asm_scanlines]
  mov eax,[asm_pixel_x]
  mov edx,[asm_pixel_y]
  mov ebx,[asm_test]
  mov ecx,[asm_length] // for (i=0; i<=length; ...
  inc ecx
    .
    .
```

Here the ecx register acts as the **for** loop counter — it is initially set to the number of pixels in the line. The eax and edx registers respectively contain the

x- and y-coordinates of the current pixel and the ebx register maintains the value
of test variable.

For each iteration through the loop the code first tests whether the more slowly
changing pixel coordinate (x or y) should be updated :

```
      .
      .
start:
   cmp ebx,0              // if (test<=0)
   jle nojump
   add ebx,[asm_update]   // test += update;
   add eax,[asm_jump_x]   // pixel.x += jump_x;
   add edx,[asm_jump_y]   // pixel.y += jump_y;
   jmp clip
nojump:
   add ebx,[asm_noupdate] // test += noupdate;
      .
      .
```

Next the line is clipped to the top and bottom of the SCENE object bitmap:

```
      .
      .
clip:
   cmp edx,0              // if (pixel.y>=0 && ...
   jl step
   cmp edx,[asm_height]   // pixel.y<Height)
   jnl step
      .
      .
```

If the pixel falls within the bounds then the appropriate Start field in the
ScanLines array is updated if necessary:

```
      .
      .
   cmp [asm_initial],0    // if (initial && ...
   jz check
   cmp eax,[esi+8*edx]    // x<ScanLines[y].Start)
   jnl check
   mov [esi+8*edx],eax    // ScanLines[y].Start=x;
      .
      .
```

And similarly the Stop field is updated if necessary:

```
      .
      .
check:
    cmp [asm_final],0      // if (final && ...
    jz step
    cmp eax,[esi+8*edx+4]  // x>ScanLines[y].Stop)
    jng step
    mov [esi+8*edx+4],eax  // ScanLines[y].Stop=x;
      .
      .
```

Now the more rapidly changing pixel coordinate is updated in preparation for the next iteration through the line-drawing line:

```
      .
      .
step:
    add eax,[asm_step_x]   // pixel.x += step_x;
    add edx,[asm_step_y]   // pixel.y += step_y;
      .
      .
```

Finally, the loop counter in the ecx register is tested and the loop continued until the end of the line of pixels is reached — when the loop eventually exits the esi register is restored and the __asm block ends:

```
      .
      .
    dec ecx                //  ... i++);
    jnz start
    pop esi
}
```

This is one situation where the loop instruction must be replaced by the dec-jnz combination — the **for** loop is simply too large for the loop instruction to work correctly.

10.8 Program Stack

One important topic concerned with assembly language programming that has not yet been discussed in detail involves the management of the program stack. The stack is a dynamic memory storage area which is intimately related to function invocations — whenever a function is called, storage space is allocated for it from the program stack and upon return from the function the stack storage is deallocated.

The following figure illustrates the state of the stack before, during and after a function call:

Before Call	During Call	After Call
Allocated Storage	Allocated Storage	Allocated Storage
Unallocated Storage	Current Stack Frame Unallocated Storage	Unallocated Storage

The current 'stack frame' provides the storage space allocated to the function — the function parameters and local variables are stored in the stack frame. A pointer to the base of the stack frame data area is typically placed in the ebp register so that the function can manipulate its variables using this register. For example, assembly language instructions such as:

```
mov eax,[asm_length]
```

are actually encoded using the ebp register to calculate the address — the asm_length variable is located at some fixed offset from the address held by the base pointer register. At the beginning of the function the stack and base pointers are identical but then as the function executes the current stack address may drop below its initial value. For example, suppose that after assigning storage space for function parameters and local variables the following instructions are executed:

```
push esi
push edi
```

In this case the contents of the stack may be depicted as follows:

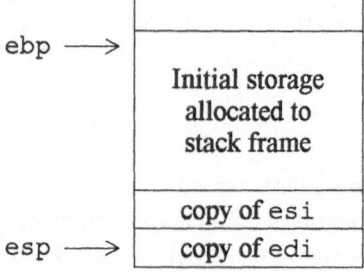

The push instruction decrements the value of the stack pointer and stores data into the newly referenced memory thus extending the stack frame — conversely the pop instruction retrieves the data referenced by the stack pointer and then increments the esp register.

10.9 Summary

This chapter has been concerned with improving the speed at which a graphics application can render images. A simple modification is to call the main drawing routine directly from the program's message loop — however, considerable gains in efficiency can be achieved by recoding selected portions of the drawing code in assembly language. The best approach is usually to concentrate maximum effort on the code which actually draws pixels — for an image with many pixels the execution of this code will constitute a high proportion of the program's overall processing. An assembly language routine is principally concerned with moving data between memory and the processor's internal registers — the 80x86 family of processors provide the data registers eax, ebx, ecx and edx as well as the address registers esi, edi, esp and ebp. The assembly language instruction set may be divided into a number of categories which include data transfer instructions, arithmetic and logical operations, flow control instructions and finally stack management instructions. The program stack provides storage for a function's parameters and local variables within a dynamically allocated stack frame — the function may manipulate its data by using address calculations which involve the base pointer register. The assembly language programming examples provided in the chapter deal with the production of an image in a SCENE object's internal bitmap — more specifically the routines erase the bitmap with a background colour, calculate the pixels forming a line and also colour-fill a polygon outline. The final image generated by the SCENE class Draw() function is displayed by blitting the contents of the bitmap to the screen — this approach avoids the technicalities associated with direct video memory programming.

11. Mathematics of 3D Geometry

The last three chapters have introduced the concept of a virtual 3D world and have shown how to generate images of this world — however, it has been assumed that the positions of the objects in the image are already known. The problem now is to calculate the image coordinates from the original locations of the objects within the virtual world — this chapter begins to construct a solution by providing a sound mathematical model of the virtual world. The essential topics include:

— vector description of the virtual world
— coordinate systems and matrix transformations
— the VECTOR class
— scalar product, vector product and triple product

Later chapters extend the foundations laid here to develop code capable of projecting a 2D image of the 3D virtual world which changes as the viewpoint is dynamically updated.

11.1 Vectors and Matrices

The xy-coordinate system used by Windows 98 can be extended into 3D by adding a z-axis that points into the screen — the following figure illustrates the arrangement of the three axes:

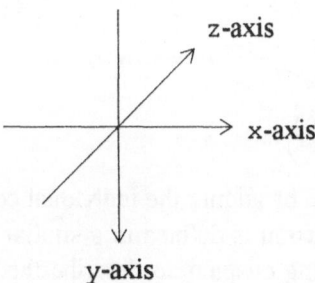

Points in 3D space may be specified by their x-, y- and z-coordinates — a general point in 3D space has the coordinates (x,y,z). In fact many different coordinate systems are possible and it is useful to define the concept of a vector as a quantity which exists independently of the coordinate system actually chosen. Vectors possess the two attributes of magnitude and direction — for example, a line with endpoints (x0,y0,z0) and (x1,y1,z1) may be represented by a vector **v** whose magnitude equals the length of the line and whose direction is set by the orientation of the line in 3D space. A change of coordinate system will alter the coordinates of the line endpoints but the vector representing the line remains fixed. Nonetheless, the components of a vector may be described with respect to a particular coordinate system through the use of delta values (see section 8.3) — for example, in the coordinate system for which the line endpoints are $(x0,y0,z0)$ and $(x1,y1,z1)$ the components of the corresponding vector $\mathbf{v}$ may be calculated as $(x1-x0,y1-y0,z1-z0)$ — this is illustrated in the following figure:

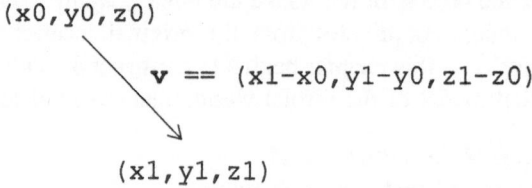

To associate a vector with a single point it is necessary to base the vector at some reference point — the vector components are then calculated as delta values relative to this reference point. If the vector is based at the origin of the coordinate system then its components equal the coordinates of the point which it represents — however, if the vector $\mathbf{v}$ is based at some other point $(x0,y0,z0)$ then vector addition must be performed to determine the point represented by $\mathbf{v}$:

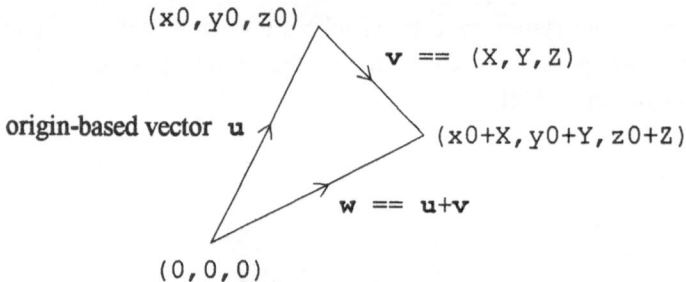

Here the vector $\mathbf{w}$ is calculated by adding the individual components of $\mathbf{u}$ and $\mathbf{v}$ — the operation of vector subtraction is defined in a similar manner. Vectors will be used extensively in forthcoming chapters to describe the construction of a virtual world — the next section introduces the VECTOR class to embody the vector concept.

So vectors exist independently of the overlying coordinate system — this means that the components of a vector change as the coordinate axes move in 3D space. Of particular interest here are transformations involving only translations and rotations of the axes — rotations alter the orientation of the axes whilst translations shift the origin. For example, if a vector $\mathbf{v}$ has the components $(L,0,0)$ in one coordinate system then a rotation can orient the new y-axis in the direction of $\mathbf{v}$ so that its components become $(0,L,0)$. Since the components of a vector represent delta values they are unaltered by a translation — nonetheless, if the vector is positioned so that its endpoints are initially at $(0,0,0)$ and $(L,0,0)$ then by shifting the origin along the x-axis to the middle of the vector the new coordinates of the vector endpoints become $(-L/2,0,0)$ and $(L/2,0,0)$ respectively. Of course, within a single coordinate system the endpoints may be associated with vectors based at the origin — however, a translation of the origin means that new vectors must be found to represent the endpoints.

The rotation and translation operations are known as 'rigid-body transformations' since they rigidly move the axes and maintain the shapes of objects in a virtual world — the rigid-body transformations specifically do not include reflections or scaling operations. Reflections flip the direction of one or all coordinate axes thus producing a mirror image of a virtual object — scaling operations stretch or shrink a virtual object and can alter its shape if different scale factors are applied along different axes. Each rigid-body transformation may be represented with a matrix M and an **offset** vector — the components of a vector are transformed by multiplication with the matrix M whilst both the matrix and the **offset** vector determine how points in 3D space should be associated with vectors. For example, if the vector **v** in the original coordinate system is transformed to a new coordinate system it becomes the vector **V** where:

```
V = M*v;
```

Suppose that **v**$==(x,y,z)$ and M has the general layout:

$$
M == \begin{bmatrix} m00 & m01 & m02 \\ m10 & m11 & m12 \\ m20 & m21 & m22 \end{bmatrix}
$$

The components of **V**$==(X,Y,Z)$ may be calculated as follows:

```
X = m00*x+m01*y+m02*z;
Y = m10*x+m11*y+m12*z;
Z = m20*x+m21*y+m22*z;
```

Both **v** and **V** represent the same underlying vector but they have different components calculated in the original and transformed coordinate systems. However, the vectors **a** and **b** associated with the endpoints of **v** are replaced with the vectors **A** and **B** in the new coordinate system:

```
A = M*a+offset;
B = M*b+offset;
```

For example, with $\mathbf{v}==(L,0,0)$, $\mathbf{a}==(0,0,0)$ and $\mathbf{b}==(L,0,0)$ then to translate the origin to the middle of $\mathbf{v}$ requires the following transformation:

$$M == \begin{bmatrix} 1 & 0 & 0 \\ 0 & 1 & 0 \\ 0 & 0 & 1 \end{bmatrix} \quad \textbf{offset} == (-L/2,0,0)$$

Here M is the identity matrix I which does not alter the vector components — hence $\mathbf{V}$ has the same components as $\mathbf{v}$ but the endpoint vectors are changed to $\mathbf{A}==(-L/2,0,0)$ and $\mathbf{B}==(L/2,0,0)$.

The rotation operations set the **offset** vector to zero — the matrix M is solely responsible for defining a rotation transformation. A common approach is to build all rotations from three basic ones — these fundamental rotations are made by fixing one of the three coordinate axes (x, y or z) and rotating about the chosen axis. For example, fixing the z-axis does not alter the z component of a vector but rotates the x and y components — here is the transformation matrix for rotation through an angle specified by the `angle_z` variable:

$$M == \begin{bmatrix} \cos(\text{angle\_z}) & -\sin(\text{angle\_z}) & 0 \\ \sin(\text{angle\_z}) & \cos(\text{angle\_z}) & 0 \\ 0 & 0 & 1 \end{bmatrix}$$

The elements of this matrix can be determined by noting the new coordinates of the points with old coordinates (1,0,0), (0,1,0) and (0,0,1). The following figure illustrates the rotation operation acting on the xy-plane:

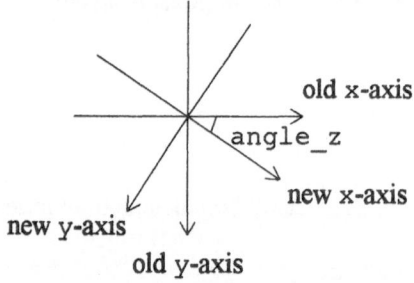

The transformation matrices for rotations about the x- and y-axes are similar but involve sines and cosines of `angle_x` and `angle_y` respectively — a matrix for a transformation requiring two or three basic rotations may be obtained by matrix multiplication. A general rigid-body transformation can be specified with the four parameters `angle_x`, `angle_y`, `angle_z` and **offset**. The transformation matrix M involved in a rigid-body transformation is known as an 'orthogonal matrix' — it has the property that the inverse transformation is represented by the transpose of the matrix M. The extra condition of a positive determinant for M is required to exclude reflections — in fact $\det(M)==1$ for all rigid-body transformations. The inverse of a matrix M representing a general rigid-body transformation may be written in two equivalent forms:

$$
M^{-1} ==
\begin{bmatrix}
m00 & m10 & m20 \\
m01 & m11 & m21 \\
m02 & m12 & m22
\end{bmatrix}
==
\begin{bmatrix}
M00 & M01 & M02 \\
M10 & M11 & M12 \\
M20 & M21 & M22
\end{bmatrix}
$$

where

```
M00 == m11*m22-m21*m12
M01 == m21*m02-m01*m22
M02 == m01*m12-m11*m02
           .
           .
```

and so on.

Chapter 15 investigates how to rigidly move an object within its virtual world. The mathematics involved are very similar to those for transforming the coordinate system but everything appears to work in reverse. For example, if the coordinate system is rotated about some axis then the effect on the vector coordinates is identical to that produced by fixing the coordinate system and rotating all the vectors about the same axis but in the opposite direction.

11.2 The VECTOR Class

The VECTOR class will represent 3D vectors — it supercedes the VERTEX structure used in chapters 8 to 10 to describe points in the virtual world. The version defined here uses integer fields to hold the 3D coordinates — like the SPRITE and SCENE classes it defines a Scale field which allows integer values to represent real numbers in fixed-point format. Here is the VECTOR class specification in outline:

```
class VECTOR {
public:
  VECTOR(int = 0,int = 0,int =0);
  VECTOR(const POINT_3D&);
  VECTOR(const VECTOR&);
  VECTOR(CHUNK*&);
     .
     .
private:
  int X;
  int Y;
  int Z;
  static int Scale;
};
```

There are a variety of ways to create a new VECTOR object and each has its own constructor — this is an example of the C++ mechanism of 'function overloading' whereby a function name can be reused provided different parameter types are involved. The first VECTOR class constructor simply assigns parameter values to the X, Y and Z fields:

```
VECTOR::VECTOR(int x,int y,int z) {
   X = x;
   Y = y;
   Z = z;
}
```

The second constructor creates a VECTOR object from a POINT_3D structure — this user-defined structure extends the Windows 98 POINT structure to 3D by adding a z field.

```
VECTOR::VECTOR(const POINT_3D& point) {
   X = point.x;
   Y = point.y;
   Z = point.z;
}
```

The constructor acts as a type conversion operator from POINT_3D type to VECTOR type — the VECTOR class also supports the reverse type conversion:

```
VECTOR::operator POINT_3D(void) const {
   POINT_3D point;
   point.x = X;
   point.y = Y;
   point.z = Z;
   return point;
}
```

A VECTOR object should be converted to a POINT_3D structure whenever the vector components need to manipulated individually.

The third VECTOR class constructor is a copy constructor — it allows the value of one VECTOR object to initialize another:

```
VECTOR::VECTOR(const VECTOR& vector) {
   X = vector.X;
   Y = vector.Y;
   Z = vector.Z;
}
```

The final constructor copies values from a virtual world file by an internal call to the VECTOR class Load() function:

```
void VECTOR::Load(CHUNK*& chunk) {
  VECTOR_CHUNK* vector = (VECTOR_CHUNK*)chunk;
  X = vector->X;
  Y = vector->Y;
  Z = vector->Z;
  chunk = (CHUNK*)++vector;
}
```

The VECTOR class similarly defines a Save() function for transferring its value to a virtual world file.

The VECTOR class also defines a number of operator functions to implement common vector operations such as assignment, addition and subtraction. For example, the VECTOR class assignment operator is:

```
VECTOR&
VECTOR::operator=(const VECTOR& vector) {
  X = vector.X;
  Y = vector.Y;
  Z = vector.Z;
  return *this;
}
```

As described in the previous section the vector addition operator adds individual components — the implementation in the VECTOR class is straightforward:

```
VECTOR
VECTOR::operator+(const VECTOR& vector) const {
  VECTOR sum;
  sum.X = X+vector.X;
  sum.Y = Y+vector.Y;
  sum.Z = Z+vector.Z;
  return sum;
}
```

The VECTOR class similarly defines functions for the − , += and −= operators. The definition of these operators allows VECTOR objects to be manipulated in an intuitive fashion — this is a very useful facility provided by the C++ language. For example:

```
VECTOR vector = ends[1];
vector -= ends[0];
```

This code calculates the vector corresponding to the line which lies between the endpoints ends[0] and ends[1].

Finally, the VECTOR class also defines the | and * product operators — these are discussed in sections 11.3 and 11.4 respectively. To implement the product operators the VECTOR class needs a static field Scale that belongs to all VECTOR objects — the value of Scale is applied to normalize products when a fixed-point format is in use. The TripleProduct() function combines the functionality of the other two product operators — the name indicates that the function accepts three VECTOR objects as parameters.

11.3 Scalar Product

The scalar product acts as a projection operation — it determines the component of one vector in the direction specified by another vector. For two vectors which maintain constant lengths but are otherwise free to rotate, the value of their scalar product is greatest when they point in the same direction and least when they point in opposite directions — actually the magnitude of the scalar product is identical in these two cases but the sign changes from positive to negative. The scalar product varies continuously between maximum and minimum values as the relative orientation of the two vectors is altered — when the two vectors are exactly perpendicular the value of the scalar product is zero. The following figure illustrates the properties of the scalar product:

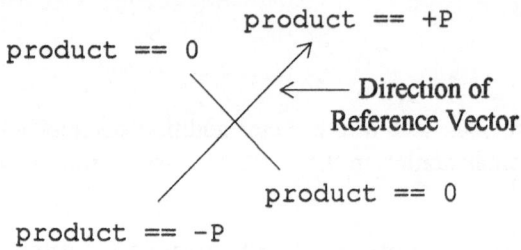

The scalar product of two vectors **u** and **v** is denoted by **u.v** — the VECTOR class uses the | operator as an alternative to the . operator. Anyway suppose that the 3D components of **u** and **v** are as follows:

```
u == (x0,y0,z0)
v == (x1,y1,z1)
```

The easiest way to define the scalar product is to rotate the vectors so that they lie in the xy-plane with the reference vector **u** pointing along the x-axis — the rigid-body transformation required to do this will have an orthogonal matrix representation M. The transformed vectors are:

```
U == M*u == (X0,0,0)
V == M*v == (m00*x1+m01*y1+m02*z1,Y1,0)
```

The scalar product of **u** and **v** measures the X component of the **V** vector as follows:

```
u.v == X0*(m00*x1+m01*y1+m02*z1)
```

But M is orthogonal so the inverse matrix is the transpose of M — applying this inverse transformation to U shows that:

```
x0  ==  m00*X0
y0  ==  m01*X0
z0  ==  m02*X0
```

Consequently the scalar product of **u** and **v** is defined as:

u.v == x0*x1+y0*y1+z0*z1

In particular, if **u**==**v** then the scalar product yields the magnitude squared of the vector **u** — the magnitude of **u** is denoted by |**u**|:

u.u == x0*x0+y0*y0+z0*z0 == |**u**|*|**u**|

The equivalence is assured by the 3D form of Pythagoras's theorem.

Furthermore, since the cos() function also performs the projection operation it is clear from a geometrical perspective that the following relation for the scalar product holds:

u.v == |**u**| * |**v**| * cos(angle)

Here angle is the angle between the two vectors. The following figure illustrates the idea:

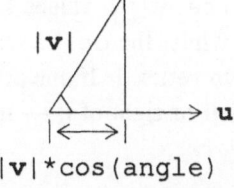

|**v**|*cos(angle)

The VECTOR class implements the scalar product operation as follows:

```
__int64
VECTOR::operator|(const VECTOR& vector) const {
    __int64 product = Int32x32To64(X,vector.X);
    product += Int32x32To64(Y,vector.Y);
    product += Int32x32To64(Z,vector.Z);
    return product/Scale;
}
```

As in section 9.3 the Int32x32To64() function is used to help avoid overflow problems — the final result is divided by Scale and returned as a 64-bit integer. The division normalizes the product vector if the original vector components have been scaled by a factor of Scale — multiplying the components produces a result scaled by `Scale*Scale` but the final division restores the original scale factor. This is an easy way to implement the function but there are more efficient alternatives.

11.4 Vector Product

The scalar product combines two vectors to yield a scalar quantity — the result is a single number that measures the projection of one vector in the direction of another. However, two vectors may also be combined to generate another vector — this action is performed by the vector product operation. Some insight into the definition of the vector product can be obtained by examining the SCENE class `IsPolygonVisible()` function that was introduced in section 9.4. This function determines the visibility of a polygon by checking if the polygon's vertices are ordered clockwise or anti-clockwise — it works by comparing the slopes of two polygon edges which share a vertex as a common endpoint:

```
BOOL SCENE::IsPolygonVisible(void) {
    .
    .
    .
    __int64 test;
    test  = Int32x32To64(delta_x[0],delta_y[1]);
    test -= Int32x32To64(delta_x[1],delta_y[0]);
    return (test > 0);
}
```

The `delta_x` and `delta_y` arrays are used to calculate the slopes of these two lines — the `delta_x[0]` and `delta_y[0]` values are for the polygon edge from vertex 0 to vertex (count-1) whilst the `delta_x[1]` and `delta_y[1]` values are for the edge from vertex 0 to vertex 1. If one of the edges is vertical then the other edge must lie either to the left or right of it — in this case the checks for visibility are as follows:

```
delta_x[0] == 0 && delta_x[1]*delta_y[0] < 0
delta_x[1] == 0 && delta_x[0]*delta_y[1] > 0
```

The following figure depicts the former case with coordinates chosen so that vertex 0 lies at the origin:

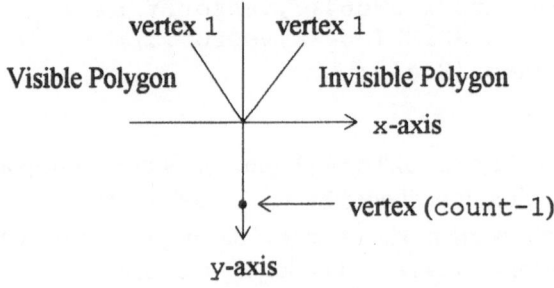

However, if neither line is vertical then there are two cases to consider:

— both edges extend horizontally from vertex 0 in the same direction
— the edges extend horizontally in opposite directions

In the first case delta_x[0] and delta_x[1] have the same sign whilst in the second case these quantities have opposite signs. The following figure illustrates the possibilities when delta_x[0]>0:

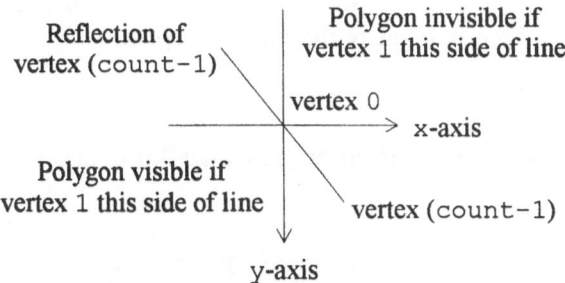

In the first case (with delta_x[0] and delta_x[1] having the same sign) the test for visibility is as follows:

$$\frac{delta\_y[1]}{delta\_x[1]} > \frac{delta\_y[0]}{delta\_x[0]}$$

Similarly, in the second case the test for a visible polygon is:

$$\frac{delta\_y[1]}{delta\_x[1]} < \frac{-delta\_y[0]}{-delta\_x[0]}$$

Here the slope on the right-hand side of the inequality refers to the line connecting vertex 0 to the reflection of vertex (count-1).

For a visible polygon with an anti-clockwise vertex ordering, vertex 1 must lie to the left of the line connecting vertex (count-1) to its reflection — similarly if the polygon is invisible then vertex 1 must lie to the right of this line.

However, all the cases are covered by a single test:

    delta_x[0]*delta_y[1] - delta_x[1]*delta_y[0] > 0

This is exactly the condition used by the SCENE class IsPolygonVisible() function to determine the visibility of a polygon. Here the test is applied to polygons which lie in the xy-plane but the remainder of this section describes how to extend the test to work with general 3D polygons. As discussed in section 11.1 the delta_x and delta_y arrays actually describe a pair of 2D vectors and so the test for polygon visibility may be rewritten using vector terminology. Suppose that the two polygon edges to be tested are represented by the vectors $u == (x0, y0)$ and $v == (x1, y1)$ so that the test quantity is:

```
test == x0*y1-x1*y0
```

The discussion of the scalar product in the previous section showed that:

```
u.v == |u| * |v| * cos(angle)
```

where `angle` is the angle between the two vectors — alternatively the scalar product may also be written in terms of the vector components:

```
u.v == x0*x1+y0*y1
```

The following figure illustrates an interesting right-angled triangle:

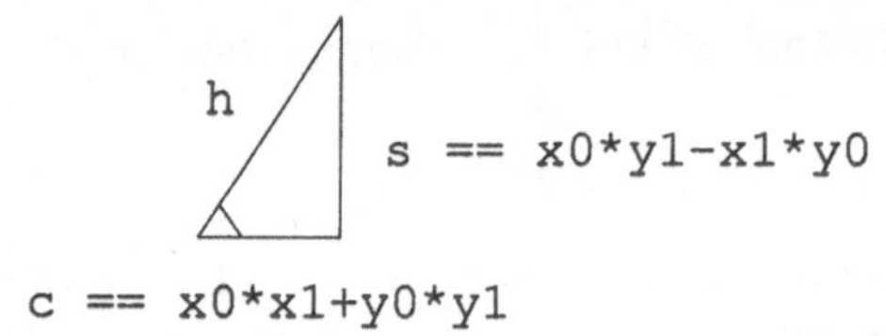

```
h
                 s  == x0*y1-x1*y0


c == x0*x1+y0*y1
```

The two shorter edges correspond to the scalar product and to the value of `test` — the length of the hypotenuse may be calculated using Pythagoras's theorem:

```
h*h == s*s + c*c
    == (x0*x0+y0*y0)*(x1*x1+y1*y1)
    == |u| * |v|
```

Hence (ignoring questions of sign) the value of `test` is actually:

```
test == |u| * |v| * sin(angle)
```

Furthermore, the previous discussion of the IsPolygonVisible() function has demonstrated that `test` is positive when `angle` lies in the range:

```
0 degrees < angle < 180 degrees
```

and `test` is negative when `angle` lies in the range:

```
0 degrees > angle > -180 degrees
```

Since this is the same behaviour as the `sin()` function the relation for `test` is correct including sign. Consequently the SCENE class IsPolygonVisible() function can be considered as testing for a positive angle between two vectors.

It is easy to extend the IsPolygonVisible() test to handle general 3D polygons by defining the vector product of two vectors — the first step is to extend the vectors **u** and **v** to 3D by setting the z component to zero:

```
u  ==  (x0,y0,0)
v  ==  (x1,y1,0)
```

The vector product of **u** and **v** is defined as follows:

```
u  x  v  ==  (0,0,test)  ==  (0,0,x0*y1-x1*y0)
```

Now take a rigid-body transformation with corresponding matrix M — the transformation will move the polygon from the xy-plane to some general location in 3D space. The transformed vectors **U** and **V** are:

```
U  ==  M*u  ==  (X0,Y0,Z0)
V  ==  M*v  ==  (X1,Y1,z1)
```

and their vector product is:

```
U  x  V  ==  M*(u  x  v)  =  (m02*(x0*y1-x1*y0),
                             m12*(x0*y1-x1*y0),
                             m22*(x0*y1-x1*y0))
```

But the matrix M is orthogonal so that:

```
m02  ==  m01*m12-m02*m11
m12  ==  m02*m10-m00*m12
m22  ==  m00*m11-m01*m10
```

Consequently, the Z coordinate of the vector product is:

```
m22*(x0*y1-x1*y0)
   ==  (m00*x0+m01*y0)*(m10*x1+m11*y1)  -
       (m00*x1+m01*y1)*(m10*x0+m11*y0)
   ==  X0*Y1-X1*Y0
```

The X and Y coordinates of the vector product may be similarly computed to yield:

```
U  x  V  ==  (Y0*Z1-Y1*Z0,
             Z0*X1-Z1*X0,
             X0*Y1-X1*Y0)
```

In the 2D case the polygons were contained in the xy-plane and the vector product always pointed along the z-axis — the polygon was visible only if the vector product pointed in the positive z direction. In the 3D case the vector product is perpendicular to the plane containing the polygon — if the polygon is visible then the vector product points in a direction which is generally away from the viewer. The new SCENE class IsPolygonVisible() function will compare the direction of the polygon's vector product with a 'viewing vector' — the viewing vector is directed from the position of the viewer towards vertex 0 of the polygon

being tested. The code for the new IsPolygonVisible() function is as
follows:

```
BOOL SCENE::IsPolygonVisible(void) {
  VECTOR u,v,w;
  u = ObjectVertices[PolygonVertices[VertexCount-1]];
  v = ObjectVertices[PolygonVertices[1]];
  w = ObjectVertices[PolygonVertices[0]];
  u -= w;
  v -= w;
  w -= ViewPoint;
  return ((u*v)|w) > 0;
}
```

The translation and scalar product operations were previously defined in sections
11.2 and 11.3 respectively — here is the definition for the VECTOR class vector
product operator:

```
VECTOR
VECTOR::operator*(const VECTOR& vector) const {
  __int64 component;
  VECTOR product;
  component = Int32x32To64(Y,vector.Z);
  component -= Int32x32To64(vector.Y,Z);
  product.X = int(component/Scale);
  component = Int32x32To64(Z,vector.X);
  component -= Int32x32To64(vector.Z,X);
  product.Y = int(component/Scale);
  component = Int32x32To64(X,vector.Y);
  component -= Int32x32To64(vector.X,Y);
  product.Z = int(component/Scale);
  return product;
}
```

The Int32x32To64() function is again used to help avoid overflow problems
associated with intermediate results.

11.5 Triple Product

The scalar quantity (u*v)|w calculated by the SCENE class function
IsPolygonVisible() is known as a 'triple product' — it combines the values
of the three vectors represented by the VECTOR objects u, v and w. In fact the
following relations hold:

```
[u,v,w] == (u*v)|w == (v*w)|u == (w*u)|v
```

Here [u,v,w] denotes the triple product operation — cycling the three vectors
does not alter the value of the triple product. The VECTOR class function
TripleProduct() will implement the triple product operation — it can be used

to rewrite the IsPolygonVisible() function as follows:

```
BOOL SCENE::IsPolygonVisible(void) {
    .
    .
    return (w.TripleProduct(u,v) > 0);
}
```

The advantage of this approach is that 64-bit integers can be used throughout the calculation of the triple product without having to truncate the intermediate results to 32 bits. The VECTOR class TripleProduct() function is defined as follows:

```
__int64
VECTOR::TripleProduct(const VECTOR& u,
                      const VECTOR& v) const {
    __int64 component,product;
    component = Int32x32To64(u.Y,v.Z);
    component -= Int32x32To64(v.Y,u.Z);
    product = X*(component/Scale);
    component = Int32x32To64(u.Z,v.X);
    component -= Int32x32To64(v.Z,u.X);
    product += Y*(component/Scale);
    component = Int32x32To64(u.X,v.Y);
    component -= Int32x32To64(v.X,u.Y);
    product += Z*(component/Scale);
    return product/Scale;
}
```

The triple product is zero if the three vectors lie in the same plane — if it is non-zero then the sign indicates the relative orientation of each vector and the plane formed by the other two. With regards to the IsPolygonVisible() function a zero value for the triple product means that the polygon is viewed end-on — positive and negative values determine the orientation of the polygon relative to the viewing vector and correspond to visible and hidden polygons respectively.

11.6 Lines and Planes

Vector notation can be applied to greatly simplify the equations of lines and planes — in both cases this requires an origin-based vector r0 that specifies one point on the line or in the plane. For a line one more vector (r1) is required to determine the direction of the line — the vector equation of the line is:

```
r == r0 + s*r1
```

The variable s changes as the general point r moves along the line — for s==0 the point is coincident with r0.

The following figure illustrates the situation:

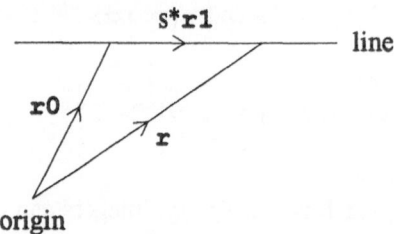

origin

Similarly, two vectors (**r1** and **r2**) are needed to describe a plane — the equation is:

```
r == r0 + s*r1 + t*r2
```

The values of s and t change independently to map out the 2D surface of the plane:

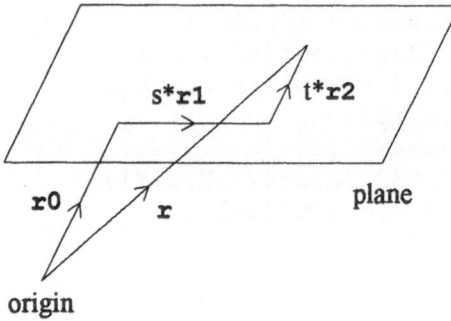

origin

The plane has an alternate description which involves vector and scalar products — the vector product of **r1** and **r2** is perpendicular to the plane and the vector **r−r0** lies in the plane so that its scalar product with **r1** x **r2** is zero. Hence the equation of the plane may also be written as:

```
(r1 x r2) . (r-r0) == 0
```

Alternatively, using the triple product notation this becomes:

```
[r,r1,r2] = [r0,r1,r2]
```

11.7 Summary

This chapter has introduced the mathematical notions essential for a sound understanding of the 3D graphics code presented in the following chapters. The most important concepts concern vectors and their application to representing points, lines and planes within a virtual world — the VECTOR class embodies the vector concept and supplies a number of functions which are useful in manipulating vectors. In particular the VECTOR class provides functions for the scalar product, vector product and triple product operations. The scalar product calculates the projection of one vector in the direction specified by another reference vector — it will be applied to a number of graphics-related problems including the calculation of the colour shading produced by a directional light source and the depth-sorting of virtual objects within a scene according to distance from the viewer. The vector product operation generates a vector which is perpendicular to a plane defined by two other vectors — it has already been applied to determine the type of vertex ordering associated with a polygon and it will later prove useful in deriving texture-mapping equations. The triple product combines the actions of the vector and scalar products — it tests for coplanarity and can quickly identify polygons which are viewed end-on. Finally, both vectors and coordinate systems can be transformed by applying rigid-body transformations. These transformations involve a combination of rotations and translations — the rotations are represented by rotation matrices and the translations by offset vectors.

12. Projection of the Viewing Volume

The last few chapters have built up a collection of routines to draw 2D images of colour-filled polygons and to represent 3D objects in a virtual world — this chapter shows how to integrate the 3D representations with the 2D drawing code by detailing the 3D-to-2D projection process. The 'viewing volume' describes a region of space which contains all the points from the virtual world that will appear in the projected 2D image. Once the projection operation is implemented it will be possible to generate realistic 3D images automatically just by calling the WORLD class Draw() function. The key topics in this chapter include:

— implementing perspective projections
— definition of the viewing volume
— world-to-camera coordinate transformations
— object-, polygon- and pixel-level clipping

The chapter defines a new CAMERA class and also updates the SCENE class Draw() function to incorporate perspective projection — a simple graphics application is developed which demonstrates this new code in action.

12.1 Perspective Projections

To create a 2D image of a 3D virtual world the objects in the world must be projected onto a screen — the following figure depicts a projected image of a cube:

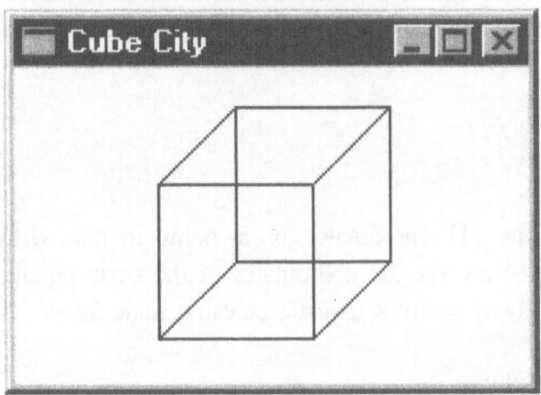

The output is produced by the wire-frame version of the Cube City program from chapter 8 — the program positions the cube vertices using an array of xy-coordinates taken from a header file. The 2D coordinates were obtained from the 3D equivalents simply by setting the z-coordinate values to zero — this type of projection is known as an 'orthogonal projection'. A more realistic image can be obtained if a perspective projection is used instead — this type of projection works by shrinking distant objects relative to nearby ones. If the virtual world is viewed from the 3D origin whilst facing along the positive z-axis then the objects which are nearby have small z-coordinates whilst those in the distance have larger z-coordinates — hence the perspective effect can be achieved by scaling the size of objects according to their z-coordinates. The following figure illustrates the idea:

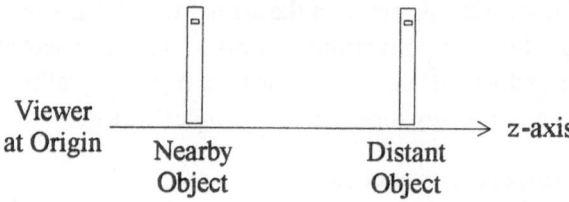

Viewer
at Origin   Nearby   Distant   z-axis
                  Object   Object

Here the viewer observes two telegraph poles which are actually the same height — nonetheless, the more distant object appears to be smaller than the nearby one. If the observed images of the two objects are drawn side-by-side they appear as follows:

Image of
Nearby Object   Image of
                                                  Distant Object

Both the x and y dimensions of the more distant object have shrunk relative to the nearby object — mathematically the perspective projection can be expressed as follows:

```
x_image = K*x/z;
y_image = K*y/z;
```

Here (x,y,z) are the 3D coordinates of a point in the virtual world and (x_image,y_image) are the 2D coordinates of the corresponding point in the projected image — the quantity K is just a constant scale factor.

12.2 The Viewing Volume

One way to visualize the projection of a 3D scene is to imagine a 2D viewing screen which stands vertically (parallel to the xy-plane) and is placed at a distance S away from the viewer along the positive z-axis.

The following figure illustrates this arrangement:

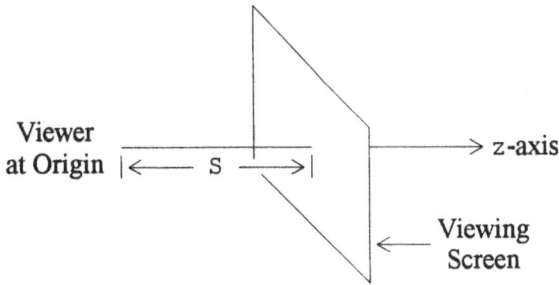

A point is projected by sending a beam of light from the point towards the viewer at the origin — the corresponding image point is determined by the position at which the light beam strikes the screen. In particular, all the points on the z-axis (with z>=S) map to the centre of the screen — the location of other image points can be calculated using the formulae given at the end of section 12.1 if the scale factor K is set equal to the screen distance S.

This arrangement clearly shows that not all points in the virtual world will appear in the projected image. For example, points with z<S are not visible — also if the screen has height H and width W then the point (x,y,z) is projected only if:

$$-W/2 \ <= \ S*x/z \ <= \ +W/2$$

$$-H/2 \ <= \ S*y/z \ <= \ +H/2$$

Finally, it may also be desirable to omit objects which lie so far away that they appear just as tiny dots — a simple approach is to set the cutoff distance by applying the condition z<=C so that for projected points:

$$S \ <= \ z \ <= \ C$$

The six conditions on the coordinates (x,y,z) define a volume of space which holds all the points that will appear in the projected image — this volume is consequently referred to as the 'viewing volume'.

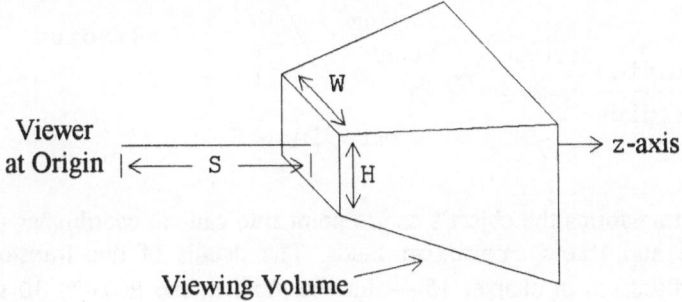

Viewing Volume

One way to speed up the rendering of a 3D scene is to perform object-level clipping — this process determines if any portion of the object lies within the viewing volume. If it does not then the object can be discarded — only if the object intersects the viewing volume need its polygons be further processed in the construction of an image. The task of performing object-level clipping is assigned to the function IsObjectVisible() defined by the new CAMERA class:

```
BOOL
CAMERA::IsObjectVisible(const VECTOR& centre,
                              int radius) {
  VECTOR vector = centre-ViewPoint;
  POINT_3D point = vector.Rotate(ViewDirection);
  int limit_x = Width*(point.z+radius);
  int limit_y = Height*(point.z+radius);
  int test_x = 2*Screen*point.x;
  int test_y = 2*Screen*point.y;
  int offset = 2*Screen*radius;
  if (point.z+radius < Screen) return FALSE;
  if (point.z-radius > Cutoff) return FALSE;
  if (test_x+offset < -limit_x) return FALSE;
  if (test_x-offset > limit_x) return FALSE;
  if (test_y+offset < -limit_y) return FALSE;
  if (test_y-offset > limit_y) return FALSE;
  return TRUE;
}
```

The IsObjectVisible() function accepts two parameters which respectively specify the location of an object in the virtual world and the object's bounding radius — the centre and radius parameters define a bounding sphere which completely encompasses the object. The function works by enclosing the virtual object's bounding sphere in a 3D box with sides of length 2*radius — the checks made on the x- and z-coordinates are illustrated in plan-view by the following figure:

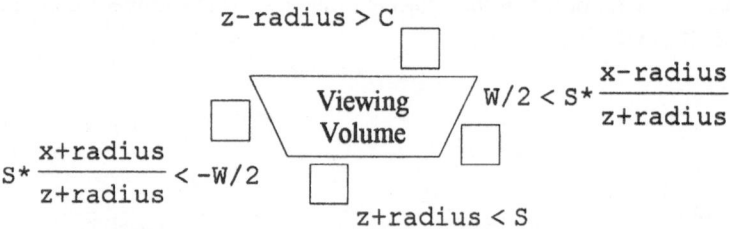

The camera transforms the object's centre point into camera coordinates using its ViewPoint and ViewDirection fields. The details of this transformation process are discussed in chapter 15 — for the moment the POINT_3D structure `point` can be assumed to hold the same 3D coordinates as the `VECTOR` parameter `centre`. To help avoid overflow problems the variables `limit_x`, `limit_y` and so on should be declared as type `__int64` and the `Int32x32To64()` function called to initialize these variables — ordinary 32–bit integers are substituted here for the sake of clarity.

An `OBJECT` object calculates its bounding radius as part of its initialization procedure — it can then query the `SCENE` object if it is visible before attempting to draw any of its polygons:

```
void OBJECT::Draw(SCENE* scene) {
  if (scene->IsObjectVisible(Position,Radius)) {
    scene->SetVertices(Vertices);
    for (int i=0; i<PolygonCount; i++)
      Polygons[i]->Draw(scene);
  }
}
```

The `SCENE` object passes the query along to its associated `CAMERA` object:

```
BOOL
SCENE::IsObjectVisible(const VECTOR* centre,
                           int radius) {
  return Camera->IsObjectVisible(centre,radius);
}
```

12.3 Taking a Snapshot

A `CAMERA` object contains a number of fields that specify the operation of the object — these include the `ViewPoint`, `ViewDirection`, `Screen`, `Cutoff`, `Width` and `Height` parameters. The `ViewPoint` and `ViewDirection` fields are controlled by the program's `VIEW` object to determine the current view of the virtual world — the `Screen`, `Cutoff`, `Width` and `Height` fields describe the camera's viewing volume and they are set by the `SCENE` object to specify how a particular view will be displayed.

The `CAMERA` object accepts a collection of 3D vertices through its `SetVertices()` function:

```
void
CAMERA::SetVertices(const VECTOR* vertices) {
  Vertices = vertices;
  for (int i=0; i<MAX_POINTS; i++)
    Transformed[i] = FALSE;
}
```

The function resets the elements in the `Transformed` array to indicate that new

vertices are available. The vertices are typically supplied by the SCENE class
SetVertices() function when it is invoked by the OBJECT class Draw()
function:

```
void SCENE::SetVertices(const VECTOR* vertices) {
  ObjectVertices = vertices;
  Camera->SetVertices(vertices);
}
```

The CAMERA class Snapshot() function is provided to take a 3D snapshot of
points in the virtual world. The function transforms a subset of the current vertices
held by the CAMERA object from world coordinates to camera coordinates — for
now this is an identity transformation and the coordinates are unchanged.

```
void
CAMERA::Snapshot(int count,const int* vertices) {
  int i,n;
  for (i=0; i<count; i++) {
    n = vertices[i];
    if (!Transformed[n]) {
      // world-to-camera transformation
    }
  }
}
```

Since every polygon typically shares its vertices with adjacent polygons belonging
to the same OBJECT object, the CAMERA object maintains the Transformed
array to ensure that each vertex is transformed at most once. The Snapshot()
function is called by the SCENE object to transform the vertices of the polygon it is
currently drawing:

```
void
SCENE::Draw(int count,const int* vertices,
                BYTE colour) {
    .
    .
    Camera->Snapshot(count,vertices);
    .
    .
}
```

The transformed points are available as part of the CAMERA object's Points array
— the SCENE object retrieves a pointer to this array just after it creates the

CAMERA object in its constructor:

```
SCENE::SCENE(int width,int height,
                    PALETTE* palette) {
    .
    .
  Camera = (CAMERA*) new CAMERA;
  Points = Camera->GetPoints();
    .
    .

}
```

The SCENE class Draw() function proceeds to project the 3D points from the Points array to form a 2D image — this is the topic of the next section.

Another important function of the CAMERA object is to maintain the current viewing volume — its dimensions are initialized to default values but these may be modified by the SCENE class SetScale() function as follows:

```
void SCENE::SetScale(int scale) {
  Scale = scale;
  int width = Width*Scale;
  int height = Height*Scale;
  int size = (Width+Height)/2;
  Screen = SCREEN_FACTOR*size*Scale;
  Cutoff = CUTOFF_FACTOR*size*Scale;
  Camera->SetViewVolume(width,height,
                    Screen,Cutoff);
}
```

The location of the viewing volume within the virtual world may be controlled by the CAMERA class SetViewPoint() and SetViewDirection() functions — these functions are typically invoked by the program's VIEW object. Chapter 15 provides a more detailed discussion of the process of selecting the current view of the virtual world.

12.4 Projecting and Clipping

The SCENE object combines the actions of clipping a virtual polygon to the viewing volume and projecting the image of the clipped polygon — in particular the x and y clipping is performed only after the polygon has been projected. To further simplify the presentation here the viewing volume is assumed to extend backwards to infinity so that there is no cutoff value — the result is that z>=S is the only remaining clipping condition which must be applied to the 3D points obtained from the CAMERA object. The clipping process may alter the number of vertices needed to describe the polygon — if no vertices remain after clipping then the polygon is invisible. The following figure illustrates the substitution of one vertex with two other vertices:

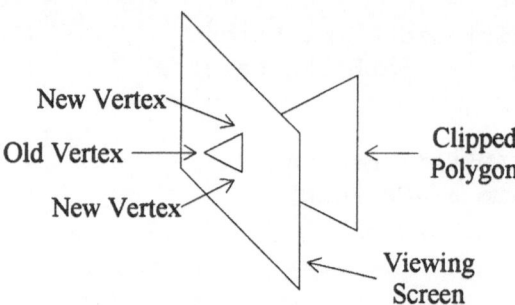

The SCENE class `Draw()` function calls the helper function `Project()` to perform the combined project-and-clip operation. The function cycles through the edges of the polygon and sets the `ends` and `test` arrays appropriately — each of the `test` elements is set to `TRUE` whenever the corresponding endpoint is beyond the plane of the screen and so potentially visible.

```cpp
int SCENE::Project(POINT* points) {
    int i,j,m,n;
    POINT_3D ends[2],delta;
    BOOL test[2];
    n = PolygonVertices[VertexCount-1];
    ends[0] = (POINT_3D)Points[n];
    test[0] = (ends[0].z >= Screen);
    int new_count = 0;
    for (i=0; i<VertexCount; i++) {
        n = PolygonVertices[i];
        ends[1] = (POINT_3D)Points[n];
        test[1] = (ends[1].z >= Screen);
```

If the current edge crosses the plane of the screen then a new vertex must be added to the projected polygon by calculating the point of intersection of the edge with the screen plane — the calculations are similar to the 2D line-clipping process described in section 8.4. The code to implement the line-clipping step follows:

```cpp
        if (test[0] != test[1]) {
            j = (i?i-1:VertexCount-1);
            m = PolygonVertices[j];
            delta = (POINT_3D)(Points[n]-Points[m]);
            points[new_count].x = ends[0].x+
                MulDiv(Screen-ends[0].z,delta.x,delta.z);
            points[new_count].y = ends[0].y+
                MulDiv(Screen-ends[0].z,delta.y,delta.z);
            new_count++;
        }
            .
            .
```

Finally, if a polygon vertex lies beyond the plane of the screen then it is projected using the perspective projection formulae discussed in section 12.1.

```
          .
          .

    if (test[1]) {
      points[new_count].x =
        MulDiv(Screen,ends[1].x,ends[1].z);
      points[new_count].y =
        MulDiv(Screen,ends[1].y,ends[1].z);
      new_count++;
    }
    ends[0] = ends[1];
    test[0] = test[1];
  }
  return new_count;
}
```

Note that the whole process maintains the correct ordering of the polygon's vertices so that the SCENE class DrawLine() function will still generate the polygon outline properly.

The Project() function returns the number of vertices in the polygon's projected image — if this is non-zero then the Draw() function calls the TransformToPixels() function for each vertex before eventually drawing the polygon:

```
void
SCENE::Draw(int count,const int* vertices,
                       BYTE colour) {
  VertexCount = count;
  PolygonVertices = vertices;
  if (IsPolygonVisible()) {
    POINT points[MAX_POINTS];
    POINT pixels[MAX_POINTS];
    Camera->Snapshot(count,vertices);
    if (count=Project.(points)) {
      for (int i=0; i<count; i++)
        TransformToPixels(points[i],pixels[i]);
      DrawOutline(count,pixels);
      ColourFill(colour);
    }
  }
}
```

12.5 A Vanishing Cube

The Vanishing Cube application will illustrate the new perspective projection routines — it draws the projected image of a cube which gradually moves off into the distance. The initial position of the cube is specified by the CubeVertices array — this is defined in a header file and contains the (x,y,z) coordinates of the cube vertices:

```
POINT_3D CubeVertices[CUBE_VERTICES] = {
   {-200000,100000,0},
   {-100000,100000,0},
   {-200000,200000,0},
   {-100000,200000,0},
   {-200000,100000,100000},
   {-100000,100000,100000},
   {-200000,200000,100000},
   {-100000,200000,100000}
};
```

The cube is moved by incrementing the z-coordinate of its Position field in each call to the VIEW class Update() function — chapter 15 provides a more detailed discussion of this method of moving objects within the virtual world. The VIEW class Update() function is implemented as follows:

```
void VIEW::Update(void) {
   VECTOR position(0,0,CUBE_STEP);
   position += Object->GetPosition();
   Object->SetPosition(position);
}
```

The following figure shows the program in action:

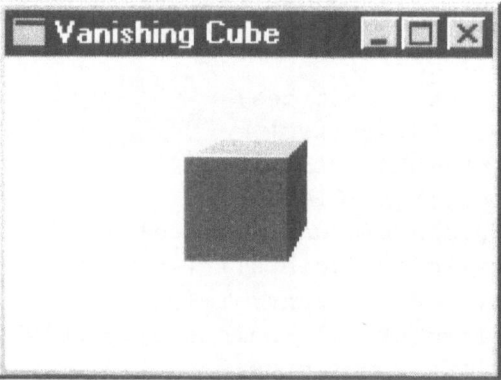

As the cube moves away its image shrinks in size until it becomes just a tiny dot — the Cutoff parameter passed to the CAMERA object can be used to make the cube vanish whenever it is sufficiently far away.

12.6 Summary

This chapter shows how the 2D drawing code from previous chapters can be integrated with the 3D representation of a virtual world. The correspondence between 3D coordinates in the virtual world and the 2D equivalents in the final displayed image is determined by a projection operation — orthogonal projection is one possibility but perspective projection produces much more realistic images. The key point concerning perspective images is that as an object recedes into the distance its image appears to shrink in size — furthermore, as the object slowly vanishes its observed position approaches the origin of the 2D image. A perspective projection may therefore be implemented simply by scaling the x- and y-coordinates of each 3D point and using the corresponding z-coordinate as the scale factor — the resultant values are the 2D image coordinates. The SCENE object further processes the image coordinates with the TransformToPixels() function — this scales and translates the image so that it fits within the SCENE object's bitmap. The projection operation is perhaps best visualized by imagining a screen onto which the 3D points are mapped. The position and size of the screen (along with a cutoff distance) define a volume which specifies the current view of the virtual world — this viewing volume contains all 3D points which will be visible in the projected image. Object-level clipping may be applied to remove any objects that are located outside the viewing volume. The CAMERA class is defined to embody the notion of a viewing volume and it provides the function IsObjectVisible() to perform object-level clipping. Furthermore, the CAMERA class allows the viewing volume to be moved through the virtual world and so can simulate a dynamically changing viewpoint. The SCENE object receives a 3D snapshot of points in the virtual world from its associated CAMERA object — these points are projected to 2D image coordinates by the SCENE class Project() function. The Project() function also performs 3D clipping to remove polygon vertices which are located on the near-side of the screen — clipping in the x- and y-directions is left until the 2D image of the polygon is actually drawn.

13. Hidden Pixel Removal

The previous chapter demonstrated how to project images of virtual world objects onto a 2D screen — the problems arise when the individual object images overlap. In the real world nearby objects will obscure those in the distance — modelling this effect in projected images of the virtual world requires that pixels projected from obscured portions of an object do not appear in the final image. This is the process of 'hidden pixel removal' and it forms the subject of this chapter — the essential topics include:

— Painter's Algorithm
— convex objects and separating planes
— Binary Space Partitioning
— drawing scenes front-to-back
— pixel level clipping and Z-buffers

The chapter also introduces the Block World application which will be further developed in chapters 14 and 15 — this program draws images of a labyrinthine world with passages and chambers.

13.1 Constructing a Scene Image

The 3D drawing code developed so far will correctly draw the image of a single object in perspective projection. However, if a scene contains a number of objects those at the front should obscure anything that is located behind them — the current software does not ensure this will happen. The pixels depicting the hidden portions of an object should not appear in the final image of the scene — this is the essence of hidden pixel removal. In fact the SCENE class function IsPolygonVisible() already provides hidden pixel removal at the polygon level — rear-facing polygons are obscured by the object's front faces and so need not be drawn. This chapter discusses more algorithms for hidden pixel removal — these mostly rely on the order in which the objects are drawn by the WORLD object. It is assumed that the virtual world contains convex objects that do not intersect — just like the convex polygons discussed in section 9.2 an object which is convex possesses the property that any two points within it can be connected by a line that does not pass outside the object. This means that convex objects do not have dents which will allow them to pack together and so complicate the drawing process.

The following figure illustrates in plan-view the problems that can arise with concave objects:

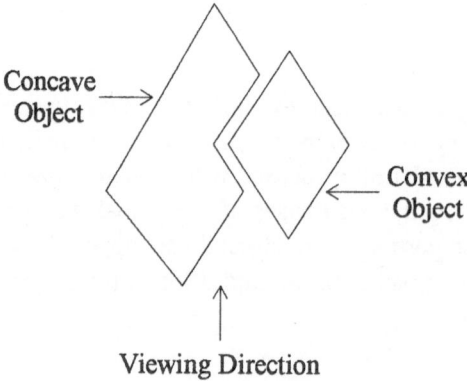

Concave Object

Convex Object

Viewing Direction

Whichever object is drawn first, the rendering of the other object image will hide pixels that are actually in front. The restriction that the virtual world contains only non-intersecting convex objects avoids such problems — one method of lessening the impact of this restriction is to split a concave object into a collection of convex objects.

13.2 The Painter's Algorithm

The simplest approach to hidden pixel removal is the Painter's Algorithm — this is modelled on the way a painter draws a scene. Firstly the background is drawn, then distant objects are painted and finally nearby objects are added — hence objects obscure one another in a natural way. To implement this algorithm the WORLD object must sort the OBJECT objects by decreasing distance from the viewpoint — the sorted list of OBJECT objects can then be drawn as before.

```
void WORLD::Draw(HDC dc) {
  SortObjects();
  Scene->BeginFrame();
  for (int i=0; i<ObjectCount; i++)
    Objects[i]->Draw(Scene);
  Scene->EndFrame();
  Scene->Display(dc);
}
```

The main difficulty is in defining the SortObjects() function — the problem is deciding how to measure distance from the viewpoint. The obvious solution is simply to choose an arbitrary point within each object and use this to compute the distance between object and viewpoint:

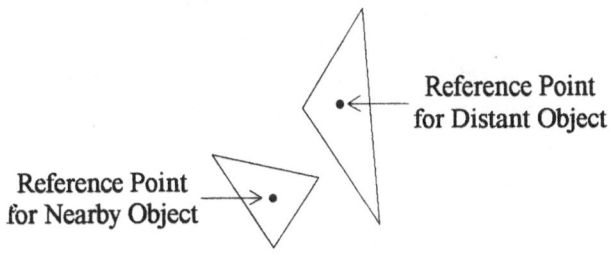

Here the choice of reference points produces the correct drawing order but it is clear that a different choice could reverse the ordering. Fortunately for non-intersecting convex objects there is a procedure for choosing the reference points so that the ordering is always correct. The basic algorithm is very slow but it can be optimized by placing an additional restriction on the virtual world — if each object is bounded by a sphere and the bounding spheres of different objects are not permitted to intersect then the centre point of an object's bounding sphere will act as a suitable reference point.

The WORLD class SortObjects() function calculates the distances between each of the virtual objects and the scene's viewpoint — the objects may then be sorted according to these distances:

```
void WORLD::SortObjects(void) {
  VECTOR viewpoint = Scene->GetViewPoint();
  VECTOR centre;
  int distances[MAX_OBJECTS]
  for (int i=0; i<ObjectCount; i++) {
    centre = Objects[i]->GetPosition()-viewpoint;
    distances[i] = centre.Magnitude();
  }
    .
    .
    .
  }
```

A standard sorting algorithm such as 'quicksort' or 'heapsort' can be used to perform the actual sort.

13.3 Separating Planes

To decide which of two non-intersecting convex objects is nearer to the viewpoint the objects must each define a reference point — the distances to the reference points determine the order in which the object images are drawn. One method for finding reference points which guarantees the correct drawing order is simply to choose a pair of points (one from each object) that are as close as possible. More specifically the points are found by calculating the distances between every point on one object and every point on the other — since the objects do not intersect there must be a pair of points for which the distance is a minimum and this pair can serve as reference points. To see why this works imagine that there is a plane placed midway between the the two reference points as illustrated in the following figure:

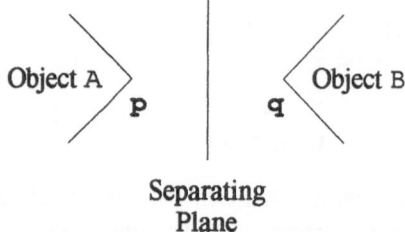

Object A p   q Object B

Separating
Plane

Here the reference points of the objects A and B are represented by the vectors **p** and **q** respectively. As described in section 11.6 the vector equation of the plane may be written as:

```
r == (p+q)/2 + s*r1 + t*r2
```

The plane cuts the line between **p** and **q** in half and the in-plane vectors **r1** and **r2** are perpendicular to the vector **p-q** pointing from one reference point to the other.

In fact the plane entirely separates the two objects A and B — object A lies on one side of the plane and object B lies on the other side of the plane. Hence if the viewpoint is on the same side of the plane as object A then this object should be drawn in front — object B is on the far of the plane and cannot possibly obscure object A. Similarly if the viewpoint lies on the same side of the plane as object B then the drawing order should place object B in front of object A. Finally if the viewpoint happens to lie on the separating plane then the drawing order is unimportant. It just remains to show that the plane really does separate the two objects — this is made reasonably obvious by imagining the analogy of two coconuts, one placed on either side of a pane of glass. However, the mathematics are straightforward and quite interesting. Firstly suppose that the plane does intersect object A at some point represented by the vector **p'** — then for some values of s and t the following equality holds:

```
p'-p == -(p-q)/2 + s*r1 + t*r2
```

Furthermore, since object A is convex all points on the line between **p** and **p'** also belong to the object — as noted in section 11.6 the vector equation of this line is:

```
r == p + u*(p'-p)
```

where u varies between 0 and 1. The distance D between the point **q** and a general point r on the line connecting p and p' may be calculated from the magnitude of the following vector:

$$
\begin{aligned}
r\text{-}q \ &== \ (p\text{-}q) \ + \ u^*(p'\text{-}p) \\
&== \ (p\text{-}q)\,[1\text{-}u/2] \ + \ u^*s^*r1 \ + \ u^*t^*r2
\end{aligned}
$$

But $r1$ and $r2$ are perpendicular to $p\text{-}q$ so that:

$$
\begin{aligned}
D^*D \ &== \ (r\text{-}q)\,.\,(r\text{-}q) \\
&== \ (p\text{-}q)\,.\,(p\text{-}q)^*[1\text{-}u/2]^*[1\text{-}u/2] \ + \ \text{terms in } u^*u \\
&== \ (p\text{-}q)\,.\,(p\text{-}q)^*[1\text{-}u] \ + \ \text{terms in } u^*u
\end{aligned}
$$

As u becomes small the terms in u^*u may be neglected — in this case D is less than the distance between p and q (i.e. the magnitude of the vector $p\text{-}q$). But D is the distance between a point in object A and a point in object B — this contradicts the fact that p and q were chosen to be as close as possible. The only possible conclusion is that the plane cannot intersect object A — similarly it cannot intersect object B and so must act as a separating plane between the two objects.

The test for deciding the drawing order of the two objects has been expressed in terms of the position of the viewpoint relative to the separating plane — more specifically if the viewpoint is located at the vector origin then the test compares the viewing direction (as defined by the $(p\text{+}q)/2$ vector) with the vector $p\text{-}q$ that is perpendicular to the plane. The viewpoint is on the same side of the plane as object A if the following condition holds:

$$(p\text{+}q)\,.\,(p\text{-}q) \ < \ 0$$

or equivalently:

$$p.p \ < \ q.q$$

But this condition states that point p is nearer to the viewpoint than point q — hence the test can be made in terms of the distances from the viewpoint to the reference points as described in the previous section.

When non-intersecting bounding spheres are introduced the WORLD class SortObjects() function can compare the distances between the viewpoint and the various sphere centres. For a pair of objects this is equivalent to determining the relative position of the viewpoint and a test plane — the test plane bisects the line between the bounding sphere centres and is perpendicular to it. If the two objects have bounding spheres of the same radius this method is identical to the previous approach and the test plane separates the two objects — furthermore, the test plane continues to act as a separating plane even if the radii of the two bounding spheres are only approximately equal. However, as the size of one object grows relative to the other the test plane between them will eventually intersect the bounding sphere of the larger object — in this case it is theoretically possible for the smaller object to be incorrectly drawn in front of the larger object but in practice this occurs infrequently.

13.4 Binary Space Partitioning

Binary Space Partitioning (BSP) is a technique which applies the notion of separating (or partitioning) planes to partially pre-calculate the drawing order for a collection of fixed objects — the exact drawing order is established by choosing a viewpoint and determining its position relative to the set of partitioning planes. The basic unit of calculation involves a single plane — this plane partitions the whole of the virtual world into two as shown below:

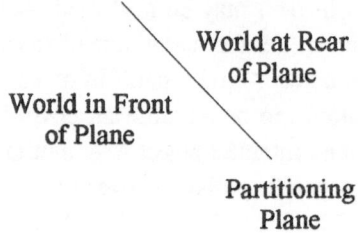

The partitioning performed by the plane may be represented as a single node in a tree structure as follows:

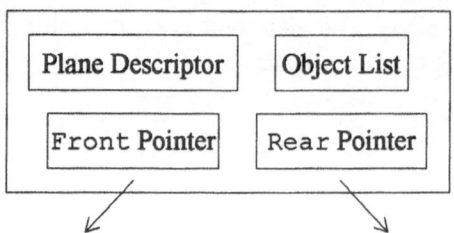

The plane descriptor is used to determine the relative position of the viewpoint and the plane represented by the node. The Front and Rear pointers reference other nodes lower in the tree — nodes in the left and right sub-trees deal respectively with the two virtual world regions in front of and behind the partitioning plane. The object list structures in each of the tree's nodes will describe how the objects within the virtual world relate to the various partitioning planes — this information can be used to speed up the object sorting process prior to drawing. For a leaf node there is no associated partitioning plane and the node's object list contains a set of objects in a particular region of the virtual world — for internal nodes the object list describes flat in-plane objects such as walls.

Of course, the two regions created by the first partitioning plane can be further sub-divided by other planes. This process is represented by extending the BSP tree — one new node is added to both the left and right sub-trees of the root node to represent the secondary planes.

The following figure illustrates the use of several partitioning planes:

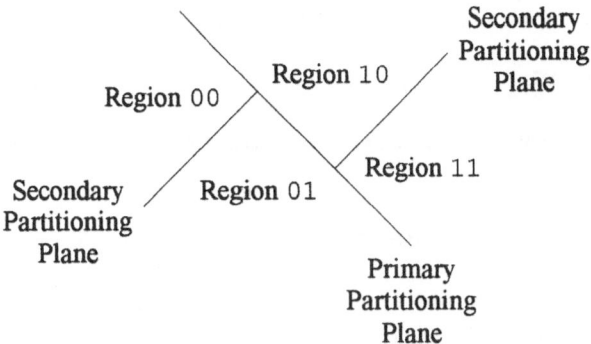

Regions 00 and 01 lie in front of the first plane whilst regions 10 and 11 lie behind this plane — each pair of regions is further sub-divided by a secondary partitioning plane. The corresponding BSP tree has seven nodes — one root node for the primary partitioning plane, two internal nodes for the secondary partitioning planes and four leaf nodes for the virtual world regions.

The partitioning process continues until the whole of the virtual world is broken up into small regions — the BSP tree then contains information detailing the layout of the partitioning planes and the arrangement of fixed objects within the various regions. The essential point is that the BSP tree can be constructed at the start of a program and need not be rebuilt with each iteration through an animation loop. The tree helps to reduce the processing required to correctly sort the fixed objects ready for drawing — the location of the viewpoint provides the key which unlocks the coded information held by the tree. If the viewpoint lies in front of a partitioning plane then the drawing order places virtual world objects which lie behind the plane at the rear of the scene, next in-plane objects are overlaid and finally objects in front of the plane are drawn last — this drawing order is reversed if the viewpoint is located behind the partitioning plane. The algorithm is recursive and descends from the root node of the BSP tree towards the leaf nodes — the WORLD class Draw() function begins the drawing process by calling the DrawTree() function and passing the TreeRoot node pointer as a parameter. Here is the code for the WORLD class Draw() function:

```
void WORLD::Draw(HDC dc) {
   Scene->BeginFrame();
   DrawTree(TreeRoot);
   Scene->EndFrame();
   Scene->Display(dc);
}
```

The `DrawTree()` function implements the recursive drawing algorithm as follows:

```
void WORLD::DrawTree(NODE* node) {
  BOOL front;
  PLANE* plane = node->Plane;
  if (plane)
    front = IsViewPointInFront(plane);
  if (plane)
    if (front)
      DrawTree(node->Rear);
    else
      DrawTree(node->Front);
  SortObjects(node->ObjectList);
  DrawObjects(node->ObjectList);
  if (plane)
    if (front)
      DrawTree(node->Front);
    else
      DrawTree(node->Rear);
}
```

The `IsViewPointInFront()` function determines the position of the viewpoint relative to the current partitioning plane. Within each region the objects are sorted and drawn as before by passing an object list to the `SortObjects()` and `DrawObjects()` functions — each region typically contains a single object so that the sorting required is minimal. Since the BSP tree is constructed before entering the animation loop, the bulk of the processing performed during each iteration is restricted to the `IsViewPointInFront()` function — the result is that the animation rate of a complicated scene will be increased considerably.

It is possible to extend this scheme to include moving objects as well as fixed objects in the BSP tree. At the start of each animation step the `WORLD` class `Draw()` function inserts the moving objects into the tree by making a call to the `InsertObjects()` function — the `DrawObjects()` function then removes the moving objects from the tree as they are drawn. The `InsertObjects()` function works by traversing the BSP tree and finding the region which currently contains the moving object — the object is then added to the object list for that region. A complication arises if the moving object is intersected by a partitioning plane — in this case the object must be sliced into two objects which lie one either side of the partitioning plane.

Finally, there is an interesting simplification of the BSP process which allows the BSP tree to be implemented implicitly — this is illustrated by the `Block World` program. For this application the partitioning planes are arranged parallel to the x=0, y=0 and z=0 planes — the planes are placed at equal intervals along each axis and so divide the whole of 3D space into a regular grid of blocks. The viewpoint will be situated within one of these blocks — the other blocks then lie at various distances from the viewpoint block as depicted in plan-view by the following figure:

3	2	1	2	3
2	1	• View Point	1	2
3	2	1	2	3

The distances are measured in grid units and are calculated by adding the x, y and z offsets from the viewpoint block — these distances determine a drawing order for the grid of block-shaped regions without having to explicitly construct a BSP tree. The Block World application contains a series of cubes that each completely fill one of the block-shaped regions of the virtual world grid. The cubes are arranged to create rooms and corridors within the virtual world — the locations of the individual cubes are specified by the following Blocks array:

```
BOOL
Blocks[GRID_SIZE][GRID_SIZE][GRID_SIZE] = {
    .
    .
    .

    {{1,1,1,1,1,1,1},
     {1,0,1,0,1,0,1},
     {1,1,1,1,1,1,1},
     {1,0,1,0,1,0,1},
     {1,1,1,1,1,1,1},
     {1,0,1,0,1,0,1},
     {1,1,1,1,1,1,1}},
    .
    .
    .
};
```

A TRUE value (1) indicates the presence of a cube and a FALSE value (0) indicates an empty block region — the data listed here describes one layer of a 7x7x7 grid.

The following figure illustrates a typical view produced by the Block World program:

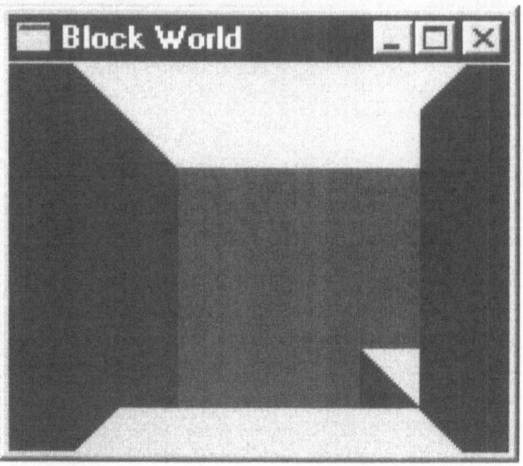

13.5 Drawing in Reverse

The hidden pixel removal techniques described so far are based on the Painter's Algorithm — distant objects are drawn first and then obscured by closer objects. This approach can involve a considerable amount of 'overdraw' as pixels are redrawn several times — the result is that the image generation process is rather inefficient. The solution is simply to reverse the drawing order and construct a scene front-to-back. In this case it is necessary to clip the background objects against any pixels that have already been drawn. The clipping process ensures that the foreground objects will correctly obscure those objects that lie behind. The implementation of the SCENE class must be updated to incorporate the necessary modifications — the starting point is the Sections array which holds a list of SCANLINE structures for each scanline in the SCENE object bitmap:

```
SCANLINE Sections[MAX_HEIGHT][MAX_SECTIONS];
int MaxSection[MAX_HEIGHT];
```

The MaxSection array indicates the number of valid entries in each scanline list — the Sections and MaxSection arrays are initialized by the SCENE class BeginFrame() function as follows:

```
void SCENE::BeginFrame(void) {
  for (int y=0; y<Height; y++) {
    MaxSection[y] = 1;
    Sections[y][1].Start = 0;
    Sections[y][1].Stop = Width-1;
  }
}
```

Hence for each scanline there is initially only one section and it covers the entire width of the bitmap — the section bounds `Start` and `Stop` are used to clip the polygon images. After a particular pixel has been drawn it is excluded from the section by updating the `Start` and `Stop` values as appropriate — in particular, if the polygon image falls in the middle of a section range then the section is split into two. The following figure illustrates the process for a single scanline:

BEFORE

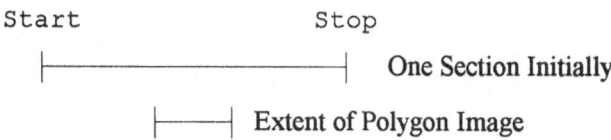

No further pixels can be drawn in the gap created by the foreground polygon — the images of background polygons will be clipped in this interval. The SCENE class `ColourFill()` function contains the relevant code — the first stage is to determine which sections contain the polygon on the current scanline:

```
void SCENE::ColourFill(BYTE colour) {
  int i,i_min,i_max,j,n;
  int start,stop,length;
  BYTE* pixel;
  BYTE* line = Dib->AcquireBits();
  for (int y=0; y<=Height; y++) {
    if (ScanLines[y].Start <= ScanLines[y].Stop) {
      for (i_min=1; i_min<=MaxSection[y]; i_min++)
        if (ScanLines[y].Start <=
              Sections[y][i_min].Stop) break;
      for (i_max=MaxSection[y]; i_max>=1; i_max--)
        if (ScanLines[y].Stop >=
              Sections[y][i_max].Start) break;
               .
               .
```

The values `i_min` and `i_max` determine the range of sections covered by the polygon — if `i_min<=i_max` then the next stage is to save sections to the left of the polygon by copying them to the Buffer array:

```
      .
      .
   if (i_min <= i_max) {
     j = 1;
     for (i=1; i<i_min; i++,j++)
       Buffer[j] = Sections[y][i];
      .
      .
```

Next the portions of the polygon falling in each of the active sections are drawn individually — this is where the polygon clipping is applied to obscure distant objects.

```
      .
      .
   for (i=i_min; i<=i_max; i++) {
     start = max(ScanLines[y].Start,
                     Sections[y][i].Start);
     stop = min(ScanLines[y].Stop,
                     Sections[y][i].Stop);
     pixel = line+start;
     length = stop+1-start;
     for (n=0; n<length; n++)
       *pixel++ = colour;
      .
      .
```

If parts of the current section remain undrawn they are transferred to the Buffer array:

```
      .
      .
   if (start > Sections[y][i].Start) {
     Buffer[j].Start = Sections[y][i].Start;
     Buffer[j++].Stop = start-1;
   }
   if (stop < Sections[y][i].Stop) {
     Buffer[j].Start = stop+1;
     Buffer[j++].Stop = Sections[y][i].Stop;
   }
 }
      .
      .
```

Finally, sections to the right of the polygon are copied intact to the Buffer array and then the entire contents of the Buffer array are returned to the Sections array in preparation for the next time this scanline is drawn:

```
                          .
                          .
                          .
        for (i=i_max+1; i<=MaxSection[y]; i++,j++)
          Buffer[j] = Sections[y][i];
        MaxSection[y] = j-1;
        for (i=1; i<=MaxSection[y]; i++)
          Sections[y][i] = Buffer[i];
      }
    }
    line += Pitch;
  }
  Dib->ReleaseBits();
}
```

The ColourFill() code is repeated for each polygon in the scene. The Sections array eventually describes the pixels not contained by any polygons — these are coloured by the SCENE class EndFrame() function using the BackgroundPixel value:

```
  void SCENE::EndFrame(void) {
    int i,n,y;
    int start,stop,length;
    BYTE* line = Dib->AcquireBits();
    BYTE* pixel;
    for (y=0; y<Height; y++) {
      for (i=1; i<=MaxSection[y]; i++) {
        start = Sections[y][i].Start;
        stop = Sections[y][i].Stop;
        pixel = line+start;
        length = stop+1-start;
        for (n=0; n<length; n++)
          *pixel++ = BackgroundPixel;
      }
      line += Pitch;
    }
    Dib->ReleaseBits();
  }
```

13.6 Z-Buffers

An alternative approach to hidden pixel removal is provided by using a Z-buffer — the Z-buffer replicates the layout of the image bitmap but instead of holding colour values it contains depth information in the form of z-coordinates. The procedure requires that each pixel value be associated with a z-coordinate value — this value corresponds to the position of the virtual world point from which the pixel is projected. Hence pixels which represent nearby points have smaller z values then those for more distant points — hidden pixel removal can consequently be implemented simply by comparing the pixel z values and determining the foremost pixel at any particular point. Furthermore, it is possible to calculate the z values for a polygon's pixels quite efficiently by interpolating the z-coordinates of the polygon's vertices. The Z-buffer technique is therefore very fast but the tradeoff is that it requires a lot of extra memory to accommodate the Z-buffer data.

The image generation process begins by filling the Z-buffer with very large z values that represent background points far away at infinity. As each pixel is projected, its z value is compared with the current contents of the Z-buffer — the pixel is only drawn if its z value is less than the corresponding value already in the buffer. Whenever a pixel is indeed drawn its z value is used to update the buffer — this means that only pixels subsequently projected from points closer to the viewpoint can overwrite the current colour information. At the end of the drawing procedure the constructed image correctly accounts for nearby objects obscuring more distant objects on a pixel-by-pixel basis — in particular the Z-buffer handles the occurrence of intersecting polygons:

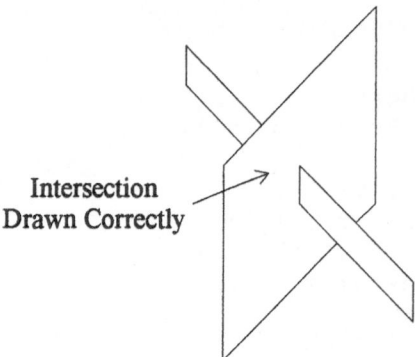

Intersection
Drawn Correctly

13.7 Summary

The construction of a virtual world image requires a strategy that will coordinate the drawing of various objects within the scene — in particular, objects in the foreground must obscure those objects that lie behind. This chapter has discussed a number of algorithms for implementing this removal of hidden pixels. Most of the techniques are based upon the order in which the objects are drawn — at the polygon level rear-facing polygons may be discarded using the function IsPolygonVisible() provided by the SCENE class. To simplify the drawing procedure the virtual world is constrained to contain only non-intersecting convex objects — more complex shapes can be constructed from these building blocks. The basic drawing algorithm is the Painter's Algorithm which simply draws objects at the back of the scene first and then overlays the images of foreground objects. To efficiently sort the objects into back-to-front order each object is surrounded by a bounding sphere centred at a reference point within the object and it is assumed that other objects are somehow excluded from the region within the sphere — the distance from the scene viewpoint to each object's reference point is then used as the criterion upon which to base the sorting decisions. The Binary Space Partitioning (BSP) process can partially pre-sort a collection of fixed objects — a BSP sorting tree is constructed by slicing up the whole of 3D space with a collection of partitioning planes. During each iteration of the animation loop, the sorting of fixed objects is completed by comparing the current viewpoint position to the collection of partitioning planes. The BSP approach can considerably increase the frame rate by reducing the amount of processing needed to generate each image frame — the process may be enhanced to integrate moving objects into the BSP tree alongside fixed objects. A simplification of the BSP technique divides the virtual world into a series of regular blocks — implementation of the BSP pre-sorting process is then possible without the BSP tree structure. The back-to-front drawing algorithm can result in the redrawing of many image pixels — to overcome this inefficiency one alternative is simply to draw in a front-to-back order but then background objects must be clipped against previously drawn pixels. Finally, an alternative approach to hidden pixel removal is to treat each pixel individually using a Z-buffer — at each image point the correct pixel to project is chosen using depth information contained in the buffer. The Z-buffer method is very fast but it does require a lot of extra memory when drawing large images.

14. Colour Shading and Textures

Shading and texture effects can add extra realism to the computer generated image of a virtual world — shading is applied to modify the basic colour of a polygon whilst texturing can add a more complicated pattern such as a brick-wall design. The underlying concepts involved are not difficult to grasp but an efficient implementation can introduce a fair degree of complexity — this chapter breaks up the process of designing a shading or texturing algorithm into a sequence of easy steps. The following topics are included:

— interaction of lights and surfaces
— common shading models
— theory and practice of texture mapping
— gloom factors and depth perception
— higher-order difference equations

The chapter also discusses a number of possible enhancements to the Block World application that will permit it to support colour shading and texture mapping.

14.1 Lights and Surfaces

The apparent colour of a surface is determined by the light shining on the surface and also by the way the surface interacts with the light — for example, a green surface seen in a red light appears to be black. In general a surface will reflect, absorb or transmit each colour in a different way — a simplification is to individually determine the effect of the surface on the light's three colour components (red, green and blue) and then to combine the results. However, even with this simplification the process is too complicated for most graphics applications — a typical solution is simply to modify the brightness of the intrinsic surface colour according to the intensity of light reflected from it. The light sources can be of three basic types:

— Point sources
— Directional sources
— Ambient lighting

Ambient lighting is the simplest to deal with — it just sets the average brightness level for an image by providing a background light intensity:

```
intensity == Intensity_Ambient
```

The light from point and directional sources shines on a surface from a certain direction — the only difference is that a point source is positioned at a definite location and so the direction of light from the point source will change over the surface:

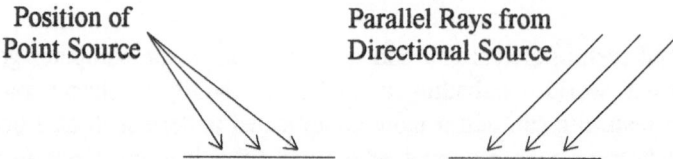

Position of Point Source

Parallel Rays from Directional Source

Light incident on a surface from point or directional sources may be reflected in two ways:

— diffuse reflection
— specular reflection

With diffuse reflection the light is reflected equally in all directions — with specular reflection the angle of reflection equals the angle of incidence.

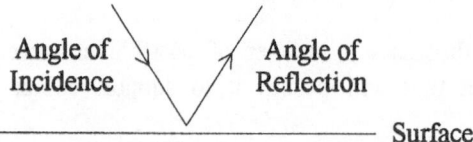

Angle of Incidence

Angle of Reflection

Surface

Directional light sources and diffuse reflection provide the simplest model for modulating the ambient lighting level. The intensity of the incident light is strongest when it hits the surface head-on and is weakest when shining directly away from the surface — in between the light intensity varies according to the scalar product between the direction vector **d** of the incident light and the normal vector **n** which points perpendicularly into the surface:

```
intensity == Intensity_Directional * n.d
```

Here both **n** and **d** are unit vectors so that when **n**==**d** the light intensity assumes its maximum value `Intensity_Directional`. The combination of ambient light and directional light defines the basic lighting model:

```
intensity == Intensity_Ambient +
                Intensity_Directional * n.d
```

14.2 Shading Options

This section shows how to calculate the colour shading applied to polygons in the image of a virtual world — it uses the basic lighting model developed in the previous section. In particular, the light intensity level modifies the brightness of each polygon's intrinsic colour through an intensity-to-brightness conversion factor. There are three shading models in current use:

— Flat shading
— Gouraud shading
— Phong shading

With flat shading the whole of the polygon is filled with a single colour shade —
this is essentially the technique developed in previous chapters but now the polygon
is coloured according to its orientation relative to the directional light source. The
SCENE object Draw() function modifies its colour parameter before
colour-filling each polygon as follows:

```
void SCENE::Draw(int count, const int* vertices,
                             BYTE colour) {
  VertexCount = count;
  PolygonVertices = vertices;
  if (IsPolygonVisible()) {
         .
         .
         .
      CalculateShade(colour);
      ColourFill(colour);
    }
  }
}
```

The SCENE class IsPolygonVisible() function now calculates the polygon's
normal vector and stores it in the Normal field:

```
BOOL SCENE::IsPolygonVisible(void) {
  VECTOR u,v,w;
  u = ObjectVertices[PolygonVertices[VertexCount-1]];
  v = ObjectVertices[PolygonVertices[1]];
  w = ObjectVertices[PolygonVertices[0]];
  u -= w;
  v -= w;
  w -= Camera->GetViewPoint();
  Normal = VECTOR(u,v,Magnitude);
  return (w|Normal) > 0;
}
```

To make the process reasonably efficient the POLYGON object must supply a scale
factor which will ensure that the normal vector is of unit length — the scale factor
is simply the geometric mean of two constant vector magnitudes and so it can be
pre-computed at the start of program execution. The relevant vectors (u and v)
define the plane of the polygon and correspond to the two polygon edges which
share an endpoint located at vertex 0 — the VECTOR class constructor invoked
here calculates the vector product of its first two parameters and then scales by the
Magnitude parameter. The polygon's normal vector is retrieved by the

`CalculateShade()` helper function when it is selecting the correct colour shade for the polygon:

```
void SCENE::CalculateShade(BYTE& colour) {
  int intensity = Intensity_Ambient;
  intensity += int(Intensity_Directional*
    (Normal|LightDirection)/Scale);
  if (intensity < MIN_INTENSITY)
    intensity = MIN_INTENSITY;
  if (intensity > MAX_INTENSITY)
    intensity = MAX_INTENSITY;
  int brightness =
    (intensity*SHADE_RANGE)/INTENSITY_RANGE;
  colour += brightness;
}
```

Here the light intensity is scaled to lie between the values MIN_INTENSITY and MAX_INTENSITY — the intensity is then converted to a brightness value that determines the colour shade of the polygon.

To add extra realism to a scene the flat shading may be replaced by Gouraud shading — this technique colours the polygon pixels individually to produce a less angular image. The algorithm starts by assigning colour values to each of an object's vertices — the object must be represented by a collection of triangular polygons and the pixel colours for each polygon are found by interpolating the values assigned to the polygon's three vertices. The following figure illustrates the idea:

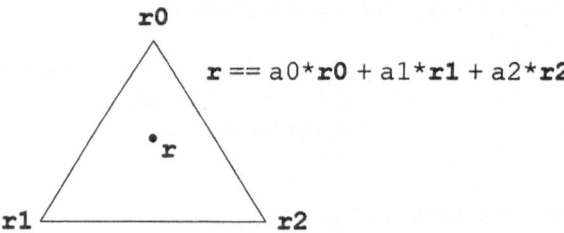

Here the vertices **r0**, **r1** and **r2** are assigned the colours stored as `colours[0]`, `colours[1]` and `colours[2]` respectively. Any point **r** within the triangle can be described by combining the three vertex vectors with a triple of weighting factors a0, a1 and a2 — these weighting factors are used to calculate the colour of the point as follows:

```
colour==a0*colours[0]+a1*colours[1]+a2*colours[2]
```

A typical approach is to combine colour values using RGB colour components. However, the question remains as to how the colours are initially assigned to the object's vertices — in fact the process is similar to that used for flat shading but now the vector **n** is an average of values taken over the set of the polygons to which a particular vertex belongs.

The extra processing required to add Gouraud shading is usually acceptable. An even more computationally intensive technique is Phong shading — this method does not rely on interpolation but instead calculates the colour values for each pixel individually. However, the algorithms involved are essentially extensions of those already presented and so they will not be discussed further here — instead the next section introduces an alternative approach to adding graphic detail to a polygon-filled scene.

14.3 Texture Mapping

Texture mapping is currently a popular way to add a sense of realism to the computer-generated images of a virtual world. A texture is essentially a 2D bitmap image pasted onto a 3D virtual object — the complicated part is determining how to map the texture image to the projection screen. The elements of the texture bitmap are referred to as 'texels' (texture elements) whilst the elements of the projection screen are pixels — hence texture mapping is the process of associating pixels with the corresponding texels. A typical case involves a rectangular bitmap pasted onto a rectangular polygon — the 2D uv-coordinate system describing points within the texture is illustrated in the following figure:

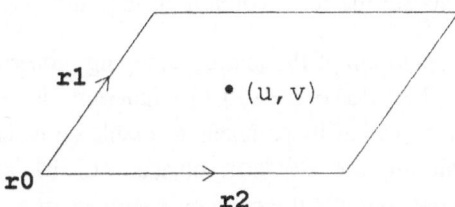

A general point **r** on the polygon is described by the following relationship:

`r == r0 + u*r1 + v*r2`

Here **r**, **r0**, **r1** and **r2** are all 3D vectors in the virtual world and the above relation is in fact the equation of the plane containing the polygon — the 2D coordinates (u, v) refer in a particular point within the texture. As described in section 11.6 the plane equation may be rewritten using the [ ] triple product notation in the following form:

`[r,r1,r2] == [r0,r1,r2]`

The new form of the plane equation may be obtained from the original by taking the scalar product of each side with the vector product **r1** x **r2** — two similar relations are generated by replacing **r1** x **r2** with the vector products **r2** x **r0** and

$r0 \times r1$ in the scalar product operations:

$$[r0, r, r2] \ == \ u*[r0, r1, r2]$$

$$[r0, r1, r] \ == \ v*[r0, r1, r2]$$

Now suppose that r projects to the point $p == (x, y, S)$ on the 2D screen then since p is just some scalar multiple of r it follows that:

$$u \ == \ \frac{[r0, p, r2]}{[p, r1, r2]} \qquad v \ == \ \frac{[r0, r1, p]}{[p, r1, r2]}$$

The denominator is positive when the polygon is visible and negative when the polygon is hidden — it is zero when the polygon is viewed end-on. These equations for $u(x, y)$ and $v(x, y)$ are the texture mapping equations — given a pixel at (x, y) on the image screen they determine the coordinates (u, v) of the corresponding texel. In fact u and v are normalized to fall in the range from 0 to 1 — to convert to indices u_int and v_int for the texture bitmap the u and v values must be scaled and truncated as follows:

$$u\_int \ == \ \textbf{int}(u*u\_max) \qquad v\_int \ == \ \textbf{int}(v*v\_max)$$

The following section discusses the interpretation of u_int and v_int as reference values used to locate the texel containing the point (u, v).

A straightforward implementation of the texture mapping process may be added to the SCENE class — the ColourFill() function is replaced by the TextureFill() function which maps texels to pixels on a scanline basis. The function starts by initializing the VECTOR objects r0, r1 and r2 from the Points array — this array contains the polygon's vertices in camera-coordinates.

```
void SCENE::TextureFill(const TEXTURE& texture) {
  VECTOR r0,r1,r2;
  r0 = Points[PolygonVertices[0]];
  r1 = Points[PolygonVertices[VertexCount-1]]-r0;
  r2 = Points[PolygonVertices[1]]-r0;
  int u_max = texture.Size.x;
  int v_max = texture.Size.y;
  int u,v,x,y;
  __int64 d;
  VECTOR p;
    .
    .
```

For each scanline the ColourBuffer array is filled pixel-by-pixel with colour information copied from the polygon's texture array and then its contents are transferred to the SCENE object image bitmap:

```
           .
           .

start = max(ScanLines[y].Start,
              Sections[y][i].Start);
stop = min(ScanLines[y].Stop,
              Sections[y][i].Stop);
for (x=start; x<=stop; x++) {
  p = VECTOR(x-Origin.x,y-Origin.y,Screen/Scale);
  d = p.TripleProduct(r1,r2);
  u = int((u_max*p.TripleProduct(r2,r0))/d);
  v = int((v_max*p.TripleProduct(r0,r1))/d);
  u = max(0,min(u,u_max-1));
  v = max(0,min(v,v_max-1));
  ColourBuffer[x] = texture.Texels[u][v];
}
colour = ColourBuffer+start;
pixel = line+start;
length = stop+1-start;
for (n=0; n<length; n++)
  *pixel++ = *colour++;
           .
           .
```

The following figure illustrates the addition of texture mapping to the Block World application:

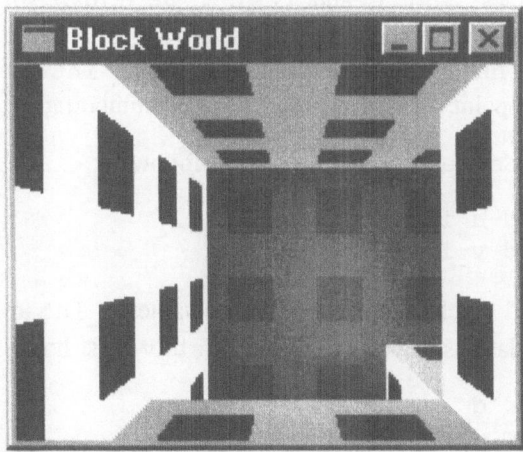

The implementation described here is very slow — this is principally due to the large number of division operations needed to compute u and v for every pixel. The following section shows how to optimize the implementation by replacing the divisions with equivalent additions and subtractions.

14.4 Implementation Optimizations

The key to optimizing the texture mapping algorithm is to calculate u and v in a stepwise manner — a similar approach was explained in section 8.3 for drawing lines in the xy-plane. In that case a decision variable `test` was defined and updated as the line was drawn — the value of the decision variable indicated when to increment the more slowly changing coordinate (x or y). Here a pair of decision variables `test_u` and `test_v` are defined and they are updated pixel-by-pixel — the values of the decision variables indicate when to modify the u and v coordinates. The following figure illustrates the relationship between u and v and the reference values u_int and v_int for a single texel:

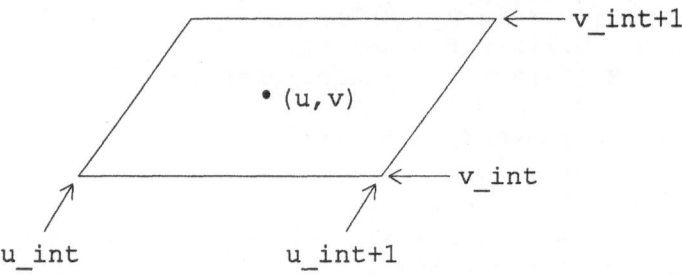

Mathematically this may be expressed as follows:

```
u_int <= u < u_int+1
v_int <= v < v_int+1
```

The decision variables `test_u` and `test_v` are defined so that they take predictable values along the boundaries of a texel. This allows the correct texel to be located simply by finding the appropriate values of u_int and v_int — the exact position of the point (u,v) within the texel is unimportant.

The definitions of `test_u` and `test_v` are as follows:

```
test_u == u*d-u_int*d
test_v == v*d-v_int*d
```

The bounds on u and v relative to the reference values u_int and v_int mean that the following relations for `test_u` and `test_v` must hold:

```
0 <= test_u < d
0 <= test_v < d
```

As the image is drawn pixel-by-pixel the decision variables are continually checked — if they move outside the desired range then the reference variables u_int and v_int must be updated to again select the correct texel. The expressions for u and v are taken from the previous section — the parameter d mentioned above is set equal to the denominator [**p**, **r1**, **r2**] so that the decision variables become:

```
test_u == u_max*[p,r2,r0]-u_int*[p,r1,r2]
test_v == v_max*[p,r0,r1]-v_int*[p,r1,r2]
```

The vector products **r1**x**r2**, **r2**x**r0** and **r0**x**r1** are constant for all pixels in the polygon and may be pre-calculated as product_d, product_u and product_v respectively — the variables incorporate the constants -1, u_max and v_max so that test_x and test_y can be expressed simply as follows:

```
test_u = p|product_u + u_int*p|product_d;
test_v = p|product_v + v_int*p|product_d;
```

Now the decision variables will change whenever the pixel coordinates (x, y) and the texel coordinates (u_int, v_int) are incremented — the delta structure holds the values of these changes:

```
delta.u_x = product_u.x + u_int*product_d.x;
delta.u_y = product_u.y + u_int*product_d.y;
delta.u_u = p|product_d;

delta.v_x = product_v.x + v_int*product_d.x;
delta.v_y = product_v.y + v_int*product_d.y;
delta.v_v = p|product_d;
```

The u_u and v_v fields are unified by placing them in an anonymous union:

```
struct DELTA {
  int u_x;
  int u_y;
  int v_x;
  int v_y;
  union {
    int u_u;
    int v_v;
  };
};
```

The delta structure fields are functions of x, y, u_int and v_int — they will also change as the texels are selected. The delta fields hold first-order differences and to describe how they should be incremented second-order differences are needed. Here the second-order differences are actually components of the product_d vector — for example:

```
delta.u_x(u_int+1) - delta.u_x(u_int) == product_d.x
delta.u_y(u_int+1) - delta.u_y(u_int) == product_d.y

delta.u_u(x+1) - delta.u_u(x) == product_d.x
delta.u_u(y+1) - delta.u_u(y) == product_d.y
```

This is an example of using higher-order differences to calculate non-linear results in a stepwise manner — another example of the technique appears in the next section.

It just remains to explain how the decision and difference variables are updated as the texture is mapped to the polygon — the following figure illustrates how the algorithm steps through the collection of pixels which make up the polygon:

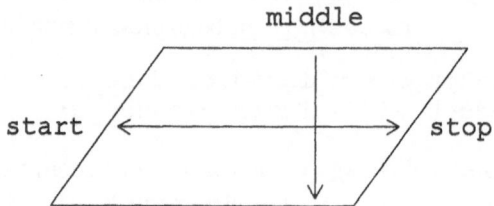

On the first scanline of the polygon a `middle` value is selected for the x-coordinate and all variables are initialized. For each subsequent scanline the values are updated as appropriate for an increment in y (with x fixed at x==`middle`). The resultant variables hold base values from which all other values for a particular scanline may be calculated — the variables have the suffix _base added to indicate this fact. To determine the pixel colours for one scanline between x==`start` and x==`stop` the base variables are copied and then updated as x is incremented or decremented from x==`middle` — now the y-coordinate is held fixed. A representative coding example is provided by the loop which steps along a scanline from x==`middle` to x==`stop` — the first piece of code makes copies of the base variables:

```
if (stop > middle) {
  u = u_base;
  v = v_base;
  test_u = test_u_base;
  test_v = test_v_base;
  delta = delta_base;
         .
         .
```

Next the appropriate decision and difference fields are updated for each step along the scanline:

```
         .
         .
  for (x=middle+1; x<=stop; x++) {
    test_u += delta.u_x;
    test_v += delta.v_x;
    delta.u_u += product_d.x;
         .
         .
```

The value of delta.u_u==delta.v_v==[p,r2,r1]==-d should be negative for a visible polygon — if this test fails through rounding errors then the pixel is drawn in black so that is will be less noticeable in the final image:

```
        .
      .
   if (delta.u_u >= 0)
      ColourBuffer[x] = BLACK;
      .
      .
```

Otherwise the values of the decision variables are used to find the correct texel for the current pixel — first the u coordinate is determined:

```
        .
      .
   else {
     while (test_u<0 && u>0) {
        u--;
        test_u -= delta.u_u;
        delta.u_x -= product_d.x;
     }
     while (test_u>=-delta.u_u && u<u_max-1) {
        u++;
        test_u += delta.u_u;
        delta.u_x += product_d.x;
     }
     .
     .
```

The v coordinate is similarly updated — the code fragment is identical to that above with u replaced throughout by v. Finally, the correct texel colour value is copied to the ColourBuffer array:

```
        .
      .
      ColourBuffer[x] = texture.Texels[u][v];
   }
  }
 }
```

The pixels in the ColourBuffer array can now be transferred to the current scanline of the SCENE object image bitmap — before the next iteration through the scanline loop the base decision and difference variables must be updated by incrementing y.

With these modifications the textured-mapped Block World program displays the same image as illustrated in section 14.3 — however, the speed at which the image is generated is now greater. Nonetheless, to obtain significant increases in the animation frame rate the code should be rewritten using assembly language — the C++ version is structured to make the conversion process as painless as possible.

14.5 Depth Perception

The final section of this chapter looks at another technique for enhancing the perception of depth provided by a 2D image — the process simply involves making the distant portions of a scene more gloomy than those that are nearby. The implementation described here relies on pre-processing a texture before it is mapped — as described in section 14.3 a general point on the textured polygon may be represented by a vector r defined as follows:

```
r == r0 + u*r1 + v*r2
```

The factor gloom(u,v) will be proportional to the length of this vector squared ($r.r$) but to implement the process efficiently first- and second- order differences with respect to u and v must be defined — this is a similar process to that described in the previous section. Stepping in the u direction with v==0 the base value of the gloom variable may be calculated as follows:

```
gloom_base(0)   == r0.r0
gloom_base(u+1) == gloom_base(u) + delta_u(u)

delta_u(0)   == 2*r0.r1 + r1.r1
delta_u(u+1) == delta_u(u) + square_u

square_u = 2*r1.r1
```

Similarly for steps in the v direction with u fixed the difference relations are:

```
gloom(u,0)   == gloom_base(u)
gloom(u,v+1) == gloom(u,v) + delta_v(u,v)

delta_v(u,0)   == delta_v_base(u)
delta_v(u,v+1) == delta_v(u,v) + square_v

square_v == 2*r2.r2
```

The base value for delta_v(u,0) may also be computed incrementally:

```
delta_v_base(0)   == 2*r0*r2 + r2*r2
delta_v_base(u+1) == delta_v_base(u) + product_uv

product_uv == 2*r1.r2
```

The first step in calculating the gloom factor is to initialize the variables — the

VECTOR objects r0, r1 and r2 should be scaled appropriately.

```
int gloom_base = r0|r0;
int square_u = 2*(r1|r1);
int square_v = 2*(r2|r2);
int product_uv = 2*(r1|r2);
int delta_u = 2*(r0|r1)+(r1|r1);
int delta_v_base = 2*(r0|r2)+(r2|r2);
```

Then the actual processing consists simply of two nested loops for the variables u and v as follows:

```
Texture.Size = texture.Size;
for (u=0; u<u_max; u++) {
  gloom = gloom_base;
  delta_v = delta_v_base;
  for (v=0; v<v_max; v++) {
    texel = texture.Texels[u][v];
    // modify texel using gloom factor
    Texture.Texels[u][v] = texel;
    gloom += delta_v;
    delta_v += square_v;
  }
  gloom_base += delta_u;
  delta_u += square_u;
  delta_v_base += product_uv;
}
```

The Texture.Texels array is now passed to the texture mapping routine instead of the original texture provided by the POLYGON object — this automatically draws distant texels in gloomier shades. The following figure illustrates the new appearance of the Block World images:

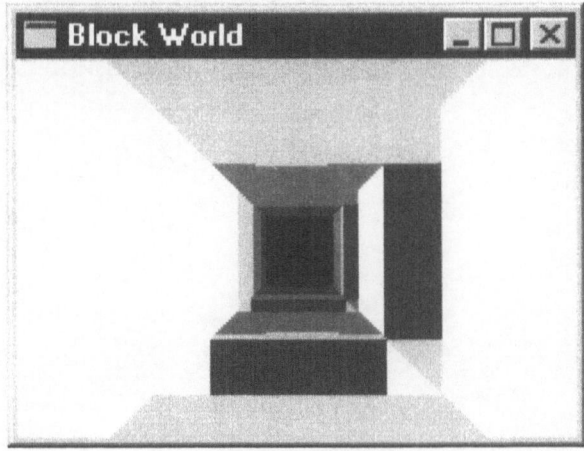

It is very easy to convert the calculation of the `gloom` factor into assembly language — the result is very rapid animation code that incorporates depth perception effects.

14.6 Summary

Shading and textures can help to add graphic realism to a polygon-filled scene. Shading routines modify the colours assigned to a polygon's pixels according to the colour and intensity of light shining onto the polygon — ambient lighting simply increases the general level of brightness whilst point and directional light sources can be used to produce more sophisticated effects. A general description of the interaction between light sources and the surfaces which they illuminate is very complicated to model — for animation applications running on home computers there is not yet sufficient processor power. A common simplification is to allow only ambient lighting plus a number of directional light sources that are reflected diffusely from the polygons within the virtual world. The flat shading model colours the whole of a polygon with the same shade of colour — this technique is best suited to angular objects which are represented accurately by a collection of flat polygons. For a more realistic representation of rounded objects the Gouraud shading model may be substituted — this interpolates the colours applied to the individual pixels from values calculated at the polygon vertices. Textures are essentially 2D bitmaps pasted onto the polygon faces of objects in the 3D virtual world — the complexity arises when the texels must be mapped to pixels on the projection screen. This chapter has derived the basic texture mapping equations and demonstrated a decision-variable approach for efficiently implementing these equations — the technique introduced the notion of using higher-order difference equations to calculate non-linear quantities in a stepwise manner. A similar procedure was also applied in the calculation of a gloom factor — by drawing more distant pixels in darker shades it is possible to enhance the impression of depth produced by the 2D projection of a 3D scene.

15. In Motion ...

Motion adds life to a computer-generated image — it is possible to animate the individual objects within a scene or alternatively to dynamically update the viewpoint from which the scene is observed. Each virtual object or observer may be assigned its own independent frame of reference defined by a local coordinate system — the local coordinate frames move rigidly through the 3D world by tracking the motion of the associated object or observer. This chapter is principally concerned with describing various coordinate system transformations — the essential topics include:

— managing the simulation of a virtual world
— collision detection
— local-to-world coordinate transformations
— world-to-camera coordinate transformations
— implementing translations and rotations
— pitch, yaw and roll
— basis and anti-basis vector sets

The chapter also outlines the techniques required to incorporate motion effects in a virtual world simulator — the `Block World` application is updated to provide an example of this process.

15.1 The Graphics Pipeline

The virtual world simulator developed in this book uses several different coordinate systems to project the images of 3D objects onto a 2D screen — there are three types of 3D coordinates (local, world and camera) and two types of 2D coordinates (image and bitmap). Bitmap coordinates are the only ones to use pixel units — the other four coordinate systems measure distances in fractions of a pixel and the `VIEW` class is free to scale these units as required. A set of local coordinates are held by each `OBJECT` object to describe the shape of the virtual object which they represent — the local coordinates are measured relative to a point specified by the object's `Position` field. An object may be placed at any location within the virtual world by a single call to the `OBJECT` class `SetPosition()` function — the local coordinates of the object's vertices are unchanged but their origin is updated. When the object is instructed to draw itself it passes absolute world coordinates to the `SCENE` object — this requires an internal transformation from local coordinates to world coordinates. The `SCENE` object uses its associated `CAMERA` object to transform from world coordinates to camera coordinates — the

camera coordinate system is described by the ViewPoint and ViewDirection
fields of the CAMERA object. The 3D camera coordinates are then projected to 2D
image coordinates and finally the image coordinates are scaled and translated to
provide bitmap coordinates which map directly to the SCENE object's DIB. The
following figure illustrates the sequence of coordinate transformations:

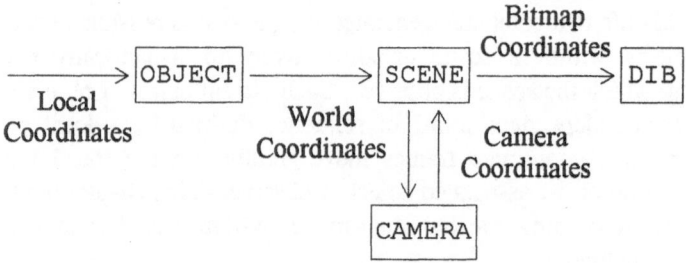

The following sections discuss the actual transformations in more detail — they
also demonstrate how to animate the virtual world objects and dynamically update
the viewpoint from which these objects are observed.

15.2 Animating the Virtual World

The WORLD, OBJECT and POLYGON classes each provide Initialize(),
Update(), Reset() and Finalize() functions — these act much like the
various Draw() functions described in section 8.2 in that a call to the WORLD class
function propagates first to each of the OBJECT objects and then to each of the
POLYGON objects. The Initialize() and Finalize() functions allow
resources to be respectively allocated and released — the Initialize()
functions may also contain code to pre-calculate constant quantities and so optimize
later iterative processing. The Reset() functions are similar to the
Initialize() functions but they do not contain start-up code that need only be
executed once. The most interesting functions here are the Update() functions —
the WORLD class version is typically called by the VIEW class Update() function
to step to the next animation frame. The OBJECT class Update() function makes
calls to the Translate() and Rotate() functions — these respectively update
the position and orientation of the object within the virtual world. Much as the
SPRITE class defines the SetPosition() and SetVelocity() functions to
control its motion in 2D (see section 7.1) so the OBJECT class provides a range of
functions to control its position and orientation in 3D:

— SetPosition(), SetOrientation()
— SetVelocity(), SetRotation()
— SetRelativeVelocity(), SetRelativeRotation()

The first pair of functions initialize the position and orientation of the object whilst
the others define the step-size used for modifying these quantities during a call to

Update(). The Position field sets the origin for the object's local coordinate system — the orientation of the object is defined by specifying (in world coordinates) the directions of the x-, y- and z-axes belonging to the local coordinate system. The pair of functions SetRelativeVelocity() and SetRelativeRotation() work only with local coordinates — the first function defines velocity components along the three coordinate axes and the second defines angular rotation rates about these axes. The SetVelocity() and SetRotation() functions are similar but they use the world coordinate system instead of the local coordinate system to provide the reference directions — both relative and absolute functions update the local-to-world transformation process but do not affect the local coordinates of the object's vertices. The next two sections present the detailed implementations of these motion-related functions from the OBJECT class.

One important problem which is closely involved with objects moving in a virtual world is collision detection — it is not strictly a graphics-related topic and so a possible solution is only sketched in outline here. Once all the virtual objects have been updated the WORLD object checks for a collision between each pair of objects — to perform the test the WORLD object simply looks for bounding boxes that overlap. If any pair of objects have collided then they both receive calls to their Collide() functions — relevant details describing the other object involved are passed in both cases. The pair of objects must decide how to handle the collision and modify themselves appropriately — for example, if a heat-seeking missile collides with a plane then the missile will explode whilst the plane should suffer damage and perhaps start to crash.

Finally, the OBJECT class provides an AttachCamera() function which allows the VIEW class to attach the SCENE object's camera to a moving object:

```
void OBJECT::AttachCamera(CAMERA* camera) {
  Camera = camera;
}
```

The OBJECT class Update() function checks for an attached camera — if one is available then the CAMERA class functions SetViewPoint() and SetViewDirection() are called to force the camera to move through the virtual world with the object. The CAMERA object sets its ViewPoint field to match the OBJECT object's Position field — the camera points in the direction of the virtual object's local z-axis.

15.3 Translations

The Position field of an OBJECT object describes its location within the virtual world — the Translate() function updates this field according to the values previously set by the SetVelocity() and SetRelativeVelocity()

functions. The influence of the SetVelocity() function is easy to understand — just like the SPRITE class version it causes the Position field to be updated for each new animation frame but now the effect is in 3D instead of 2D:

```
void OBJECT::Translate(void) {
  Position += Velocity;
    .
    .
```

The influence of the SetRelativeVelocity() function is a little more complicated — the RelativeVelocity vector must be transformed to world coordinates before it can be added to the Position vector. The transformation is actually a rotation and it is performed by calling the VECTOR class Rotate() function:

```
    .
    .
  VECTOR velocity = RelativeVelocity;
  velocity.Rotate(Basis);
  Position += velocity;
}
```

The Rotate() function may be defined as follows:

```
VECTOR& VECTOR::Rotate(const VECTOR* basis) {
  __int64 x,y,z;
  x  = Int32x32To64(X,basis[0].X);
  x += Int32x32To64(Y,basis[1].X);
  x += Int32x32To64(Z,basis[2].X);
  y  = Int32x32To64(X,basis[0].Y);
  y += Int32x32To64(Y,basis[1].Y);
  y += Int32x32To64(Z,basis[2].Y);
  z  = Int32x32To64(X,basis[0].Z);
  z += Int32x32To64(Y,basis[1].Z);
  z += Int32x32To64(Z,basis[2].Z);
  X = int(x/AngularScale);
  Y = int(y/AngularScale);
  Z = int(z/AngularScale);
  return *this;
}
```

The Basis array is a collection of three unit vectors which describe the x-, y- and z-axes of the local coordinate system in world coordinates — the Basis array is used to specify the orientation of the OBJECT object. For example, if the RelativeVelocity vector is directed along the local z-axis then the velocity vector in the SCENE class Translate() function will have its components set respectively to basis[2].X, basis[2].Y and basis[2].Z scaled by the magnitude (Z) of the RelativeVelocity vector. The VECTOR class maintains an `AngularScale` field in addition to its `Scale` field — just as the `Scale` field allows an object's position to be specified to the nearest fraction of a pixel so the `AngularScale` field permits a set of basis vectors to accurately represent a particular orientation in 3D space.

15.4 Rotations

The `SetOrientation()` function specifies the initial directions of the local x-, y- and z-axes in world coordinates — the `Rotate()` function will subsequently modify these settings by updating the `Basis` array of VECTOR objects. One possibility is to rotate the object about the axes of the world coordinate system — this type of rotation is initiated by calling the `SetRotation()` function to set the `OBJECT` object's `AngularVelocity` field. As in the previous section the rotation is actually performed by the VECTOR class — section 11.1 discusses the derivation of the associated transformation matrix.

```
void OBJECT::Rotate(void) {
  for (int i=0; i<3; i++)
    Basis[i].Rotate(AngularVelocity);
  VECTOR::InvertBasis(Basis,AntiBasis);
     .
     .
}
```

The VECTOR class `Rotate()` function is overloaded to allow a POINT_3D structure to act as a parameter instead of a set of basis vectors — the x, y and z fields define the angles through which the vector will be rotated about the three coordinate axes:

```
VECTOR& VECTOR::Rotate(const POINT_3D& angle) {
  POINT_3D cos,sin;
  CalculateComponents(angle,cos,sin);
  Rotate(X,Y,cos.z,sin.z);
  Rotate(Y,Z,cos.x,sin.x);
  Rotate(Z,X,cos.y,sin.y);
  return *this;
}
```

Here the sine and cosine functions are implemented within the helper function `CalculateComponents()` by using a look-up table. The table can be pre-defined in a header file and this will considerably reduce the amount of processing required during program execution — the header also defines the HYPOTENUSE constant to allow the sine and cosine values to be represented in fixed-point integer format. The individual rotations about the various axes are actually performed by an internal VECTOR class Rotate() function:

```
void
VECTOR::Rotate(int& x,int& y,int cos,int sin) {
  __int64 u,v;
  u  = Int32x32To64(x,cos);
  u -= Int32x32To64(y,sin);
  v  = Int32x32To64(x,sin);
  v += Int32x32To64(y,cos);
  x = int(u/HYPOTENUSE);
  y = int(v/HYPOTENUSE);
}
```

The VECTOR class InvertBasis() function is called to calculate the AntiBasis array of vectors — the anti-basis describes the orientations of the x-, y- and z-axes for the world coordinate system using local coordinates. Whenever a camera is attached to the virtual object the AntiBasis array is passed to the CAMERA object by calling its SetViewDirection() function — the CAMERA object uses the anti-basis to transform from world coordinates to camera coordinates. The next section covers the InvertBasis() function in more detail.

The SetRelativeRotation() function initiates rotations relative to the local coordinate axes — this is especially useful when the virtual object is carrying the SCENE object's camera. In this case the animation images generated by the SCENE object give the impression of travelling with the virtual object — relative rotations allow the motion of the object to be controlled in a natural way. With the local z-axis pointing ahead and the local x-axis pointing out to the right, the rotations about the local x-, y- and z-axes are referred to as 'pitching', 'yawing' and 'rolling' respectively — these motions are common for real-world objects such as ships and planes. Whereas the SetRotation() function results in the Basis vectors being rotated, the AntiBasis array is affected by the function SetRelativeRotation() — instead of rotating the object's vertices relative to the world coordinate system, the object is considered as fixed and the world coordinate system is apparently rotated in the opposite direction. The relative rotation is implemented as follows:

```
void OBJECT::Rotate(void) {
      .
      .
  for (i=0; i<3; i++)
    AntiBasis[i].Rotate(-RelativeAngularVelocity);
  VECTOR::InvertBasis(AntiBasis,Basis);
}
```

Another call to the VECTOR class InvertBasis() function is needed to update the `Basis` array since the object is now oriented differently relative to the world coordinate system.

15.5 Transforming Coordinates

Section 15.1 described the sequence of coordinate transformations that must be applied to project the image of the 3D virtual world onto a 2D screen. The general implementation of these transformations has already been discussed in previous chapters — in particular sections 12.4 and 8.3 define the `Project()` and `TransformToPixels()` functions provided by the `SCENE` class to perform the camera-to-image and image-to-bitmap coordinate transformations. The local-to-world and world-to-camera coordinate transformations are applied by the `OBJECT` class `Transform()` function and the `CAMERA` class `Snapshot()` function respectively — section 12.3 introduced the `Snapshot()` function but omitted the transformation details. The `OBJECT` class `Draw()` function calls the `Transform()` function to refresh the `TransformedVertices` array — this array contains the world coordinates of the object's vertices and is passed to the `SCENE` object:

```
void OBJECT::Draw(SCENE* scene) {
  if (scene->IsObjectVisible(Position,Radius)) {
    if (!Transformed)
      Transform();
    scene->SetVertices(TransformedVertices);
    for (int i=0; i<PolygonCount; i++)
      Polygons[i]->Draw(scene);
  }
}
```

The `OBJECT` class `Transform()` function actually transforms from local to world coordinates:

```
void OBJECT::Transform(void) {
  Transformed = TRUE;
  for (int i=0; i<VertexCount; i++) {
    TransformedVertices[i] = Vertices[i];
    TransformedVertices[i].Rotate(Basis);
    TransformedVertices[i] += Position;
  }
}
```

The `Transformed` flag indicates that the `TransformedVertices` array is up-to-date — the flag is set to `FALSE` by any `OBJECT` class function such as `Translate()` or `Rotate()` that alters the `Position` or `Basis` fields.

Similarly the CAMERA class Snapshot() function performs the world-to-camera coordinate transformation:

```
void
CAMERA::Snapshot(int count,const int* vertices) {
  int i,n;
  for (i=0; i<count; i++) {
    n = vertices[i];
    if (!Transformed[n]) {
      Points[n] = Vertices[n]-ViewPoint;
      Points[n].Rotate(ViewDirection);
    }
  }
}
```

The OBJECT class Update() function sets the fields ViewPoint and ViewDirection within an attached CAMERA object as follows:

```
        .
        .
if (Camera) {
  Camera->SetViewPoint(Position);
  Camera->SetViewDirection(AntiBasis);
}
        .
        .
```

The one remaining point to cover is the implementation of the VECTOR class InvertBasis() function which converts between a basis and its inverse — a basis is simply a collection of three unit vectors pointing along the x-, y- and z-axes of a coordinate system. As demonstrated by the VECTOR class Rotate() function from section 15.3 the transformation from local to world coordinates is represented by the following matrix:

$$
M == \begin{bmatrix} \texttt{Basis[0].X} & \texttt{Basis[1].X} & \texttt{Basis[2].X} \\ \texttt{Basis[0].Y} & \texttt{Basis[1].Y} & \texttt{Basis[2].Y} \\ \texttt{Basis[0].Z} & \texttt{Basis[1].Z} & \texttt{Basis[2].Z} \end{bmatrix}
$$

Note in particular that the Basis vectors form the three columns of the matrix. Furthermore, the matrix represents a rigid-body transformation as defined in section 11.1 — the inverse of the matrix can therefore be obtained simply by transposing rows and columns. However, the inverse matrix represents the transformation from world to local coordinates and so its columns correspond to the AntiBasis vectors — equivalently the AntiBasis vectors are defined by the rows of the original matrix M. The InvertBasis() function may consequently be implemented as follows:

```
void VECTOR::InvertBasis(const VECTOR* basis,
                         VECTOR* anti_basis) {
  int VECTOR::*t = &VECTOR::X;
  for (int i=0; i<3; i++) {
    anti_basis[i].X = basis[0].*t;
    anti_basis[i].Y = basis[1].*t;
    anti_basis[i].Z = basis[2].*t;
    t = (i?&VECTOR::Z:&VECTOR::Y);
  }
}
```

Here the pointer variable t is used to select the X, Y and Z fields from the appropriate VECTOR objects — the .* operator is needed to dereference the pointer.

Once the modifications described in this chapter are incorporated in the Block World application, the images of the virtual world can be animated to simulate motion. In particular the VIEW class can supply code to allow the user to pilot a virtual object through the 3D world — by attaching the SCENE object's camera to this object the world is viewed from a dynamically changing viewpoint. The following figure shows the latest Block World program in action:

15.6 Summary

Many of the graphics algorithms described in this book are intended to increase the speed at which an image can be rendered — there is little point in taking so much trouble if the application will draw only a single static image. To see the real benefits of optimizing the drawing code the image must be updated dynamically — this chapter has discussed the techniques necessary to animate the images generated by a virtual world simulator. In particular, the WORLD object can make each virtual object move by invoking its Update() function — if the SCENE object's camera is attached to a moving object the viewpoint of the displayed image will also change. The image generation pipeline involves a number of transformations between coordinate systems. The OBJECT class uses a local coordinate system to describe the vertices of each virtual object — the local coordinates are transformed to world coordinates according to the current position and orientation of the object within the world. The CAMERA class performs the world-to-camera coordinate transformation and so provides uniform input to the SCENE object. Finally, the SCENE object projects 3D camera coordinates to 2D image coordinates and then transforms to bitmap coordinates measured in pixels. The VECTOR class provides the functions necessary to implement the coordinate system transformations. In particular, the VECTOR class deals with triples of unit vectors that describe the directions of the coordinate axes — each triple is known as a 'basis' since any other vector can be obtained as a weighted sum of the basis vectors. The OBJECT and CAMERA classes use basis vectors to perform rotations between coordinate systems — in each case the inverse transformation may be represented by an anti-basis that is obtained from the original basis set simply by transposing rows and columns in the transformation matrix.

Postscript

This book has described many of the graphics facilities provided by Windows 98 — it has also presented a variety of algorithms that may be applied to generate images using the basic building blocks. The journey has been a long one with many new topics being encountered along the way:

— message-based programming
— window management
— working with C++ objects
— Windows 98 Graphics Device Interface
— pens, brushes, bitmaps and palettes
— sprite animation
— wire-frame and polygon-fill images
— assembly language programming
— 3D vector geometry
— perspective projections
— hidden pixel removal
— colour shading and texture mapping
— virtual world simulation

Nevertheless, this is just the beginning of the adventure — armed with the essential knowledge contained within these pages you are now ready to create a Windows 98 graphics application of your very own ...

Index